COMPUTER CONFIDENCE:
A Challenge for Today

JAMES F. CLARK

Fulton County Schools
Atlanta, Georgia

KATHY BRITTAIN WHITE

University of North Carolina at Greensboro
Greensboro, North Carolina

Published by

JO1 **SOUTH-WESTERN PUBLISHING CO.**

CINCINNATI   WEST CHICAGO, IL   DALLAS   PELHAM MANOR, NY   LIVERMORE, CA

ISBN: 0-538-10010-9

Library of Congress Catalog Card Number: 84-51520

4 5 6 7 8 9 10 D 2 1 0 9

Printed in the United States of America

PREFACE

The use of computers has become an important part of our lives. Computers, from small electronic devices to giant rooms full of circuitry, are affecting the way we live. As time goes by, almost everyone will be dealing with computers on a frequent basis. The interaction with computers may be on a daily basis at work doing such tasks as typing memos. The interaction may be part of personal activities, such as withdrawing money from an electronic teller machine. It may even be driving your car and listening to an on-board computer tell you that the engine requires coolant. Whatever the particular person's situation, the computer is having a large impact on all of us as a society. The primary goal of this book, therefore, is to help you develop a high degree of computer confidence—the confidence that comes from understanding the many uses of computers and the ways in which people use them and instruct them.

Computer literacy means to become acquainted with the computer and its uses well enough to be able to read or talk about it without misunderstanding. The computer is not magical or mysterious. It was designed to be a time- and labor-saving device. This book will help you to better understand it and to accept it as part of daily life, like the automobile or the telephone.

The entire field of computers and information systems is so broad that only a small part of it can be covered in any book. With this book, you should be able to develop a good understanding of the basics of computers. Your level of confidence with computers should be high, and you should be ready to pursue additional studies if you have a strong interest in this area. While you will not become a computer programmer from reading this book, you will become aware of the programming process and develop some familiarity with simple programming in the BASIC language. The BASIC programming examples shown in this book are compatible with the following microcomputers: Apple,®[1] IBM,[2] TRS-80,™[3] and Commodore.[4] They may also be easily adapted to use with most other microcomputers.

Each chapter in the text concludes with review questions and a list of vocabulary words. The questions and vocabulary words should be used to help you check your understanding of the material from the chapter. If the questions about a particular subject seem difficult, or you do not understand the meaning of a vocabulary word, go back and restudy the subject or word.

The workbook that is available for the text contains a rich assortment of study guides and exercises designed to reinforce your understanding of the topics discussed in each chapter. Applications diskettes are also available for popular microcomputers. The activities on the applications diskettes will also help reinforce your understanding.

The book contains a variety of interesting topics which relate to the use of computers in our society. Each chapter also contains a short special-interest story to help make you aware of some of the ways in which computers are being used in today's world. In addition, the appendixes in the back of the book will help you understand the history of computer-related devices and acquaint you with the skill of keyboarding. The keyboarding materials were prepared by Dr. T. James Crawford, Dr. Lawrence W. Erickson, Dr. Lee R. Beaumont, Dr. Jerry W. Robinson, and Dr. Arnola C. Ownby. They are reprinted here with the permission of South-Western Publishing Co.

If your goal is to be confident in using computers for personal productivity, you will find that this text and its accompanying materials will fulfill your need. If you want to learn programming or pursue a career in information systems, these materials will help develop the foundation upon which to base additional study. If your goal is to be prepared for this new technology, the text will provide confidence in your understanding of the computerized world around us.

---

[1]Apple® II Plus, Apple® IIe, and Applesoft® are registered trademarks of Apple Computer, Inc. Any reference to Apple II Plus, Apple IIe, or Applesoft refers to this footnote.

[2]IBM is a registered trademark of International Business Machines. Any reference to the IBM, IBM Personal Computer, or IBM PCjr refers to this footnote.

[3]TRS-80® is a trademark of the Radio Shack Division of Tandy Corporation. Any reference to the TRS-80 Model III or Model 4, or to the Radio Shack Microcomputer, refers to this footnote.

[4]Commodore is a registered trademark of Commodore Business Machines, Inc. Any reference to the Commodore computer refers to this footnote.

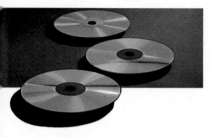

CONTENTS

PART 1 The Computer in Your Life

PART 2   Framework of a Computer System

PART 3 Hardware

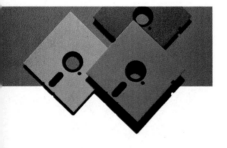

PART 4   Software

PART 5   Processing

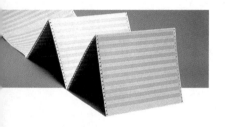

PART 6   **Programming**

ACKNOWLEDGMENTS

Illustrations on the pages indicated by Steve McInturff © 1985:
pp. 14, 17, 32, 33, 35, 48, 51, 70, 73, 88, 89, 91, 114, 117, 136, 139, 158, 161, 180, 181, 183, 196, 199, 222, 225, 244, 245, 266, 267, 269, 288, 289, 291, 310, 313, 330, 333

For permission to reproduce the photographs on the pages indicated, acknowledgment is made to the following:

Cover Photo © Henry Ries
1	© Melvin L. Prueitt, Los Alamos National Laboratory
2	Standard Oil of California
8	Photograph from Hazeltine Corporation 1979 Annual Report
9	Port of Seattle
11	Digital Equipment Corporation (top)
11	Courtesy of Merck & Co., Inc. (bottom)
16	© Costa Manos/Magnum Photos Inc.
18	© David Wagner/Phototake
19	IBM Corporation
22	Photo courtesy of Satellite Business Systems
24	Cincinnati Milacron, Inc.
26	Photo courtesy of NASA
29	IBM Corporation
32	IBM Corporation
34	John Colwell from Grant Heilman
36	© Melvin L. Prueitt, Los Alamos National Laboratory
39	Zenith Electronics Corporation (top)
39	Cray Research (bottom)
40	IBM Corporation
44	Hewlett-Packard Company
49	Chrysler Corporation
50	General Motors Corporation
54	IBM Corporation
56	Digital Equipment Corporation (bottom)
58	Recognition Equipment Incorporated (bottom)
60	TRW Inc.
61	Photograph courtesy of Intel Corporation
63	Hewlett-Packard Company

64	Courtesy of The Upjohn Company
74	Heath Company
76	© Dan McCoy/Rainbow
82	A. T. & T. Bell Laboratories
83	Courtesy of The Nielsen Lithographing Co.
94	© Melvin L. Prueitt, Los Alamos National Laboratory
96	Digital Equipment Corporation
97	Figgie International
100	NCR Corporation
101	The Southland Corporation (top)
102	Albertson's, Inc.
103	NCR Corporation
104	Recognition Equipment Incorporated
105	The Central Trust Company
106	Courtesy of Cadillac
107	Courtesy of UNIMATION INC., a Westinghouse Company (bottom)
108	Hewlett-Packard Company
110	1983 Steve Dunwell
115	Courtesy of Apple Computer, Inc.
116	IBM Corporation
118	© Phototake
120	Courtesy of Lundy Electronics & Systems, Inc. (top)
120	Courtesy of Lundy Electronics & Systems, Inc. (middle)
120	Courtesy of Lundy Electronics & Systems, Inc. (bottom)
121	IBM Corporation
122	Radio Shack, A Division of Tandy Corporation
125	Centronics Data Computer Corporation (top left)
126	Exxon Office Systems
127	Courtesy, DatagraphiX® (top)
127	Courtesy, DatagraphiX® (bottom)
129	Bell & Howell
130	Bell & Howell
131	Hewlett-Packard Company
132	Photo courtesy of McDonnell Douglas Corporation
137	Photo Courtesy of American Airlines
138	Delta Air Lines, Inc.
140	© Melvin L. Prueitt, Los Alamos National Laboratory
145	Control Data Corporation
148	Courtesy of BASF Systems Corporation (top)
148	Storage Technology Corporation (bottom)
150	Control Data Corporation
152	Storage Technology Corporation (top)
153	A. T. & T. Bell Laboratories
154	Photo courtesy of 3M
161	Federal Express Corporation
162	Federal Express Corporation/Photography by Dana Duke
166	© Melvin L. Prueitt, Los Alamos National Laboratory
172	NCR Corporation

180	Carnegie-Mellon University
182	Photo Courtesy of Cincinnati Milacron, Inc.
184	TRW Inc.
185	Photo courtesy of The Future Now Shops
197	Hewlett-Packard Company
198	Courtesy of Apple Computer, Inc.
202	© Melvin L. Prueitt, Los Alamos National Laboratory
203	Wang Laboratories, Inc.
208	Simplex Time Recorder Co.
213	Photo courtesy of Satellite Business Systems
224	© Ray Nelson/Phototake
226	© Paul Jablonka/International Stock Photography Ltd.
246	© Bill Smith, 1985
247	© Dan McCoy/Rainbow
248	© Melvin L. Prueitt, Los Alamos National Laboratory
251	Sperry Corporation
252	Delta Air Lines, Inc.
253	Hewlett-Packard Company
254	Standard Oil of California (top)
254	Ted Kawalerski/THE IMAGE BANK (bottom)
261	Cincinnati Milacron, Inc.
266	Courtesy of UNIMATION INC., a Westinghouse Company
268	The DeVilbiss Company
272	© Melvin L. Prueitt, Los Alamos National Laboratory
288	Florida Division of Tourism
290	Florida Division of Tourism
292	© J.T. Hoffman/Phototake
311	Conoco Inc.
312	Carnegie-Mellon University
314	© Dan McCoy/Rainbow
331	Carnegie-Mellon University
332	Heath Company
334	© Steven F. Grobe/The Picture Cube
337	Photo courtesy of Ramtek Corporation
340	Courtesy of Planning Research Corporation
341	Courtesy of Planning Research Corporation
342	Courtesy of Planning Research Corporation (top)
342	Courtesy of Planning Research Corporation (bottom)
343	Courtesy of Planning Research Corporation
344	Courtesy of Burroughs Corp.
345	Courtesy of Planning Research Corporation
346	IBM Corporation
348	IBM Corporation (top)
348	IBM Corporation (bottom)
350	Courtesy of Planning Research Corporation
352	Sperry Corporation
353	UPI/BETTMANN ARCHIVE
354	Sperry Corporation
355	IBM Corporation

356   IBM Corporation
357   Intel Corporation
358   IBM Corporation
365   © Paul Jablonka/International Stock Photography Ltd.
366   IBM Corporation (bottom)
367   IBM Corporation (top left)
368   Courtesy of Lundy Electronics & Systems, Inc. (top left)

REVIEWER ACKNOWLEDGMENT

The authors would like to acknowledge the contributions of the following people in reviewing the manuscript and recommending excellent changes for revisions.

David Damcke
Jefferson High School
Portland, Oregon

Jon Lewis
McMinnville Public Schools
McMinnville, Oregon

LaVelle Reed
Roseburg Senior High School
Roseburg, Oregon

PART 1
The Computer in Your Life

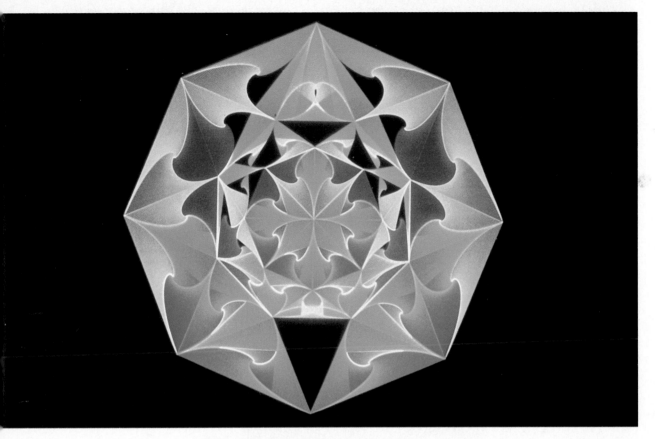

CHAPTER 1

The Computer and You

Objectives

1. Describe the benefits of the computer in your daily life.
2. Describe the uses of the computer in the community.

The computer may be the most important invention affecting your life. Some people compare it to the discovery of the wheel or the invention of the printing press. Some say that its effects will totally change life for the better. An opposite view is that computers threaten our way of life. Why do these different opinions exist? The computer is a tool that does tasks, and the way it is used depends on the individual. As with any tool, however, people make the choice to use the computer, either for good or for bad.

BENEFITS OF THE COMPUTER TO INDIVIDUALS IN THEIR DAILY LIVES

You are probably aware of many ways in which the computer affects your daily life. Figure 1.1 shows one of the ways you might use the computer. There are other ways of which you are probably not aware. Let's take a look at some of the benefits of the computer to you as an individual.

FIGURE 1.1

Many gas stations now use computers.

Information Sources

Businesses known as **information utilities** have large computers that store huge groups of information about many different subjects. These groups of information are known as **data bases** and are available for your use. You can use them to obtain information on many topics, read the daily news, play games, make your own airline reservations, obtain the latest stock market reports, or perform other activities. The range of services provided by such businesses is continually increasing.

To get information from such a service, you can use a small computer. A device known as a **modem** attaches the small computer to a phone line. This device allows your computer to communicate with the large computer. You pay a fee to the utility for the amount of time your computer is connected to their computer. Some services available from the utility also require payment of extra fees.

Electronic Banking and Shopping

Banks have used computers for years. Nearly every bank offers an automatic teller, such as the one shown in Figure 1.2, that is in service 24 hours a day. Many banks have started issuing cards that allow their customers to also use other banks' 24-hour tellers nationwide. A large number of customers prefer the machine to a human teller, even during hours when the bank is open.

Bill-Payment-by-Phone Services

Growing numbers of banks are giving customers an opportunity to pay bills by phone. To use one of these services, you tell the bank the name and address of each business that you pay on a regular basis, along with your account number at each business. Payments that are the same every month, such as rent or mortgage payments, can be scheduled for automatic payment. Items that vary in amount, such as the phone bill or electric bill, are paid when you instruct the computer to do so. To tell the bank's computer to pay your bill, you simply dial the computer's phone number. Then, using a push-button phone, you enter your bank card number and a secret password, and the codes for the transfer of payment to the business from either your checking or savings account. Then you enter the business' code number (provided by the bank), the amount of money to be paid, and the date on which the payment should be made.

FIGURE 1.2

The automatic bank teller is an electronic banking service available at most banks.

Debit Cards

Debit cards have also been introduced. These cards look just like credit cards, but cause the amounts of purchases to be immediately subtracted from the checking account instead of a bill being sent days or weeks later. Since items must be paid for immediately, persons who use debit cards to purchase items will be less likely to buy items they cannot afford.

In addition to the use of debit cards, computers are changing shopping in many other ways. Many stores have joined forces with the information utilities discussed earlier. After "browsing" with your computer, and perhaps watching someone demonstrate products, you may immediately place your order using the computer. Figure 1.3 shows a person shopping by computer.

FIGURE 1.3

Some people do their shopping by computer.

Household Control

Most likely, you or your friends do not yet live in a house run by a computer. However, you may be surprised by the number of household devices that now may be computer controlled. Refrigerators, ranges, microwave ovens, washers and dryers, stereos, televisions, video disk players, and thermostats, for example, may contain small computers. Figure 1.4 shows one of these devices. Some houses, however, have all of their operations under the supervision of computers. The air-conditioning system is under computer control to produce the most comfort at the lowest cost. Lawn sprinklers are turned on automatically whenever needed. Fire alarms and burglar alarms keep a constant watch. The control unit can automatically call the fire department or police department if an emergency develops.

FIGURE 1.4

A microwave oven is one of many computer-controlled household devices.

Household tasks such as grocery shopping and cooking may be computerized. At least one major appliance manufacturer has built a kitchen supervised by a computer. The system uses the **Universal Product Code** (UPC), which is a series of bars of different widths. Also known as bar codes, these bars are printed on grocery items by the products' manufacturers to identify the items. As you unpack groceries to store them, you move a scanner across the bar codes. The **scanner** is a device that reads the numbers represented by the bars and feeds the numbers into the computer. Bar-code scanners are also used at grocery store checkouts.

All of your recipes may also be stored in the computer. You tell the computer what recipe you are using, and it deducts from its records all the ingredients you will need. As you plan the next week's meals, the computer checks to see what items you need to purchase. It will prepare your grocery list and transmit your order to a grocery store computer, where the order will be prepared for immediate pickup or delivery. If you have some leftover meat loaf, onion soup, and green beans, the computer can show you the recipes for several food dishes you can make using these leftovers. The computer can even weigh ingredients for you and watch over the cooking process.

Learning Aids

The computer is also used to help students learn. Perhaps the most common are learning toys such as shown in Figure 1.5.

FIGURE 1.5

Computerized learning toys can be a lot of fun.

Some learning aids are called **computer-assisted instruction** (CAI). There are many computer-assisted learning programs for use on home computers. There are learning programs that will help you with multiplication, English, and many other subjects. Data bases, such as those discussed in the first part of this chapter, can make research for school projects much easier. There are also many personal improvement computer programs, such as one that analyzes your writing style and helps develop your writing skill.

One advantage of computer-assisted instruction is that each student can learn at his or her own pace. When a student is finished with a lesson at the computer, the computer "remembers" how far the student has progressed. The next lesson can then pick up exactly where the student left off. Another advantage of CAI is immediate feedback. The computer can tell you whether an answer is right or wrong without any delay.

Weather and Environment

Probably every commercial television station in the country uses some type of computer to provide information to help predict the weather. This equipment may show temperature ranges, rainfall, and wind flow. What is not obvious in watching a television weather report, such as the one shown in Figure 1.6, however, is the great amount of computing that goes into the forecasts. Even though weather forecasting is still far from being 100 percent accurate, forecasts are now much more accurate than ever before.

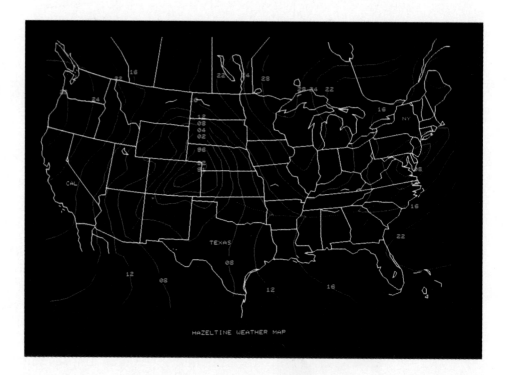

FIGURE 1.6

Weather reports require a great amount of computing.

In addition to weather forecasting, various other environmental successes are possible due to computers. The tracking of oil spills and other pollution in streams, for example, has helped overcome environmental hazards. The paths that water currents will take, changes in the wind, and changes in water temperature affect the direction in which pollution will travel. When computers predict the direction of travel, action can be taken to quickly clean up the mess.

Transportation

Almost every kind of transportation has been affected by computers. Trains operate with no crew members, as shown in Figure 1.7. Many airlines can fly to their destinations and land under the control of the computer, making flight safer and more efficient. The captain serves as a manager, telling the computer what to do. For a number of years, computers have provided controls in your car, such as ignition spark control and fuel control. Each new model introduced seems to have more computer controls added. Systems are already developed that keep cars from running into each other, as well as computerized road maps that always "know" where a particular car is and show its location.

FIGURE 1.7

With the help of the computer, some trains can operate with no crew members.

Community Service

Fire fighting and the saving of lives are aided by the computer. Computerized mapping systems can quickly point out the location of a problem and identify the emergency crew closest to the scene. Computerized mapping can also help decide where to place equipment and personnel to ensure the shortest response time. In some communities, computers can provide fire fighters with floor plans of buildings in which they may need to fight fires.

Crime Control

Crime control is another area in which computers help to organize information. States have agreed, for example, to share driver's license records for persons whose licenses have been taken away. These people cannot go to neighboring states to obtain licenses. Other records of crimes committed are kept by the FBI's National Crime Information Center. For example, this information has been used to find stolen cars that have been driven across state lines. In other cases, computers have been used to analyze the details of a series of crimes that seemed to be committed by the same person, eventually leading to the arrest of the criminal. Officers may have **terminals** (keyboards and screens) in their cars to quickly get to information stored in the computer. Figure 1.8 shows such a terminal. All of society is better protected when the computer helps in the arrests of persons involved in crimes.

Health Promotion

Computers have long been used for routine record keeping by hospitals. However, today many people also owe their lives to the computer. A modern hospital is a showroom of computerized equipment. **Sensors** (devices that detect changes) can be attached to patients to tell when there are changes in temperature, heart rate, blood pressure, or other vital signs. If there is a negative change, the hospital staff is alerted immediately. This has saved many lives. Medical tests that were once very time-consuming or impossible are now completed quickly by computer. Machines can scan the body and provide information never before thought possible. Computers are thus able to help doctors diagnose illnesses. Figure 1.9 shows one application of computers in a medical setting.

FIGURE 1.8

Police officers use terminals in their cars.

FIGURE 1.9

Computers help diagnose illnesses.

All the medical uses of computers discussed thus far have dealt with diagnosing diseases and saving lives. An equally exciting area in the medical use of computers, however, is the direct use of computers in the treatment of patients. Pumps controlled by computers can already inject drugs into the bloodstream. Computers also perform the full-time measurement of chemicals within the body, with the computer making second-by-second decisions on how much of the drug is required. Such uses of the computer should provide much better treatment for diabetes, for example.

Persons who have lost the use of their legs through spinal cord injuries are now somewhat able to walk through computer stimulation of their leg muscles. Important beginnings have been made toward artificial vision for the blind. Computer-controlled wheelchairs and robotic arms that respond to the spoken word are proving to be of tremendous value to the disabled.

SUMMARY

The computer is a powerful tool. Used properly, it can vastly improve the quality of life. Computers are providing faster and more accurate information than ever before. Areas such as information utilities, banking, household operation, learning, public safety, transportation, health care, and the environment benefit from the use of computers.

REVIEW QUESTIONS

1. What is an information utility? A data base? (Obj. 1)
2. Describe how computers can provide better service for bank customers. (Obj. 1)
3. How may computers be used in the home? (Obj. 1)
4. List two ways the computer is used in dealing with the weather and environment. (Obj. 2)
5. How have computers affected transportation? (Obj. 2)
6. How have computers improved community services? (Obj. 2)
7. Describe four ways in which computers improve health care and the quality of life for those who are ill or disabled. (Obj. 2)

8. How is the computer used as a learning tool? (Obj. 2)

9. What is CAI? How does it benefit students? (Obj. 2)

10. What is the function of a modem? (Obj. 2)

VOCABULARY WORDS

The following terms were introduced in this chapter:

information utility	scanner
data base	computer-assisted
modem	instruction
debit card	terminal
Universal Product Code	sensor

WORKBOOK EXERCISES

Complete all exercises in Chapter 1 of the workbook before proceeding to Chapter 2 in this text.

DISKETTE EXERCISE

Complete the diskette exercise for Chapter 1 before proceeding to Chapter 2 in this text.

Computers Add Zest to Camps

In the olden days, summer camps provided youngsters a chance to get away from home for a little while. They provided lots of fun things to do such as arts and crafts, sports, and outdoor activities. Camp settings themselves were generally rather rustic, presenting somewhat of a back-to-nature environment.

Today, camps may still be all those things, but a new wrinkle has been added. More and more camps are adding computers to their lists of activities. At the same time, additional camps are being set up that build their entire programs around the use of computers. All the other activities are the frosting on the cake, while computers make up the heart of the entire camp. Some camps are day camps, in which participants work during the day at camp and go home each evening. Others are boarding camps, complete with lodging facilities and food services.

The amount of time spent on computers versus the amount of time spent on other activities varies depending on the camp. In some day camps, the entire day is spent on computers. In some boarding camps, by comparison, computers may be used by a camper for only a couple of hours a day. The remainder of the day may then be devoted to more traditional activities such as baseball, boating, or swimming.

Just as the time spent on computer activities may vary, so may the ages of students attending the camps. Many camps are for younger students, frequently those who are in elementary school. Other camps concentrate on providing activities for teenagers. The amount of computer knowledge learned in camp also

varies tremendously. For many younger children, the use of prewritten programs is the primary computer activity. For others, beginning programming in the LOGO or BASIC languages may be introduced. For high school students, some camps (usually those sponsored by colleges or universities) challenge the participants to dig deeply into the subject of computers. After attending some of these camps, participants may have learned about the same amount as if they had enrolled in regular college courses in computers.

As an example of a computer camp, consider one operated by the University of North Carolina at Greensboro. There are several things the university wants students to learn at the camp. One of the main things is to make sure that kids have a knowledgeable and realistic view of what computers can do and what they cannot do. Another is that the students should learn to use a computer to perform useful work. A third thing students should learn is the effect computers have on society. The last thing students work on is to improve their understanding, reasoning, and problem-solving skills.

To help students learn these desired things, the university set up a program for elementary and high school students. The program is set up as a day camp, with students spending three hours each day for five days in a computer lab on the college campus. Several different camps are set up so that students can be grouped by grade level while they receive instruction in using computers. The fourth, fifth, and sixth graders are grouped together, and the seventh, eighth, and ninth graders are grouped together. Each of the groups of 27 to 30 students are handled by two teachers and four assistants. Students work together on the computers in groups of two to three students per computer.

On each topic studied during the camp, students are first given information. Then they go to the computers and experiment with the information they have learned. During this experimentation, they key in programs and run them, discovering what the computer can do in given circumstances. Following this discovery phase, they perform a problem-solving activity. In the problem-solving activity, each student develops a set of steps necessary to solve a problem. Usually the problem is one that can be worked on the computer, but non-computer problems are

also used to help stress the importance of communicating precisely. For example, students may be asked to write down the steps for making a peanut butter and jelly sandwich. The instructors would then follow the students' instructions in order to point out their weaknesses. For instance, an instructor may put on a big show banging on the top of the jelly jar when the instructions fail to mention opening the jar. Or the instructor may spread the peanut butter with a finger when no utensil is specified for the work. This kind of activity is both fun and worthwhile for developing an appreciation of the importance of being precise.

While the University of North Carolina's day camp provides only computer experiences, it is somewhat typical of many camps. As the number of computers in homes and schools grows, the number of camps devoted only to learning about computers will probably decrease. More and more, however, the old-style boarding camps will probably add computer activities to their schedules.

CHAPTER 2

The Computer and Society

Objectives

1. Describe the impact of the computer on society.
2. Describe the negative uses of the computer.
3. Describe the impact of the computer on privacy.

OMNIPRESENCE

The term **omnipresence** means the state of being present everywhere. Certainly, omnipresence is an appropriate term to use when describing the impact of the computer on society. We cannot turn on the television without seeing all types of computer advertisements. Newspapers and magazines are full of advertisements about computers as well as articles concerning computer use. You and your friends may talk about computer games and buying computers. Many communities offer special programs so that young people and adults can learn more about the computer. Most schools have computers that are available for students to use in some of their classes. Courses on computers are taught in many schools. The computer has become such a major part of our society that it is hard to imagine our lives without the influence of the computer. Figure 2.1 shows one example of the widespread use of computers.

FIGURE 2.1

A computer can be combined with specialized equipment, enabling it to time swim meets.

ARTIFICIAL INTELLIGENCE

Artificial intelligence is a term used in reference to the development of "thinking computers." **Artificial intelligence** describes a field of study in which people are attempting to develop computers that can be used for intelligence and imagination. Society has been thinking about such intelligent computers for some time. In the last 40 or 50 years, books, movies, and science fiction programs have featured computers that were smarter than the people who built them.

There are emotions and ways of thinking that the computer does not understand. Love and happiness are very much a part of being human. At this time, those emotions are not possible for the computer to understand.

The earliest form of study in artificial intelligence involved using the computer to solve puzzles and play chess. So far, artificial intelligence has not yet come close to reproducing human intelligence. Who can say what promise artificial intelligence offers? The study of artificial intelligence is limited only to the extent of the human imagination.

NATURAL LANGUAGE PROCESSORS

To communicate with the computer involves writing a series of instructions in special languages called **programming languages**. Although most of these programming languages use English words, there are specific rules to follow so that the computer can understand the instructions. These instructions look very different from the instructions you would give to a friend explaining how to perform a job. Yet in the future, the use of **natural language processors** may allow us to communicate with the computer just like we now communicate with another human being. A translation device in the computer will then be able to translate the natural language into machine language. This machine language is further discussed in Chapter 5. A typical natural language communication between the computer and a person could go something like this:

Person: I want to learn about a sport.

Computer: What sport would you like to learn about?

Person: Baseball.

Computer: What do you want to learn about baseball?

It is believed that by the end of the 1980s many computers will be able to use natural language processors to some extent, making it easier to learn to use the computer. Figure 2.2 shows one way of using natural language processors.

FIGURE 2.2

This computer is asking medical questions on the screen.

NEW TECHNOLOGIES

The term **technology** refers to applied science (a way of achieving a practical purpose). In the computer field, new technologies mean new uses for the computer. Some new uses of computer technology are in the office. Many office workers are using computers instead of typewriters. **Electronic mail** is a way of sending messages by computer system. This has affected the way many office workers communicate.

Teleconferencing

Another way that communication is being affected is in the area of teleconferencing. **Teleconferencing** is a way to hold business meetings without people leaving their offices. Persons holding a teleconference can see each other by way of television monitors and talk to each other by using the telephone. The use of teleconferencing actually improves productivity because it saves travel time and expenses. Figure 2.3 shows a teleconference in progress.

FIGURE 2.3

The use of teleconferencing improves productivity.

Telecommuting

Telecommuting is another trend made possible by the computer. **Telecommuting** is a term to describe the act of a worker using a computer at home to perform a job. Telecommuting capabilities allow workers the flexibility of working at home if they choose. Many workers feel they can be more productive by working at home without the types of interruptions found at the office. Telecommuting might not be for everyone, but it allows workers the freedom to choose where they want to work.

Computer Output Microfilm

Another new technology that many offices are using is **computer output microfilm** (COM). Instead of keeping large files in traditional file cabinets, many offices are storing recordings of the files on microfilm in order to save space. Figure 2.4 is a sample of how microfilm looks. These same offices then use another new technology to be able to retrieve those same records. **Computer-assisted retrieval** (CAR) is the technology that assists the office worker in finding the microfilmed records. These technologies have made office work much more efficient than when it was done without the computer.

FIGURE 2.4

Computer output microfilm is similar to the film shown above.

Robotics

Robotics is another current technology that is being used extensively in manufacturing. It deals with the construction and maintenance of robots. One of the most sophisticated robots available is the PUMA 500. It is a small robot that weighs 120 pounds and has an arm that can reach three feet. It actually looks like a giant arm more than it looks like the science fiction robots shown on television. PUMA 500 is used by General Motors on assembly lines to perform a variety of tasks like welding, painting, spraying, assembling parts, and other routine tasks. There are many other robots that are similar to PUMA 500. Figure 2.5 shows such a robot.

FIGURE 2.5

Robots are used widely in manufacturing.

Entertainment

It is predicted that because of new computer technology, the computer will become the entertainment center of the home. If you already play video games, you might say that it is already the entertainment center. But it is going to be able to provide a greater variety of family-type entertainment that is not available today.

The Cashless Society

Use of the new computer technology may result in what is called the **cashless society**. Such a term describes a society that does not require cash to buy and sell items. The technology is already available to have an instant cash transfer whenever a purchase is made. If you are making a purchase, your bank account code can simply be entered into the computer. Then the correct amount will be transferred from your bank account to the store's account where you are making your purchase.

Communications by Satellite

Other recent technology has been developed in the area of communications. Satellites will be used more extensively in space to aid in sending information from one place to another. With the use of satellites, many weather problems that in the past affected telephone lines will be avoided. Figure 2.6 shows a communication satellite.

Computer Size

Computers have been introduced that are so small they can be held in your hand. Some cost less than $300, yet they can perform the functions of larger computers. It certainly seems that new technology is making it easier and less expensive to use computers. Figure 2.7 shows a small portable computer.

NEGATIVE USES OF THE COMPUTER

You would probably not want to return to a society in which computers were not used in your everyday life. However,

FIGURE 2.6

The INTELSAT satellite was one of the first satellites to have ship-to-shore and shore-to-ship communications capabilities.

FIGURE 2.7

This small portable computer can easily be held on your lap.

there are some very real problems that have resulted from computer use.

Computer Crime

No one knows the extent of computer crime. However, you only need to read the newspapers to learn about the persons who get caught for illegal computer use. Figure 2.8 shows newspaper and magazine stories dealing with computer crime. Computer crime may involve changing computer records for personal gain, such as a student changing a course grade. Other criminals may use the computer to steal. For example, they may have merchandise shipped to a phony business at no charge, or they may add money to a bank account by transferring a few cents into it from each of thousands of other accounts. In addition, there are persons who damage computer systems or data. For instance, a

FIGURE 2.8

Computer crime is one of the negative uses of the computer.

programmer who gets mad at an employer may cause the computer to erase vital records from the system. There are also cases of what might be called "spying" by computer, where a criminal will "listen in" on data being transmitted from one business location to another. Fortunately, computer users have become more aware of the dangers of computer-related crimes and are beginning to take more steps to protect their computer systems and data.

Computer Ethics

Computer ethics refers to a code of conduct regarding the proper use of computers. Perhaps you cannot imagine committing a computer crime such as the ones just described. Even so, it is good to be aware of computer ethics. Have you ever copied video games that were copyrighted or not supposed to be copied? Have you looked at computer printouts that were private? It is very important for all individuals to develop a code of ethics that helps promote honesty in the use of computers.

Loss of Privacy

Many persons have a concern about the possible loss of privacy caused by computers. Information on millions of people is stored in thousands of computers across the country. Personal privacy begins to disappear whenever a person opens the first charge account or checking account, or with the first filing of an income tax return. Personal privacy is lost when businesses collect too much information about a person, as shown in Figure 2.9. Privacy is lost when that information is obtained by people who do not have the right or the need to have it.

The problem of privacy is even greater when incorrect information is passed on. Charge account billing errors, for example, can give persons bad credit ratings. Even after the billing errors have been corrected, the credit ratings may not be changed because of an oversight.

The idea of ethics is important in protecting the privacy of others. Just because information is available does not mean that it

FIGURE 2.9

Loss of privacy can be a result of computer use.

is right to give it to others. Many people are concerned that information will be given to the wrong people. Laws continue to be introduced to protect the privacy of individuals in this matter.

Our country was built on the idea of an individual's rights and freedom. It is the responsibility of everyone to make sure that the computer is used in such a way that rights and freedom are protected.

SUMMARY

The computer is here to stay. It is hard to imagine a day that is not influenced by the computer in some way. It is being used in artificial intelligence studies to try to develop "thinking computers." As yet, no computer can be programmed to use emotions, such as happiness and love, when making decisions. Many new technologies will further affect our lives in the office, in the community, and at home. Not all people believe these changes are good. Some people have used the computer to commit crimes. Many fear that there will be a loss of privacy because of the computer's capability to store large quantities of data.

REVIEW QUESTIONS

1. Why is the term *omnipresence* used in describing computer use? (Obj. 1)
2. What does artificial intelligence mean? (Obj. 1)
3. Describe the benefits of teleconferencing. (Obj. 1)
4. How are natural language processors used? (Obj. 1)
5. What is CAR? (Obj. 1)
6. Name one use of robotics discussed in this chapter. (Obj. 1)
7. What is meant by the term *cashless society*? (Obj. 1)
8. Discuss two ways that computer crimes are committed. (Obj. 2)
9. Why are computer ethics important? (Obj. 2)
10. Why are many people concerned that the computer will cause a loss of privacy? (Obj. 3)

VOCABULARY WORDS

The following terms were introduced in this chapter:

omnipresence
artificial intelligence
programming language
natural language
  processors
technology
electronic mail

teleconferencing
telecommuting
computer output microfilm
computer-assisted retrieval
robotics
cashless society
computer ethics

WORKBOOK EXERCISES

Complete all exercises in Chapter 2 of the workbook before proceeding to Chapter 3 in this text.

DISKETTE EXERCISE

Complete the diskette exercise for Chapter 2 before proceeding to Chapter 3 in this text.

Computers Down on the Farm

The computer is just as much at home on the farm as it is in an office downtown. Many of the uses of the computer are the same on the farm as in the downtown office, since farming is also a business. There is accounting work to do, as well as word processing, and these two functions are carried out using the usual kinds of computer software. The farmer also must do a tremendous amount of planning and forecasting. For example, possible income might be computed under different sets of circumstances. What if there is a drought resulting in a low yield, but the price of the product goes up because of the low yield? Or what if there is an excellent growing season, but the price goes down because every farmer has harvested a bumper crop? What

happens to profits if money for seeds, fertilizer, and fuel can be borrowed at a 1 percent lower rate? The answers to these kinds of questions can be explored by using one of the many computer programs available on the market.

The really interesting applications of computers in farming, however, are in those areas where there is no equivalent in the office. For example, on many dairy farms the computer has become what might be called a full-time worker. Such applications of the computer are becoming more and more common as those in the dairy industry realize the impact the computer can have on their operations. In these operations the cows have been deprived of their privacy, so to speak. Each cow has been equipped with a transponder. The transponder is a small radio transmitter that the cow wears around her neck.

Let's look in on a typical day at the farm. Various cows come to the feeding barn to eat. The catch is, some cows ought to eat more and some cows ought to eat less, based on how much

milk they are producing. With old, traditional dairy farming, each cow ate either as much as she wanted or as much as was in the feed trough, whichever came first. Now the computer calculates how much food each cow should have and lets the cow eat only that much. Now, you ask, how does the computer know which cow is which? Well, remember that transponder around the cow's neck? When the cow enters a feed station, the transponder radios the computer and tells it which cow is in the feed station. The computer then quickly looks up how much food that cow should get and slowly dispenses it, delivering the food no faster than the cow can eat it. This way, if the cow gets tired of eating and leaves the feed area, the transponder tells the computer of the exit, and the computer stops releasing food. No food is left over in the trough for some other cow to eat.

Before the computer was installed, dairy operators guessed at how much food should be given to the cows in total. There was certainly no way to control how much each individual cow ate. Since the cost of food might be 50 percent of a dairy operator's costs of producing milk, waste in feeding can eliminate profit very quickly. With the computer-controlled system, one dairy reports that after three months it was saving six pounds of grain per cow per day. Assuming a typical herd of 250 cows, that is 250 times 6 pounds times 365 days per year, for a total savings in grain of 547,500 pounds per year. Along with the savings in grain, milk production also increased. The computer can calculate this gain, which may average 10 pounds per cow per day, or 912,500 pounds of milk per year for a herd of 250 cows. Combine the grain savings with the increased production, and the computer has a very large effect on the amount of profit that can be made. Even when the cost of the computer system (about $140 per cow for a typical installation) is figured in, the figures still look good.

There are other advantages to the computerized operation. For example, the computer tells the operators when a cow is off her feed. When a cow fails to eat as much as she should, something is usually wrong. Therefore, each morning the computer prints out a "flag list" showing the identification of all cows that did not eat at least 62.5 percent of the expected amount. These cows are checked to see what is wrong. They may be sick, they

may be having trouble adjusting to being new in the herd, or they may have been prevented from eating by the other cows.

Another computer use is in the area of tracking milk production. Each cow must earn her keep by producing an expected quantity of milk. Cows that are not performing up to expectation in milk production are permanently "put out to pasture" earlier because of the detection ability of the computer. Previously, it might have been weeks before the operators realized a cow was not giving enough milk. Now the computer points out the problem immediately. Rather than continuing to feed a cow that is not producing much, the operator can now remove her from the herd promptly. The cow then becomes a meat producer instead of a milk producer.

Farming will never be the same now that computers are becoming commonplace. The use of computers helps improve the efficiency of farming and should help keep the cost of food from going up as much as otherwise would be the case.

CHAPTER 3

Jobs and the Computer

Objectives

1. Describe jobs which use the computer as a tool.

2. Describe various career opportunities in the computer industry.

3. Describe how the use of the computer has changed existing jobs.

The computer industry has created many new jobs while changing many others. Some manufacturing jobs and routine jobs no longer exist because they are now done by computers. Most people agree that the computer will change the way we do our jobs even if we do not choose a career in the computer industry. In this chapter, several careers in the computer field will be discussed, as well as the impact the computer has had on existing jobs.

PEOPLE WHO USE THE COMPUTER AS A TOOL

Many people who have jobs outside the computer industry now depend on the computer as a tool to perform their work. For example, many office workers use the computer to write letters or other types of documents. The computer makes it much easier to save these materials. Also, there is no need to rewrite or retype them every time changes need to be made. Jobs such as checking at the grocery stores have been made much simpler because of the use of the computer. Workers who once had to write a company's payroll with pens or pencils now use the computer as a tool in their jobs. Many advertising companies use the computer to keep track of mailing lists to send to customers. It is hard to think of many jobs that could not benefit from using the computer as a tool. Figure 3.1 shows a person using the computer to prepare a mailing list.

The manuscript for this book was prepared using a computer. Many authors have replaced their pens or pencils with the computer. Using the computer makes it easier and faster to write textbooks and also makes it easier to make any changes that might be needed.

PEOPLE WHO DESIGN COMPUTERS

An engineer designs and plans all of the parts needed to build the computer. Usually a design is first drawn on paper with detailed plans so that each computer part can be carefully assembled. Later, other workers will need to check a parts list produced by a computer before the actual manufacturing of the new com-

FIGURE 3.1

The computer can be used for many tasks, including the preparation of a mailing list.

puter begins. Figure 3.2 shows an engineer planning a computer design.

People who design computers usually have college degrees in engineering or computer science. Many have more advanced degrees to better prepare for this job. A person who designs computers must be very good at detail work, must enjoy working somewhat alone, and must be able to complete tasks within a given time limit. This career usually pays very well and such workers are currently in high demand. It is difficult to predict how great the demand for computer designers will be during the decade of the 1990s.

PEOPLE WHO MAKE COMPUTERS

There is another group of workers that manufacture and build computers. This work is similar to the work performed in other manufacturing companies. Figure 3.3 shows workers building a computer.

These workers assemble computer parts and actually build computers to be marketed. They can either make a specific item

FIGURE 3.2

Many engineers use computers to plan the designs of products.

FIGURE 3.3

These workers are hand-wiring a CRAY-1 computer system.

for the computer or assemble the parts to put the computer together. The people employed in the manufacturing of computers usually do not need college degrees. Technical or vocational training in high school would usually be adequate. Many of these workers are trained on the job. People who work in the manufacturing of computers must enjoy working with their hands.

PEOPLE WHO REPAIR COMPUTERS

People who repair computers have the job title of **computer service technician** or **customer engineer**. These workers are trained to replace parts and to check for problems in the operation of the computer. They are very much like mechanics who repair automobiles. Figure 3.4 shows a service technician repairing a computer. Demand for these workers is estimated to double during the 1980s. The increase in the number of computers has increased the need for workers trained to repair them. Many computer service technicians have a high

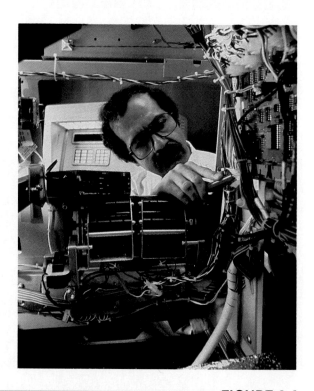

FIGURE 3.4

Service technicians repair computers.

school education only, and they are trained on the job to fix specific kinds of computers. However, employers prefer these employees to already have a general knowledge about computers. Such knowledge is usually obtained from technical schools or community college programs.

People who repair computers must enjoy working with their hands and troubleshooting (finding problems and fixing them). As new computers are designed and manufactured, these workers must have additional training to be able to repair the new machines.

PEOPLE WHO SELL COMPUTERS

Another career related to computers involves selling computer hardware and the supplies used with computers. **Hardware** is the physical equipment that makes up a computer system. Every computer manufacturer has salespeople that talk with potential customers about the features of the computer. To be successful as a computer salesperson, you must understand what the computer can do and what it cannot do. You must also understand what the customer wants. Figure 3.5 shows several computer salespersons demonstrating various features of microcomputers being sold.

To be successful as a computer salesperson, you need some technical knowledge and the ability to communicate with potential customers who may know very little about the computer. The benefits of such a job are an opportunity to learn about new computer products and to meet new people. The potential rewards are very high because there are many people interested in buying computers.

The educational background of computer salespeople varies. Many salespeople have only a high school education. However, if you are interested in such a career, some high school or college marketing courses would be helpful, as well as an educational background that includes some courses on computer technology.

PEOPLE WHO WRITE SOFTWARE

People who write **software** (instructions that tell the computer what to do) are called programmers. Programmers

FIGURE 3.5

Computer salespersons must know what the computer can do so that they can demonstrate the computer's various features.

write instructions, or programs, to the computer so that it is able to execute a task or operate properly. There are two types of programmers: systems and applications.

A **systems programmer** writes instructions that tell the computer how to operate. Instructions such as how to get words from the screen and how to put the words into the computer's files are necessary for the computer to operate. Systems programmers usually write their instructions to enable the computer to run other jobs. Figure 3.6 shows a programmer at work.

The other kind of programmer is called an **applications programmer**. These programmers write instructions to solve problems. For example, a program that would instruct the computer to add three numbers and calculate an average would be an applications program because it accomplishes a specific job. Also, a program to calculate the payroll for a business would be an applications program to solve a business job.

FIGURE 3.6

Programmers write instructions, or programs, to the computer
so that it is able to execute a task or operate properly.

A systems programmer usually has a computer science
degree from a college or university. Such a degree involves a
mathematical understanding of the functions of the computer.
The applications programmer usually has a business data processing degree that emphasizes an understanding of business. Both
types of programmers must also have an understanding of the
computer as well as an understanding of programming languages.

There has been a big demand for both types of programmers, but this demand is expected to level off during the 1980s.
There will, however, continue to be a need for programmers to
write new programs and fix other programs. The job of programmer can also help you move into other technical jobs in data
processing or data processing management.

A programming career requires an individual who enjoys
solving problems using the computer. If you are interested in a
career as a programmer, you must enjoy working alone, detail
work, and writing and testing programs.

PEOPLE WHO TRAIN COMPUTER USERS

With so many people using the computer, a relatively new career area is that of training computer users to operate the computer. Many companies have training departments to assist new users in learning to use the computer. The trainers must understand computer technology and enjoy teaching other people. For that reason, many companies hire former teachers or people with good communication skills. They then train these individuals in computer technology. Most companies also feel that people with educational and employment backgrounds similar to the users are better trainers.

The educational background needed varies in this area. If you enjoy teaching others and like working with computers, this might be a career field to consider. In Figure 3.7, a trainer is showing a new user how to operate the computer.

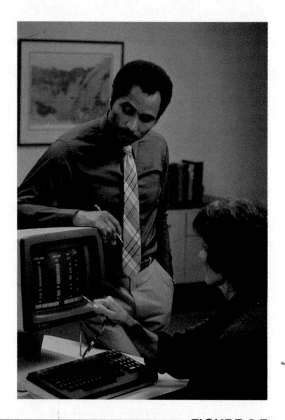

FIGURE 3.7

Trainers show computer users how to operate the computer.

PEOPLE WHO ARE
TECHNICAL WRITERS

Another recent career field in the computer industry is that of technical writing. A **technical writer** prepares written manuals to explain how to use the computer and how to run programs that may come with the computer. Since most people think computer manuals are difficult to read, technical writers are responsible for taking computer material and writing step-by-step instructions to make the material easier for users to understand. Many companies have hired workers with good writing skills and trained them to write computer manuals.

There is an increasing demand for people who possess writing skills. There is no specific educational background required for technical writing. However, if you are interested in such a career, take computer courses as well as English courses so that you may better qualify for these jobs.

HOW THE COMPUTER HAS
CHANGED EXISTING JOBS

The tremendous increase in the number of computers has definitely caused changes within the employment market. Certain jobs in factories have changed because of the computer. Some factories have replaced workers with robots. Certain jobs on assembly lines can now be done by computer, and assembly workers are no longer needed for these jobs. This worries many people. Some are concerned that the computer will completely replace the individual worker. However, many factories have given workers an opportunity to learn new skills and perform more interesting jobs.

CAREERS AND THE FUTURE

It is very hard to plan a career in the computer field. Changes occur so rapidly that it is difficult to predict what new job opportunities will be available when you are ready to enter the work force. The most important factor at this time is that you are aware that there are many career opportunities in the computer field.

SUMMARY

The computer has definitely changed the work force. Many people who do not directly work in the computer industry use the computer as a tool in their present jobs. There are many other people who are directly involved in designing, manufacturing, repairing, and selling computers. Programmers write instructions to tell the computer how to operate and how to perform specific tasks. Systems programmers usually have computer science backgrounds, while applications programmers usually have business data processing backgrounds. The use of the computer has also created other positions to help users run the computer. Two examples of such careers are computer training and technical writing. It is hard to predict what the job market will be in the future. However, it is safe to say that there will be many jobs involving the use of computers.

REVIEW QUESTIONS

1. Describe a job that uses the computer as a tool. (Obj. 1)

2. Discuss two of the newer careers in the computer industry related to working with users of computers. (Obj. 2)

3. What educational background might a worker who designs computers have? (Obj. 2)

4. Describe a job in the computer industry that requires only a high school education. (Obj. 2)

5. In what career in the computer field is the demand for trained workers expected to double in the next few years? (Obj. 2)

6. What are the job skills required in selling computers and computer-related supplies? (Obj. 2)

7. Discuss the job duties of an applications programmer. (Obj. 2)

8. Compare the educational backgrounds of an applications programmer and a systems programmer. (Obj. 2)

9. What job skills are very important for people who train computer users? (Obj. 2)

10. Discuss one job that has changed because of the computer. (Obj. 3)

VOCABULARY WORDS

The following terms were introduced in this chapter:

computer service	software
technician	systems programmer
customer engineer	applications programmer
hardware	technical writer

WORKBOOK EXERCISES

Complete all exercises in Chapter 3 of the workbook before proceeding to Chapter 4 in this text.

DISKETTE EXERCISE

Complete the diskette exercise for Chapter 3 before proceeding to Chapter 4 in this text.

Computers Aid in Creating Cars

The creation of a car is not what it used to be. In the good old days, automotive stylists worked on the design of a new car. They concentrated on being creative and coming up with something different. They drew rough sketches of each design idea on paper. Every change in an idea required a new sketch. Eventually, the designs resembled what the stylists were after. Then drafters produced finished drawings of the designs. These drawings, requiring long hours of work to complete, included every minute detail of each design. Hundreds of hours might be consumed just drawing exactly the right shape for a bar in the grill of the proposed automobile.

Hand-powered drafting, though, was not the end of a process requiring tremendous amounts of labor. Once the detailed drawings were finished, model makers went to work carving models of the designs from lumps of clay. To save labor, one side of a model might be one design, while the opposite side might be a different design. Many times, the first models created were done to small scale. For designs still surviving after the evaluation of the small-scale models, full-sized models were frequently carved. These activities consumed thousands of hours of work.

Not unlike the designers and model makers, engineers also worked manually to design the working parts of the car. New body designs might require changes in the chassis, and the engineer's job was to design those changes. Working with slide rules (old-fashioned computational devices), intuition, and guesswork as engine and chassis details were tackled, the engineer trudged onward, making sure the car would function once it was assembled. Nobody ever heard of a drag coefficient or wind tunnel

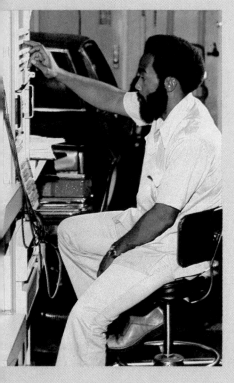

testing (tests for wind resistance). In the days of less expensive gasoline, it wasn't very important whether a car cut smoothly through the air.

In contrast, take a look at the way a car is designed now. The stylist creates a design on a computer display. With simple commands, the drawing on the screen can be turned for viewing from any angle. Selected dimensions can be changed, immediately changing the appearance of the design on the screen. If, for example, the stylist chooses to reduce the height of the car, the change will be made immediately. In this manner, the stylist can create a visually pleasing design and have the computer calculate interior and exterior dimensions of the vehicle. Since smooth designs that cut easily through the air are necessary in today's world, the computer can simulate the amount of wind resistance that will be encountered by the designer's latest scheme. Either large or small changes may be made to improve the aerodynamic performance of the vehicle. This is done mathematically, with no physical creation of any kind. Any required drawings can be produced immediately by plotters attached to the computer system, doing in a few moments what previously required hundreds of hours.

Computer calculations can be made to determine whether a proposed method of constructing the automobile will be strong enough to withstand the wear and tear of years of day-to-day use. Instead of using slide rules, engineers now use computers to help them determine what the performance of engine and drive train components will be. Computers help determine how strong the springs should be, for example, or how thick the roll bar should be to produce the desired handling characteristics for the automobile.

If models of the design are produced, computer-controlled tools can help produce each model directly from the design stored in the computer. As in the olden days, many special tools and dies must be created to help produce the vehicle. Dies are molds which must be created to stamp the metal parts into the correct shapes. In this work as in so many other jobs, though, the computer now plays a major role. Computer-controlled machines can take the computer-stored designs of different parts of the vehicle and help design the necessary tools and dies.

Under CAD/CAM, which stands for computer aided-design/computer-aided manufacturing, the computer performs two major functions. It aids in the design of the tools and dies, and then controls the milling machines and other equipment used to produce the tools and dies. Then, when all the special tools and equipment are in place and the vehicles are rolling down the assembly line, computers come into play again. Those uses of the computer will be the subject at the end of a later chapter.

In summary, the use of computers helps stylists and engineers design safer, more economical, higher quality vehicles. The vehicles can be designed in less time and with less labor. Also, the use of the computer in designing vehicles helps hold down the price increases by making the manufacturing process as efficient as possible, with little wasted material. This helps make cars more affordable to their buyers.

PART 2
Framework of a Computer System

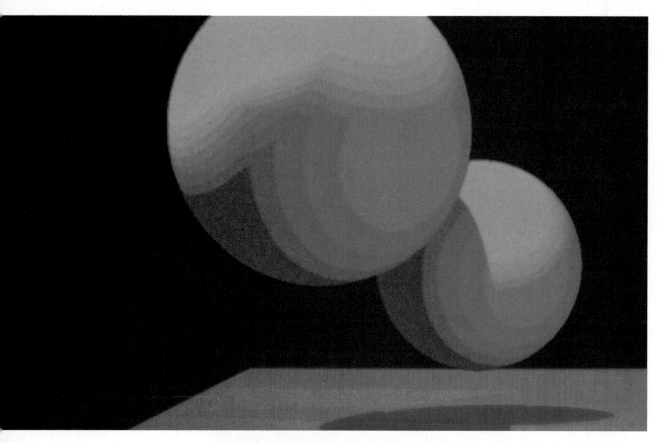

CHAPTER 4

The Computer System–How It Works

Objectives

1. Identify and describe the components of a working computer system.

2. Describe the roles of input, processing, and output in an information system.

THE WORKING COMPUTER SYSTEM

Our society has many complex devices, such as cars, calculators, and televisions, that we use every day without actually knowing how they work. The computer can be used in just that way. But if you understand the parts of the computer and their functions, your understanding will assist you in controlling the operations of the computer in a more effective manner.

A working computer system consists of hardware (equipment), software (instructions that tell the computer what to do), and **data** (information that is processed by the computer system). These different parts of the computer that work together are called **components** of the computer system. To understand how these components fit together into a working computer system is very important. Figure 4.1 is a diagram of a working computer system. It will be expanded in future chapters as we learn more about the different components that make up a computer system.

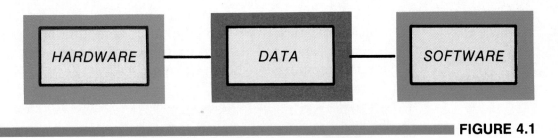

FIGURE 4.1

Diagram of a working computer system.

HARDWARE OF COMPUTER SYSTEMS

In this section, we are going to learn about the hardware of a computer system. Today we hear a great deal about the equipment that makes up a computer system. All of the names that are used to describe the hardware of the computer fit into one of four categories as shown in the illustration in Figure 4.2. This section describes the four main categories of hardware. These are (1) input devices, (2) processor, (3) auxiliary storage devices, and (4) output devices.

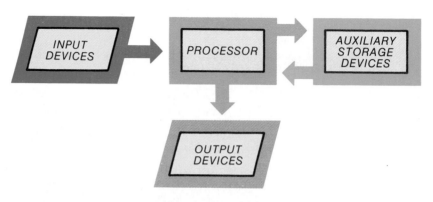

FIGURE 4.2

The four main categories of hardware.

Different Kinds of Computers

Computers come in a wide range of capabilities and speeds. Years ago, all computers were large in size and were called **mainframe** computers. An example of a mainframe is shown in Figure 4.3.

A smaller, less powerful computer was later invented and called a **minicomputer**. Then the "computer on a chip" was invented and called the **microcomputer**. Examples of microcomputers are shown in Figure 4.4.

FIGURE 4.3

Mainframe computers are large in size.

FIGURE 4.4

Microcomputers are much smaller than mainframes.

The problem with these names, all based on the physical size of the computer, is that microcomputers have become more powerful than minicomputers used to be, and minicomputers have become more powerful than many mainframes used to be. All three categories of machines have become smaller in size. To add to the confusion, a very fast and powerful computer known as a **supercomputer** was created. Figure 4.5 shows an example of a very small microcomputer.

FIGURE 4.5

This portable computer is a very small microcomputer.

The following is a detailed look at the hardware of computer systems, as well as the steps in information processing.

Input Devices

All computers have one or more input devices. An **input device** receives data and feeds it to the processor. Commonly used input devices include keyboards such as the one in Figure 4.6. A **keyboard** sends data to the processor each time a key is struck. An **optical scanner** sends data to the processor as it "looks at" data in printed or written form. An optical scanner is shown in Figure 4.7. Several input devices will be discussed in detail in Chapter 6.

FIGURE 4.6

The keyboard is a commonly used input device.

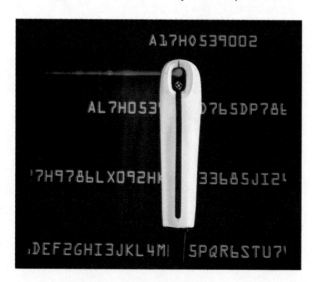

FIGURE 4.7

Optical scanners relay data to the computer.

Processing

There are two main parts involved in the processing of data. These are the processor and memory. Although the computer does not have memory in the same way we think of human memory, it has locations in which to place data while the data is being processed. The two main parts of memory will be discussed in more detail later in this section.

Processors

All computers do processing by following a series of instructions in a program. The computer system unit that receives and carries out these instructions is the **processor**. All computer systems, regardless of size or manufacturer, have processors (also referred to as central processing units or CPUs). The processor performs many different functions. It receives and temporarily stores instructions as well as the data to be processed. It moves and changes stored data. It does arithmetic calculations. It makes decisions of logic, such as determining if two numbers are equal. It directs the action of the input and output devices. Therefore, the processor may be defined as that part of a computer system that receives and stores instructions and data, performs arithmetic and logic operations, and directs the actions of the input and output devices.

The processor shown in Figure 4.8 is a **microprocessor**. All of the processing circuits are contained in one piece known as an integrated circuit. The term **integrated circuit** (IC) refers to any electronic "chip" that contains large numbers of electronic components. The chip is a small piece of material that is used for memory and other applications in a computer. All small computers and many larger computers use microprocessors. Some supercomputers are made from many microprocessors working together.

The different functions of the processor are regulated by a clock. The idea of the clock is somewhat similar to installing a pacemaker in a human; pulses from the pacemaker keep the human heart beating in the proper rhythm. In the same way, the clock pulses keep the processor functioning in the proper rhythm. Within the processor, these pulses are called electronic impulses. Typical clock speeds for microprocessors are 5 megahertz and 8 megahertz. A **megahertz** is a million cycles,

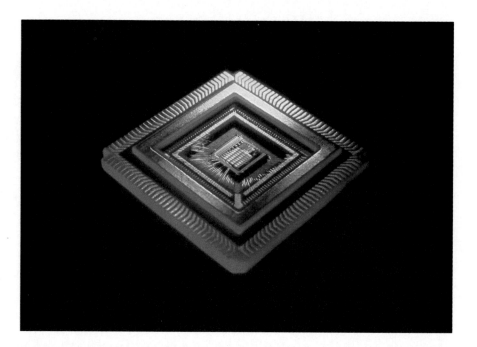

FIGURE 4.8

Microprocessors contain all of the circuits in one piece known as an integrated circuit.

or pulses, per second. The fact that a particular processor may be running at a clock speed of five million cycles per second does not mean it can do five million arithmetic calculations per second. Many processing operations require more than one clock cycle to be performed.

Memory

The instructions being processed by a computer do not all remain in the processor. Most of the time, they are stored in locations known as **memory**. Memory may also be referred to as main memory or **main storage**. From there, each instruction is copied into the processor and carried out. The data being processed is not loaded into the processor all at once. It, too, spends most of its time in memory, being moved into the processor when necessary for processing. The processed data is then returned to memory for further use or output.

The memory of a computer is made from electronic circuits that, like the processor, are contained on integrated circuit chips. Figure 4.9 shows such a chip. Memory can accept, hold,

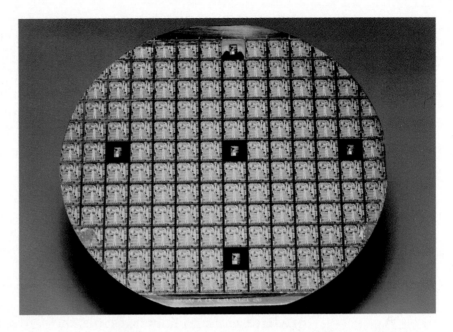

FIGURE 4.9

This wafer will produce over one hundred memory integrated circuit chips.

and release data, as well as the instructions for processing the data. Data and instructions are stored as electronic impulses in specific locations in memory. You can imagine memory as being like a large number of mailboxes, each box being labeled with a number. This number is known as a **numeric address**. Any desired "mail" (data) may be placed in specified locations.

There are two main types of memory used by computer systems. These are called random-access memory and read-only memory.

RAM   **Random-access memory** (RAM) is used as a temporary location in memory while processing is taking place. This type of memory is erased when the computer is powered down (turned off). In other words, all the information in RAM is erased when the computer is turned off. Rapid progress has been made in placing more storage locations onto one RAM circuit chip. Chips that can hold the equivalent of over 32,000 characters were introduced in 1983. Chips capable of holding over 128,000 characters are now being produced.

ROM   **Read-only memory** (ROM) does not lose its data when the power is turned off. Therefore, it is frequently used to store instructions necessary for getting the computer started when it is powered up (turned on). The term read-only memory is appropriate since the computer can only read data from a ROM chip; it cannot write or store data in the chip. With ROM, the data or instructions contained in a memory chip are placed there (programmed) during the manufacturing process. Once the data is in, it cannot be changed. The amount of data that can be stored in one ROM memory chip varies depending on the type of chip.

Auxiliary Storage

Nearly all general-purpose computers include the ability to connect to additional storage devices that hold data outside the memory of the computer. These additional storage devices are known as **auxiliary storage**. Auxiliary storage devices are **on-line** to the computer; that is, they are connected directly to the computer. They are, therefore, under the control of the processor and can be used at all times. Figure 4.10 shows a **disk drive**, the most common form of auxiliary storage. The disk drive records data in a method similar to that used by a cassette tape recorder.

Auxiliary storage is used to hold computer programs so they may be read into the computer's random-access memory when they are needed. Large amounts of data may also be stored on

FIGURE 4.10

Disk drives are the most common form of auxiliary storage.

auxiliary storage. Remember from an earlier section that data stored in RAM is temporary. Therefore, any data that needs to be kept for future use is usually recorded on a magnetic disk before the computer is powered down. Chapter 8 will explain in detail the operation and use of auxiliary storage.

Output Devices

Just as a computer system must have at least one input device, it must also have at least one output device. An output device records, prints, or displays information in usable form. The most common output devices are the **video display**, commonly known as a **monitor**, and the **printer**. Monitors display output on televisionlike screens. Printers produce output in the form of written characters on paper. Figure 4.11 shows a monitor, while Figure 4.12 shows a printer. Output devices will be discussed in detail in Chapter 7.

FIGURE 4.11

Monitors display output on televisionlike screens.

FIGURE 4.12

Output can be produced on paper by using a printing device.

INFORMATION PROCESSING

The job of putting data into usable form is called **information processing**. A **system** is simply a group of devices and procedures for performing a task. Therefore, a system that processes data is called an **information system**. In an information system, data is created or collected and fed into the system. Data that enters the system is known as **input**. Useful information leaves the system as **output**; that is, processed information. In between the input and output, the data is processed. **Processing** consists of steps set up to make sure everything that should be done to the data is completed.

Input

What is the origin of the data that is input into information systems? It comes from many sources. Information about students in a school, for example, comes from registration, grade reports, and similar sources. Data regarding hours worked by an employee is taken from forms or time cards. Information on test scores is obtained from graded tests. The data to be processed is referred to as **raw data** or **original data**. If raw data is first written on forms, the forms are known as **source documents**. Figure 4.13 shows an example of a source document. Many applications do not use source documents, however; the data is input directly to the computer. Frequently part of the input is data that has been collected and processed in an earlier period.

FIGURE 4.13

A computer in a bank would view this check as a source document.

Processing

Once data has been input, it must be processed. Processing includes such things as doing arithmetic, making comparisons, and putting data into the desired order. Computers follow processing steps in much the same way that the human mind does. For both, each step leading to the desired result must be included in the processing plan, and these steps must be in logical order. When steps are left out or when steps are out of order, the computer will not produce the desired result. When the same is true of people, wrong answers are also given and wrong decisions are made.

Output

Once the processing of data is finished, output takes place. Output is the process of storing the information or showing it to a user. If stored, the information is available whenever needed. In either case, the information is ready for the user.

There is nothing unusual about the cycle of input, processing, and output. You have used it many times in making purchasing decisions or writing term papers. In making a purchasing decision, you collect information about a product and its prices in various stores. This is the input stage, which passes the data along to your brain. Your brain processes the data and decides at which store you should make your purchase. When you go to the store and purchase the item, you complete the output phase of the cycle. These steps are shown in Figure 4.14. Similarly, in writing a paper, you first decide on the subject and consider an outline of the kinds of things you want to say about the subject. You collect many facts from reading, from interviews, and from expert opinions. These facts are the input. Then you put the facts in the order you want them in your paper, which is the start of processing. The processing plan also includes writing a first draft, checking the first draft for accuracy and good English skills, and making corrections. The finished paper is the output of the system.

The steps of input, processing, and output are necessary in an information system. Regardless of the kind of information being produced, or whether the system is manual or computerized, the processing of data uses these three functions. Data enters the processing system, various operations are done on the data to convert it to useful information, and the useful information leaves the system. Names of students are facts. Arranging the names in alphabetic order so a certain name can be found quickly is a form of information processing. Recording test scores made by students, preparing bills for customers, and classifying the kinds of jobs obtained by high school graduates are other examples of information processing.

FIGURE 4.14a

This is Fred. He is collecting information about a sweater he would like to buy (INPUT).

FIGURE 4.14b

Now Fred is checking out similar sweaters and prices at a different store (ADDITIONAL INPUT).

FIGURE 4.14c

Fred is comparing prices and quality of different sweaters in his mind (PROCESSING).

FIGURE 4.14d

Fred now returns to the original store to buy the original sweater (OUTPUT).

A WORKING COMPUTER SYSTEM

The outline of a working computer system has been expanded below to include the information covered in this chapter. Figure 4.15 shows the details in this chapter categorized under the correct component: hardware, software, and data.

A WORKING COMPUTER SYSTEM

I. HARDWARE

    A. Input devices

    B. Processing
       1. Processor
       2. Memory (RAM and ROM)

    C. Output devices

    D. Auxiliary storage

II. DATA

III. SOFTWARE

FIGURE 4.15

Outline of a working computer system with emphasis placed on the hardware component.

SUMMARY

A computer system consists of hardware, software (programs), and data. The hardware is made up of input devices, the processor, output devices, and auxiliary storage devices. These parts are common to all computers, from hand-held units to extra fast supercomputers.

The purpose of a computer system is to process raw data, converting it into useful information. The information processing cycle includes the steps of input, processing, and output. These steps are the same whether the processing is being done manually or with the aid of a computer.

REVIEW QUESTIONS

1. Name the three main components in a computer system. (Obj. 1)

2. What is the function of an input device? Name two commonly used input devices. (Obj. 1)

3. What is the function of the processor? (Obj. 1)

4. What is the function of memory? (Obj. 1)

5. What is the function of auxiliary storage? Name a commonly used auxiliary storage device. (Obj. 1)

6. What is the function of an output device? Name two commonly used output devices. (Obj. 1)

7. What are the two types of memory? How do they differ? (Obj. 1)

8. How is a source document used? (Obj. 2)

9. What is raw data? (Obj. 2)

10. Name and describe each of the steps in the information processing cycle. (Obj. 2)

VOCABULARY WORDS

The following terms were introduced in this chapter:

data	random-access memory
components	read-only memory
software	auxiliary storage
mainframe	on-line
minicomputer	disk drive
microcomputer	video display
supercomputer	monitor
input device	printer
keyboard	information processing
optical scanner	system
processor	information system
microprocessor	input
integrated circuit	output
megahertz	processing
memory	raw data
main storage	original data
numeric address	source document

WORKBOOK EXERCISES

Complete all exercises in Chapter 4 of the workbook before proceeding to Chapter 5 in this text.

DISKETTE EXERCISE

Complete the diskette exercise for Chapter 4 before proceeding to Chapter 5 in this text.

Building a Computer Adds Insight

Building your own computer can add a lot of insight into how computers work. It can also help you figure out what is wrong if your computer breaks down. There are two ways in which you can build a computer. The first is to build it from circuit designs you can find in various magazines. If you take this route, you must find and purchase all the different parts required. The second, and far easier, method is to build a computer from a kit. The most popular kits are versions of commercially available microcomputers. When one of these is assembled, you are assured of being able to find an adequate amount of software to use with the computer once it is finished. Given the advantages of building a computer from a kit rather than

building one from scratch, let's take a look at how a typical computer might be put together from a kit.

After buying the kit in a huge pasteboard box, you rush home from the store. Arriving home, you open the box only to find several smaller boxes inside. Opening the boxes, you find several completed electronic circuit boards. Upon seeing the boards, you decide that there's not much to put together, so it will be very easy. But you've not yet noticed the quantity of other parts in the boxes. There are hundreds of small electronic parts, nuts, bolts, screws, wires, and so forth.

Your first step is to find all the parts and check them off against the parts list to make sure you have everything. If you

don't know what the different parts look like, don't be too concerned, for the manual shows you detailed drawings of every part. You will probably find this step of the kit-building process a lot easier if you put the small parts into a muffin tin or other organizer-type container. If any parts are missing, return to the store and get replacement parts for the missing ones. If you've never soldered electronic parts together, you'll need to learn how to do that first. To make this possible, the kit includes complete instructions for you to follow as you practice the technique. If you proceed with the computer's assembly and do a poor job of soldering, the kit will not work. Once you have mastered the soldering, you are ready to begin assembly.

Carefully follow each step in the instruction manual one at a time. When you finish each step, check it off in the manual. Work carefully and make sure you do each step correctly. You will find that many of the steps are mechanical in nature. That is, they involve fastening pieces of hardware together. Most of the more complex and sensitive electronic circuitry has already been factory assembled for you. For example, the circuit board containing the actual microprocessor chip of the computer may already be assembled. Likewise, the circuit card designed to control the disk drives may already be assembled.

Having the more complex circuit cards already put together and tested has a couple of big advantages to the kit builder. The first advantage is that the kit builder knows the cards will work; assembly and adjustment of these cards is somewhat difficult when done at home. The second advantage is that the kit builder is not required to have the instruments that would be necessary to calibrate (adjust) some of the circuits. In fact, the only electronic measuring instrument the kit builder needs is a simple VOM (volt ohm meter). This meter is used at various points during the assembly process to ensure that voltages and resistances are correct. When the instructions say to test the unit in some way, make sure the test comes out right. If it does not, fix whatever is wrong before continuing to the next step. Continuing with assembly when a test does not come out right can result in ruining some of the parts of the computer. There is a reasonably large amount of mechanical assembly as well as electronic wiring, so methodically plow your way through.

The most exciting part of building the whole kit is when you turn on the power at the end of assembly and expect the thing to work. Usually it will, and you will have the thrill of having created a complex electronic device. If it does not work, you have three options. First, try to figure out for yourself why it doesn't work. Second, have a friend who is very knowledgeable about computers try to figure it out. Or, third, return the computer to the dealer where you bought the kit and let the dealer's service department figure out why it won't work.

Once your computer is complete, you will have a unit just as capable as a factory-assembled unit. In addition, you will know a lot about how it works. The manuals explain the theory of its operation, and you will know firsthand how the parts went together. Depending on pricing at the time you buy your kit, you might even save some money over the cost of a factory-assembled unit. For many people, putting a computer together is a very exciting and valuable activity.

CHAPTER 5

Data: Information for the Computer

Objectives

1. Define character, field, record, and file.
2. Describe memory locations inside the computer.
3. Describe how data is stored in memory.

In Chapter 4, the hardware of the computer system was discussed. It was also learned that the main purpose of a computer system is to process data into useful information. This chapter explores in more detail how data is defined and stored in memory locations for processing.

DATA CATEGORIES

A **character** is the smallest element of data processed by a computer system. A character is any letter of the alphabet, a number, or any special character such as a dollar sign ($) or a percent sign (%). Figure 5.1 shows examples of an alphabetic, a numeric, and a special character.

Alphabetic Character	A
Numeric Character	5
Special Character	%

FIGURE 5.1

Examples of an alphabetic, numeric, and special character.

Data Fields

Characters are often grouped together into an individual item of data known as a **field**. Usually data fields contain several characters that make up words. A person's name is a field. A person's street address is another field. Examples of two data fields are shown in Figure 5.2.

Records

Suppose that we have the following fields of data about a person: name, street address, city, state, ZIP code, and telephone

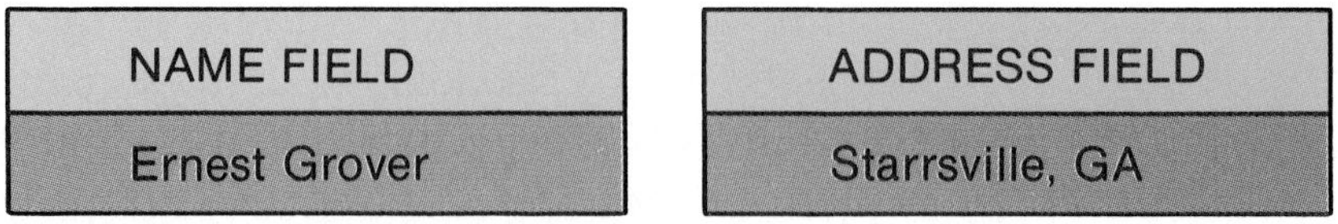

NAME FIELD		ADDRESS FIELD
Ernest Grover		Starrsville, GA

FIGURE 5.2

Two different fields.

number. The information about one person may be written on a card as shown in Figure 5.3. When grouped this way, the data becomes a record. A **record** can be defined as a group of related fields. Therefore, all the fields of data about Ernest Grover make up one record.

```
Ernest Grover
1057 Bramblegate Drive
Starrsville, GA   30209-6428
(912) 379-5443
```

FIGURE 5.3

The related fields on this card make up one record.

Files

A **file** is a collection of related records treated as a unit. An example of a file might be students' records. A teacher often has a file for the students in a class. The records of all students enrolled in one class would be found in that particular file. On each record, there might be fields that would contain a student's name, test grades, and possibly grades from daily assignments. Another example is a group of cards containing customer names and addresses. They may be grouped into a file as shown in Figure 5.4. Note that the file is made up of two or more records. Note, also, that all of the records contain the same kinds of data. Each record contains a customer's name, address, and telephone number.

When a file is processed, one or more records may be placed in RAM at a time. Therefore, each record in a file must be distinguished in some way from all other records in the same file. This is a necessary requirement in processing records. In Figure 5.4, you will note that each record can be identified by the customer's

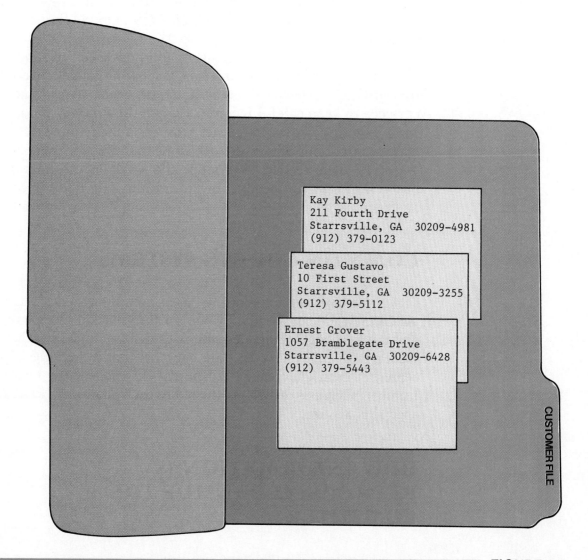

Kay Kirby
211 Fourth Drive
Starrsville, GA 30209-4981
(912) 379-0123

Teresa Gustavo
10 First Street
Starrsville, GA 30209-3255
(912) 379-5112

Ernest Grover
1057 Bramblegate Drive
Starrsville, GA 30209-6428
(912) 379-5443

CUSTOMER FILE

FIGURE 5.4

A customer file where each record contains the same kind of data.

name. The data in these fields is different on each record. A name or number is used to identify each record to the computer. This identifying name or number is used to find a specific record.

The primary goal in information processing is to create and use records. Records take the guesswork out of decision making. Because incorrect decisions can ruin a business, it is very important that correct records be ready when and where they are needed.

For example, a florist must know how many flowers and plants will be needed during the year. If too many are ordered, the florist loses money. If too few are stocked, business is lost. Last year's files on purchases and sales will help the florist make decisions.

An insurance company needs to know when to send out notices (bills) to its policyholders. A teacher needs to know what final grades have been earned by students in each class. A taxpayer needs to keep careful records of how much money he or she earns and how it is spent. In these cases and many more, records play an important role in the decisions that must be made.

The data needed to produce the kinds of information a business or a person needs is organized into data fields, records, and files.

COMMON CODING SYSTEMS

The two most commonly used computer codes are the **ASCII** (American Standard Code for Information Interchange) and the **EBCDIC** (Extended Binary Coded Decimal Interchange Code). Both codes serve the same purpose, but the numbers that represent each character are different. In each of the codes, a number, such as 8 or 124, is assigned to each character, digit, and special character.

HOW INFORMATION IS REPRESENTED INSIDE THE COMPUTER

To help you understand how the computer works, imagine that each character is represented inside the computer by a series of electronic switches. In many ways, these electronic switches can be compared to the light switches in our homes. A light switch can be in only one of two states: on or off. The circuits inside the computer can be thought of in much the same way as the light switches. The electronic switches can be either on or off. Since on and off represent only two conditions, it is impossible to directly store numbers and letters, such as ASCII code 65. Instead, they are converted into **binary numbers**. Binary means consisting of two things, so a binary number is made by using only two digits, 0 and 1. The binary number system is the only coding system the computer actually understands.

Imagine eight on/off switches grouped inside the computer. These eight switches can store one character. By turning various switches on and off, there are 256 different combinations possible. These eight switches are known as a **byte**. Each switch is an on or off condition (a 1 or 0) known as a **bit**. Eight bits make a byte. It takes one byte to store one character of data. In the binary number system, there can be as many 0's and 1's as needed within the eight switches to represent a particular number. Each 0 can be thought of as representing a switch that is turned off, while each 1 represents a switch that is turned on.

Each time a key on a keyboard is struck (Figure 5.5), the ASCII or EBCDIC code number for that key is generated and

FIGURE 5.5

Each time a key on a keyboard is struck, the ASCII or EBCDIC code number for that key is generated and converted into a binary number which is input into the computer.

converted into a binary number which is input into the computer. Inside the computer, the binary number is stored in a memory chip as in Figure 5.6. When output is to be produced, the code number of each character is sent to the output device, such as the printer in Figure 5.7. In addition to ASCII or EBCDIC code numbers for all the visible characters, there are also numbers for various control functions, such as tabulating and backspacing. Regardless of the coding system being used on any computer system, data is represented inside the computer by the use of binary numbers.

FIGURE 5.6

Binary numbers are stored in memory chips.

FIGURE 5.7

When output is to be produced, the code number of each character is sent to the output device which converts it into a readable character.

THE PROCESSING OF DATA

We have discussed the categories of data: character, field, record and file. We have also discussed the way data is represented in memory. Let us now look at the processing that would take place in the computer system if we wanted to process the customer file with the records that were previously illustrated in Figure 5.4.

A diagram of the computer system that was discussed in Chapter 4 is shown in Figure 5.8. We have now learned that the processor and memory (both ROM and RAM) are made up of electronic circuits that represent information by turning switches off and on. Eight switches or bits make up a byte. Each byte can store one character of data.

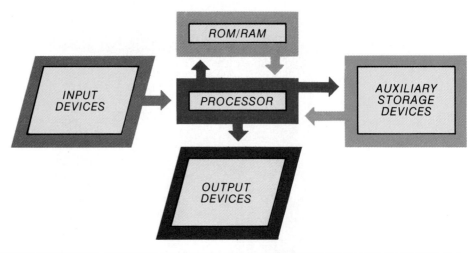

FIGURE 5.8

Diagram of a computer system showing the addition of memory.

If we were to key in the name *Ernest Grover*, it would take thirteen bytes to store the name in RAM as shown in Figure 5.9. The space between the first and last name would require one byte, and the twelve letters of the name would require twelve bytes.

Even though in this example we see the actual letter in a byte, there would actually be a code (either ASCII or EBCDIC) that would store the letters in numeric form. These codes can be learned and many programmers use them in their work. For our purposes, it is enough to understand that there is a coding system and that each character takes a byte of RAM memory.

Computer manufacturers express the capacity of memory in terms of the letter *K. K* is short for **kilobyte**, which means 1024 bytes of computer memory. Many times you hear a computer owner say his or her computer has 64K of memory. This means that the computer has approximately 64,000 bytes of memory and has the capacity to store up to 64,000 characters during processing. Figure 5.10 shows such a computer.

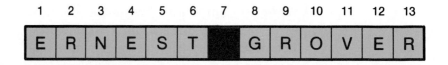

FIGURE 5.9

This name requires the use of thirteen bytes of memory.

FIGURE 5.10

This computer can store 64K of memory during processing.

A WORKING COMPUTER SYSTEM

As we present additional information, it is important to remember which computer component is being discussed: hardware, software, or data. This chapter discussed the data component. Figure 5.11 adds the information about data to the outline of the working computer system.

A WORKING COMPUTER SYSTEM

I. HARDWARE

   A. Input devices

   B. Processing
      1. Processor
      2. Memory (RAM and ROM)

   C. Output devices

   D. Auxiliary storage

FIGURE 5.11a

Partial outline for a working computer system.

II. DATA

    A. Categories
        1. Character
        2. Field
        3. Record
        4. File

    B. Common coding systems
        1. ASCII
        2. EBCDIC

III. SOFTWARE

FIGURE 5.11b

Continuation of outline for a working computer system with emphasis placed on the data component.

SUMMARY

This chapter explores how data is defined and placed in memory for processing by the computer. Four categories of data are defined. The smallest data element is a character. Characters are combined to make fields. Examples of data fields would be name and address fields. Data fields can hold information about an individual. All the fields about one person make up a record. Several records make up a file. These categories make it possible for the computer to process data.

A character of data is stored in a byte. A byte is made up of eight bits, which are actually on and off conditions inside the computer. Each on and off condition is represented by a 1 or a 0 in the binary number system. By combining various on and off conditions, 256 different combinations are possible. Two common computer codes are the ASCII and EBCDIC codes.

REVIEW QUESTIONS

1. What is a character? Give an example of an alphabetic character and an example of a numeric character. (Obj. 1)
2. What is a field? (Obj. 1)
3. What is a record? (Obj. 1)
4. What is a file? (Obj. 1)
5. Give an example of two files that might be processed in a business. (Obj. 1)
6. What is a byte? (Obj. 2)
7. How many bits does it take to represent one character of data? (Obj. 2)
8. How many switches make up a bit? (Obj. 2)
9. What are two commonly used computer codes? (Obj. 2)
10. What does it mean when a computer system has 64K of memory? (Obj. 3)

VOCABULARY WORDS

The following terms were introduced in this chapter:

character	EBCDIC
field	binary number
record	byte
file	bit
ASCII	kilobyte

WORKBOOK EXERCISES

Complete all exercises in Chapter 5 of the workbook before proceeding to Chapter 6 in this text.

DISKETTE EXERCISE

Complete the diskette exercise for Chapter 5 before proceeding to Chapter 6 in this text.

Hacker—a Good Word Gone Bad

A hacker is a person who is very good with computers; that is, that used to be the definition. Now the word *hacker* has come to mean a person who is very good with computers and uses them to commit criminal actions. Some hackers do not realize the seriousness of their actions. They look upon the challenge of breaking into computers belonging to other persons or companies somewhat as a game. Whether or not they change valuable data, steal information, or use the computer to illegally get money or merchandise for themselves, however, they are still committing serious wrongdoings.

There are quite a few reports of schools and colleges in which students have broken into computerized grade files and changed course grades. Some of these students claim they were just looking for the challenge. Others were purposely going about raising their grade point averages or were selling their services to other students for a fee.

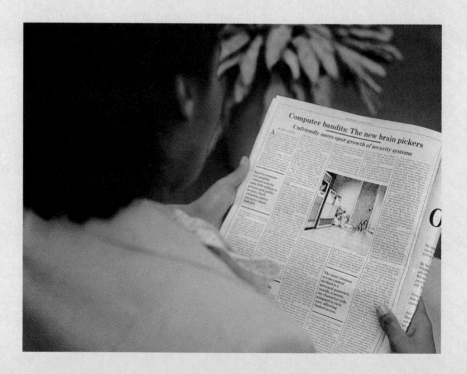

There are several cases of revenge against reporters who
have investigated and reported on the activities of hackers. In at
least two cases, reporters have been threatened with death. In the
case of a *Newsweek* reporter who did a story on hackers, some of
the subjects of the story sought revenge. They broke into a computerized file at the credit bureau, obtained the numbers of the
reporter's credit cards, and posted the numbers on a computerized bulletin board where anyone who so desired could obtain
them. In addition, the reporter was put on "teletrial" on a bulletin board system in Gainesville, Texas. In the teletrial, various
hackers could make accusations, agree with the accusations of
others, or enter defenses for the person "on trial." Eventually the
reporter was "acquitted" by the mock trial.

In the case of illegally using computers for personal gain of
money or possessions, there are numerous examples. Many of
the persons who commit these crimes are employed by the orga-
nizations they are cheating. There are cases, for example, of bank
employees who have programmed the computer to take a penny

or so from each of thousands of accounts and transfer it to their accounts. Employees have had paychecks made out to nonexistent people they have entered on the payroll. They then cash the checks themselves. There have been employees of merchandising firms who have instructed the computer to ship goods to them at false addresses without ever billing them for the merchandise.

It might be easier to deal with computer crime if we knew how much of it was going on. Unfortunately, no one knows exactly how much computer crime there is. A report from the American Bar Association, however, gives some clues. Twenty-five percent of the thousand largest businesses in the U.S.A. say they have been the victims of computer crime sometime in the previous year. The amount of money lost to such crime was estimated to be between $145 million and $750 million.

Many businesses and individuals are now taking a much harder stand against computer crime. The business that might have overlooked a minor case of computer trespassing in the past is now likely to prosecute the hacker to the full extent of the law. Also, more and more states are modifying their laws to make computer crime a more serious offense with much harsher penalties than before. These revised laws address many of the unique characteristics of data being in the form of electronic impulses rather than in the form of material objects. The laws rightfully make it much easier for persons to win court cases against computer criminals. Along with the much greater emphasis on making sure computer criminals are prosecuted and punished, there is growing concern on the part of many expert computer hobbyists who would like to see the definition of *hacker* returned to its previous honorable position.

Also, more and more security safeguards are being built into computer systems to protect them from criminals. For years, many large computers could be called by anyone with a terminal. Later, passwords protected all the programs and data from illegal users. These passwords could be defeated by the persistent person. There are still systems protected only by passwords, but more and more computers are being protected by what is known as a call-back system. In these systems, the computer containing valuable data is supplied with a list of all the phone numbers with which it is allowed to "hold a conversa-

tion." Anytime the computer receives a call, it immediately asks the caller for its phone number and then hangs up. There is never a chance for the caller to deal with passwords. If the caller leaves its number (many illegal callers will not), the computer that received the call then looks at its stored list of numbers to see if the caller's number is on the list. If the caller is on the list, the computer dials back and sets up communication, still perhaps using a password as a second safeguard. If the caller is not on the authorized list, no return call is made. Also, the unauthorized number is stored in a file of illegal attempts to get on the system. Such stored data may serve as an important clue in detecting persons trying to make use of the computer for criminal purposes and can serve as evidence to help convict the criminal.

PART 3
Hardware

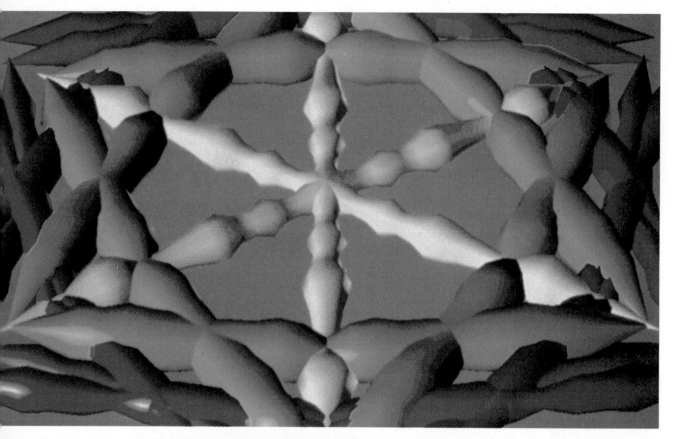

CHAPTER 6

Input Devices and Media

1. Describe input devices and their characteristics.
2. Describe ways in which each input device is used.

Input provides the bridge between data and processing. It is here that the programmers' old saying "garbage in, garbage out" (GIGO) applies. GIGO indicates the importance of accurate input. This chapter goes into detail about the input devices. Remember, regardless of the input device used, the data must be accurate for the processing and output to be accurate.

An input device receives data and communicates it to the processor. Input begins with a command from the processor to the input unit. The command is given because an instruction in a program tells the processor to do so. Once the command is given, the input device sends data to the processor as discussed in Chapter 5. As the data is received, the processor generally stores it in RAM so it will be available for use.

Some input devices use media; others do not. **Media** refers to the materials that data is recorded on before it is sent to the computer. For example, characters may be written on paper, in which case paper is the **medium** (the singular form of media). As another example, data may be recorded on a strip of magnetic tape, in which case the tape is the medium.

VIDEO DISPLAY TERMINALS

A **video display terminal** (VDT) consists of a keyboard and a display device. Used as both an input device and an output device, the VDT remains the most popular method of "holding a conversation" with a computer. When any system is set up for two-way communication between the user and the computer, it is said to be **interactive**. The VDT is frequently used in airline reservation systems because it is interactive. There are many other systems that use the VDT for that reason.

More attention has been paid in the last few years to the **ergonomic** design of input devices, such as video display terminals and the desks on which they are used. This means that the devices should be comfortable and nontiring, allowing the operator to produce more work. Many manufacturers provide a wide selection of color combinations for the screens, as shown in Figure 6.1. Many other manufacturers produce a wide variety of furniture, such as chairs and desks, that can be tailored to the persons using them.

FIGURE 6.1

Many displays have a wide selection of color combinations.

SPEECH RECOGNITION DEVICES

For many applications, the ability to instruct a computer by voice command or voice response is valuable. This can be done by use of a **speech recognition device**. For example, in many applications, both hands are needed to work. A parts salesperson may speak over the phone to a computer in the parts warehouse to determine the availability of a part. You may command your voice-controlled telephone to make a call for you. Figure 6.2 shows a voice-controlled telephone in use. Handicapped persons can command wheelchairs or robot arms through the spoken word.

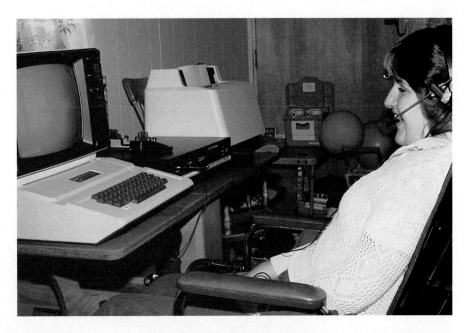

FIGURE 6.2

Susie is a quadriplegic as a result of a broken neck she suffered in 1979. She uses this voice-controlled computer system to write papers for school.

As valuable as these applications are, the ideal would be a computer input device that could recognize ordinary everyday speech. Present systems, however, can only recognize several hundred words. They must also be trained to recognize one or, at most, a few different voices. There are so many differences in speech from one person to another that it is very difficult for a computer to accurately recognize words. Research in advanced voice recognition is under way in many labs, but experts think it will be a while yet before large-scale speech recognition becomes a reality.

OPTICAL-CHARACTER READERS

An **optical-character reader** (OCR) is one type of scanner, or input device. The way it works is similar to the reading method that humans use. When light is placed on a printed form, the human reader scans the form. Images of the letters, numbers, or marks are reflected to the eye. The images are then changed into nerve impulses and sent to the brain. The brain has been programmed through learning and experience to recognize the images. In a similar fashion, a character reader can read numbers, letters of the alphabet, and symbols directly from a typed, printed, or hand-printed page.

An optical-character reader requires only one column per digit or character. It is, therefore, very suitable for handling large quantities of data. Hand-printed optical-character reading has many uses; one area where it is often used is in libraries (Figure 6.3).

FIGURE 6.3

Many libraries use optical-character readers.

The use of OCR forms makes it possible to have on-the-spot data recording at a low cost. A worker can record the amount of time it takes to complete a job. A customer's purchases can be recorded, and so on. The only equipment needed for this kind of recording is a pencil and an OCR form. Figure 6.4 shows an OCR form. Note that the directions show the proper way to print numbers so that the computer will accept them. The numbers must be a close match to the model characters stored by the scanner, or reading errors will occur.

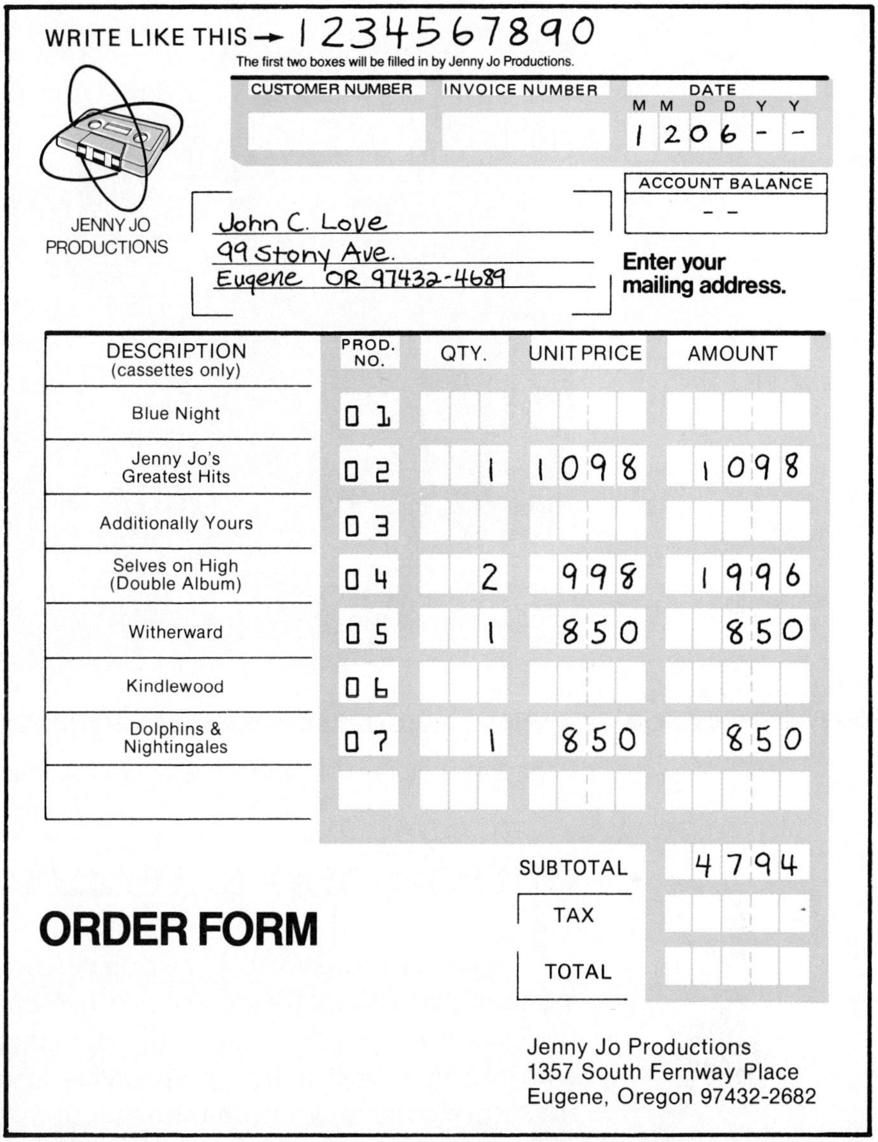

WRITE LIKE THIS ➔ 1 2 3 4 5 6 7 8 9 0

The first two boxes will be filled in by Jenny Jo Productions.

JENNY JO PRODUCTIONS

CUSTOMER NUMBER	INVOICE NUMBER	DATE M M D D Y Y
		1 2 0 6 - -

ACCOUNT BALANCE
- -

John C. Love
99 Stony Ave.
Eugene OR 97432-4689

Enter your mailing address.

DESCRIPTION (cassettes only)	PROD. NO.	QTY.	UNIT PRICE	AMOUNT
Blue Night	0 1			
Jenny Jo's Greatest Hits	0 2	1	1 0 9 8	1 0 9 8
Additionally Yours	0 3			
Selves on High (Double Album)	0 4	2	9 9 8	1 9 9 6
Witherward	0 5	1	8 5 0	8 5 0
Kindlewood	0 6			
Dolphins & Nightingales	0 7	1	8 5 0	8 5 0

ORDER FORM

SUBTOTAL	4 7 9 4
TAX	
TOTAL	

Jenny Jo Productions
1357 South Fernway Place
Eugene, Oregon 97432-2682

FIGURE 6.4

An OCR form makes it possible to have on-the-spot data recording.

OCR equipment is frequently used in department stores. Figure 6.5 shows an optical scanner being used to read the price ticket on an item. Usually the scanner reads a stock number rather than the price. The computer to which the scanner is attached then looks up the stock number in a price table to determine the amount to charge for the item. This makes it easy to ensure that customers receive the sale prices on items that are specially priced, or to change the prices when necessary.

FIGURE 6.5

Department stores frequently use optical scanners to read price tickets.

OPTICAL-MARK READERS

The **optical-mark reader**, shown in Figure 6.6, is a scanner that senses the presence or absence of marks made by regular pencil or pen on specially designed forms. Optical-mark recognition is frequently used for test scoring, data collection, inventory control, and other applications where the number of different responses and volume of data are somewhat limited. Figure 6.6 also shows one input medium that may be used. Note that the locations for recording each kind of data are already defined on the form before the form is marked in pencil.

BAR-CODE SCANNERS

A **bar-code scanner** can read bars, or lines, that are printed on the package of a product. These bars, which represent data, are generally printed in a code known as the Universal Prod-

FIGURE 6.6

Optical-mark readers sense the presence or absence of marks on specially designed forms.

uct Code (UPC). The code is printed on a product by the manufacturer and is made up of a series of bars that reflect a laser beam from a scanner. In Figure 6.7, a typical bar code is shown. The type of scanner that reads bar codes is shown in Figure 6.8.

FIGURE 6.7

The UPC is printed on the packages of most products.

FIGURE 6.8

Bar-code scanners read the bar codes on products.

Retail stores (especially grocery stores) use bar-code scanners to speed up the check-out process. Bar-code scanners transmit the product's coded numbers directly to a computer. The computer then looks up the correct prices and descriptions in data which it has previously stored in memory. Each customer gets a sales slip listing the names of the items purchased, and the items are automatically subtracted from the store's inventory. Store managers thus have a system of instant inventory control. In addition, the store does not need to prepare price tags. Also, since the cashiers do not need to key in prices, time is saved and errors are reduced. Figure 6.9 shows a checker using a bar-code scanner.

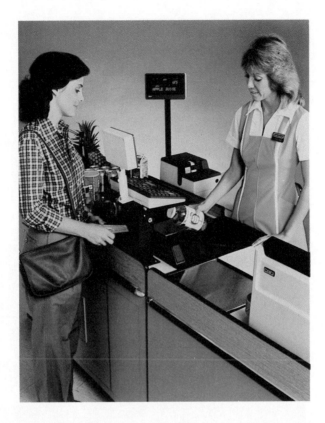

FIGURE 6.9

Many grocery store cashiers use bar-code scanners.

MICR READERS

Banks in the United States use **magnetic ink character recognition** (MICR) for much of their data input. An MICR reader is an input device that is used to process data printed in magnetic ink in the form of specially designed numbers and symbols.

In MICR, checks and deposit slips have all necessary data printed on them in magnetic ink when the checks and deposit slips are first printed up. The numbers and special symbols (there are no alphabet letters) appear in an unusual-looking style. This style gives each character a different magnetic code when the documents go through a reader. The reader can transmit the data directly to a computer system for immediate processing or store it on disk or tape for later processing. Figure 6.10 gives one example of MICR code.

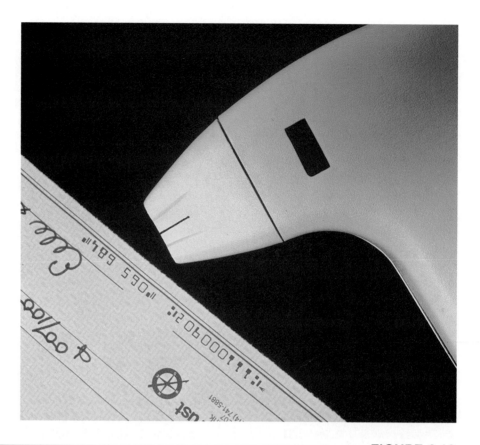

FIGURE 6.10

The code on this check is being read by an MICR reader.

MAGNETIC SCANNERS

A **magnetic scanner** operates on the same principle as a tape recorder. The tape it reads, however, is usually only a short piece of tape no more than a few inches long. Some retail stores use price tags on which short strips of magnetic tape contain the stock numbers of the products. The largest use of magnetic scanners, however, is to read coded information on the backs of credit cards and 24-hour teller machine cards used by banks. For the latter, a magnetic strip on the back of each customer's identification card contains the person's account number and other needed information. This identification card is shown in Figure 6.11. When the card is inserted into the teller machine, the magnetic scanner reads the tape on the back of the card and transmits the customer's account number to the processor.

FIGURE 6.11

Bank identification cards are read by automatic teller machines.

REAL-TIME SENSORS

The **real-time sensor** is one of the newest developments in computer input. Real time means "while it is happening." Therefore, a real-time sensor sends information to the computer processor about an event while it is happening without the need of human assistance. There are many applications for real-time sensors, so we will look at just a few. The computer that controls the ignition and fuel systems in a car uses several real-time sensors for input. While a car is running, real-time sensors are constantly measuring such things as engine speed, vehicle speed, and the level of carbon monoxide in the exhaust. This data is constantly input to the computer. After processing the information, the computer produces output in the form of commands to the ignition and fuel systems. These commands keep efficiency as high as possible while, at the same time, keeping air pollution produced by the engine within a certain limit. Figure 6.12 shows an automobile that uses real-time sensors.

FIGURE 6.12

This automobile uses real-time sensors.

A computer can be used in a burglar alarm. When a burglar alarm is controlled by a computer, several real-time sensors observe the area and feed the computer information as to whether or not an intruder is present. Figure 6.13 shows such a real-time system.

One of the most exciting developments in real-time sensors is the creation of robots with senses of vision and touch. This development makes it possible to use robots in applications previously not possible. The robot in Figure 6.14 is inputting what it "sees" to the computer that is controlling its operation.

OTHER INPUT DEVICES

There are several kinds of input devices that have not yet been discussed in this chapter. The following paragraphs describe some of them.

Light Pen

A **light pen** is one of several types of input devices that may be used to point out locations on a VDT. For example, if there are four items to choose from on the screen, the user will

FIGURE 6.13

Computer-controlled burglar alarms are very efficient.

FIGURE 6.14

The robot (the small device in front of the man who is standing) is connected to a computer that is also connected to a camera. The camera is being used as an input device to "learn" motions. The computer will then command the robot to copy the motions taught by what the camera "sees."

press the light pen against a dot printed on the screen in front of the desired item. Then the computer will calculate the position against which it is pressed. Figure 6.l5 shows a light pen in use. Depending on the computer program with which a light pen is used, the operator may draw shapes, move images from one part of the screen to another, and so on.

FIGURE 6.15

A light pen is being used on this display screen.

Mouse

The **mouse** is a pointing device used with a video display. Like a living mouse, a computer mouse has a body and a tail. The tail is a wire connecting the body to the computer. The body contains one or more push buttons. As the body of the mouse is moved, a marker known as a **cursor** moves on the video display. When the mouse is moved up, the cursor moves up; when the mouse moves left, the cursor moves left, and so on. Once the cursor is in the desired location, pressing a button on the mouse causes an action to be taken. The type of action depends on the computer program in use at the time. Figure 6.16 shows a picture of a mouse.

FIGURE 6.16

The mouse in this picture (small box with the cord) was used to draw the images shown on the screen.

Digitizer

The **digitizer** changes shapes into numbers for storage by computers. For example, if you have a favorite cartoon picture you would like to transfer to a computer for display, you can trace the picture with a digitizer. The digitizer transmits the proper numbers to copy the picture on the VDT. The picture you trace is **two-dimensional**. That is, it is flat and has a length and a width. All digitizers can handle two-dimensional objects. Some can also handle three-dimensional objects. **Three-dimensional** objects have depth as well as length and width. Artists, advertising companies, and engineers could all benefit from the use of digitizers. Figure 6.17 demonstrates one use of a digitizer.

FIGURE 6.17

This digitizer is transmitting the dimensions of a map to the computer for display.

A WORKING COMPUTER SYSTEM

The hardware component of the functional computer system contains input, processing, output, and storage devices. This chapter discussed the input devices. Figure 6.18 adds the input devices discussed in this chapter into the working computer system outline.

A WORKING COMPUTER SYSTEM

I. HARDWARE

A. Input devices
   1. Video display terminal
   2. Speech recognition device
   3. Optical-character reader
   4. Optical-mark reader
   5. Bar-code scanner
   6. Magnetic ink character reader
   7. Magnetic scanner
   8. Real-time sensor
   9. Light pen
   10. Mouse
   11. Digitizer

B. Processing
   1. Processor
   2. Memory (RAM and ROM)

C. Output devices

D. Auxiliary storage

II. DATA

A. Categories
   1. Character
   2. Field
   3. Record
   4. File

B. Common coding systems
   1. ASCII
   2. EBCDIC

III. SOFTWARE

FIGURE 6.18

Outline of a working computer system with emphasis placed on input devices.

SUMMARY

Many kinds of input devices exist. Each type has capabilities that make it appropriate for particular applications. Video display terminals are useful for just about any applications that require interactive communication between the user and the computer. Speech recognition devices allow workers to do other things with their hands while inputting data into the computer. Various kinds of scanners are appropriate for applications that require the reading of data written on the packages of products, price labels, checks, identification cards, and so on. Real-time sensors allow efficient control of automobiles, home appliances, and airplanes, just to name a few. The mouse is becoming more popular as an input device. Also, there are many input devices designed for special uses. Regardless of the needs of a business, there is probably an input device to meet those needs.

REVIEW QUESTIONS

1. Give one common use of VDT input devices. (Objs. 1, 2)
2. What is ergonomics? (Obj. 1)
3. What are speech recognition devices? (Obj. 1)
4. Compare optical-character readers and optical-mark readers. (Obj. 1)
5. When would an optical-character reader be used as an input device? (Obj. 2)
6. How is a bar-code scanner used in a grocery store? (Obj. 2)
7. How is a mouse used as an input device? (Obj. 2)
8. What are two applications of magnetic scanning? (Obj. 2)
9. What is the main difference between real-time sensors and the other input devices you are familiar with? (Obj. 1)
10. Compare the main uses of a light pen and a digitizer. (Obj. 2)

VOCABULARY WORDS

The following terms were introduced in this chapter:

media	magnetic scanner
medium	real-time sensor
video display terminal	light pen
interactive	mouse
ergonomic	cursor
speech recognition device	digitizer
optical-character reader	two-dimensional
optical-mark reader	three-dimensional
bar-code scanner	
magnetic ink character recognition	

WORKBOOK EXERCISES

Complete all exercises in Chapter 6 of the workbook before proceeding to Chapter 7 in this text.

DISKETTE EXERCISE

Complete the diskette exercise for Chapter 6 before proceeding to Chapter 7 in this text.

Working at Home by Computer

For years some persons have been predicting that the computer would allow many individuals to work at home avoiding the necessity of traveling to a workplace. Now the technology to allow many people to work at home is readily available. Take a look at several kinds of jobs that might be done at home as easily as at an office.

Mail-order businesses employ many persons whose duty is to take phone orders from customers. When a customer calls, the employee asks what merchandise is desired, then enters the stock number of the merchandise into the computer. The computer can immediately tell whether the item is in stock. If it is not in stock, it can tell when new stock is expected to be received. By

using such a computer system, the business is able to provide the customer with better service. Not only is the customer more aware of when an order will be received, but the initial entry of the order by the person answering the phone is all that is required in the way of data entry. From that point on, the printing of the invoice and shipping papers is done by the computer. From a technological standpoint, there is no reason a mail-order company should maintain an office large enough to hold perhaps 50 or 100 operators to take orders. There is no reason each of the employees could not have a terminal in his or her home. Customers would still dial the one published phone number for ordering, but the calls would be automatically rerouted to phones and computer terminals in the operators' homes. Since the computer is recording the orders of customers handled by each operator, keeping tabs on how much work each person does is not difficult.

For many other customer service jobs, a similar situation to that of the mail-order company exists. For example, computer software companies frequently employ software experts to answer customer questions. All day long, these persons do noth-

ing but answer phones and guide customers through problems they are encountering in using the company's software. There is no technological reason these persons cannot work at home, with the calls being automatically rerouted to the phones in their homes. Likewise, persons who handle reservations for hotel chains or airlines could easily work at home. Since their tool is a computer terminal, there is no reason a terminal and a phone could not be located in each employee's home. For many other kinds of employees, there are occasions when working at home would be appropriate. For example, an executive who is working on a budget (plan of income and expenditures) for the business might have far fewer interruptions at home during this phase of the work.

By working at home, persons can sleep later, and they have no traffic problems to contend with. Also, they do not have the expense of driving an automobile or taking public transportation to work. The effect of all this is that the person can work the same number of hours and produce the same amount of work. Less money is spent on transportation, however, and the person has more time to devote to personal activities.

Working at home sounds like a great idea for many employees. It is technologically possible. It makes sense for many businesses who could reduce expenses by having employees work at home. In spite of all these advantages, however, few employees actually work at home. Given a choice, few people want to work at home. In fact, it seems unlikely that there will ever be many persons working at home through the use of computer terminals.

Why is working at home so unpopular? It certainly cannot be the working hours. Remember that the employee has more leisure time because of time saved in not commuting to work every day. It certainly cannot be the expense. The employee has more money left to spend since there is no expense involved in commuting to work. Rather, the answer to the riddle seems to lie in human nature. By nature, people are social beings; that is, people need people. Being able to see fellow workers and talk with them face to face is a very important part of the workday for most people. It is not that employees have to see each other to perform their work. Instead, it is the support mechanism that

exists in the workplace. Everyone needs someone to talk to. For example, if you had a very bad night, you might be able to talk to fellow workers about it during a break time or at lunch. Their listening to your explanation of the problem would make you feel much better. Or suppose something really good happened to you the night before. You know that having good news and no one to tell it to is very frustrating. Again, being able to tell good news to those you work with is a very satisfying experience. None of these human interactions are possible in a work-at-home setting.

In spite of years of predictions, it is very unlikely that large numbers of people will be employed in jobs in which they work at home through the use of computer terminals. The need to be around other people is simply too great to be ignored by most persons.

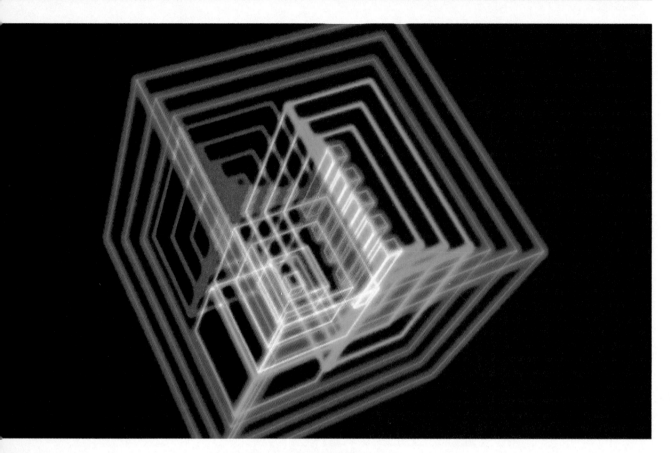

CHAPTER 7
Output Devices and Media

Output devices have the job of delivering the final product for the computer system. Data is input into the computer system, as discussed in Chapter 6, and processed. Useful information is produced and output in a variety of ways. In this chapter you will learn about the most commonly used types of output devices. You will learn their characteristics and the kinds of applications for which they are best suited.

VIDEO DISPLAYS

The **video display** is one of the most common devices used for computer output. It is especially well suited for interactive applications requiring both input and output, such as in banking systems or word processing. Most video displays use CRTs, although other methods of displaying the data are becoming more common. As you learned in Chapter 6, a video display is frequently combined with a keyboard to form a video display terminal.

Some computers may be attached to standard television sets, which then serve as video displays. Most televisions, however, are unsuitable for use with many computer systems. Due to the way they are made, television sets can display only a limited number of characters on the screen. That number is too limited for businesses to use. Video displays used in business to process information usually contain either 24 or 25 lines of 80 characters or columns each. Displays with 132 columns are becoming more common, as are those that can display up to 60 lines. A few can display the same amount of information as several printed pages of text.

Video displays may be either monochrome or multicolored. **Monochrome** means only one color. Common display colors are green, amber, and white. They can do an excellent job of presenting information in an easy-to-understand form. A **graphic** (a chart, drawing, or picture) looks much better in multicolor. For applications involving words and numbers, however, multicolor displays may be harder to read. For that reason, some displays can easily switch between monochrome and multicolor. In Figure 7.1, note the different appearances of the graphics on the different displays.

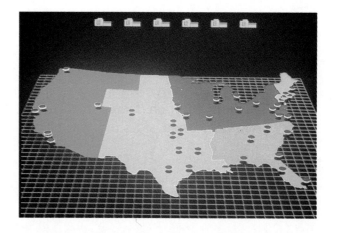

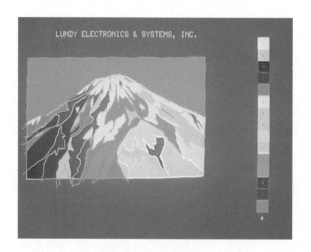

FIGURE 7.1

Graphics can be used for all kinds of displays.

PRINTERS

Printers are commonly used devices that place output on paper. Placing output on paper is generally called making a hard copy of the information. With the exception of video displays, printers are the most common output device. Nearly every computer application uses a printer in some way. Just a few uses are printing bills, letters, and accounting records. When examining available printers, you find tremendous differences: differences in speed, print quality, price, and special features. Some printers can only produce characters; others can print detailed graphics. Some printers can use only one color, while others can print in several colors. Figure 7.2 shows one of the newer printers.

Two common methods used to place characters on a sheet of paper are the impact and nonimpact methods. With some printers, the paper is struck to form the images; these printers are known as **impact printers**. With impact printers, the part of the printer that does the printing is known as a **printhead**. Impact printers are best used when more than one copy of the same document is needed. **Nonimpact printers**, on the other hand, form characters without actually striking the paper. Regardless of the method of printing, a character code is received from the computer. The printer then translates the character code and prints the character.

FIGURE 7.2

The IBM 3800 represents a high-technology printing device.

Impact Printers

This section discusses some commonly used impact printers. Four common impact printers are the daisy wheel printer, dot-matrix printer, band printer, and chain printer.

Daisy Wheel Printers

A **daisy wheel printer**, such as the one shown in Figure 7.3, is an impact printer. It gets its name from the fact that it uses a print wheel that looks like a daisy. Figure 7.4 shows the actual printing mechanism. The print wheel rotates until the desired character is in position in front of the paper. Then a hammer strikes the character. An inked ribbon between the daisy wheel and the paper causes an image to be printed.

Daisy wheel printers produce what is known as **letter-quality** print; that is, the characters are made from unbroken lines and look as if they were produced by good typewriters. This is important when printing letters and other documents that must be of high quality. In exchange for such letter-quality printing, however, the user pays a price in the form of low speed. In fact, some daisy wheel printers are extremely slow, around ten characters per second.

FIGURE 7.3

The daisy wheel printer is an impact printer.

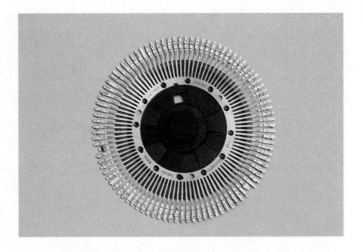

FIGURE 7.4

The daisy wheel printing mechanism has "petals" that resemble a daisy.

Dot-Matrix Printers

A **dot matrix** is simply a row and column arrangement of dots. Therefore, a dot-matrix printer, like·the one shown in Figure 7.5, produces a character by forming it from rows and columns of dots. As the printhead moves across the paper, tiny pins or wires in the printhead tap the paper through a ribbon to form the image of each character. There are wide differences in the number and arrangement of the pins or wires used to do the printing. The more dots that are used to form each character, the higher the quality of print. The quality, however, is still not as high as with a daisy wheel printer. Many printers that are used with microcomputers are dot-matrix printers.

The print speed of dot-matrix printers ranges from around forty characters per second to several hundred characters per second, which is fast enough for most small computer systems. A few dot-matrix printers use more than one printhead to achieve even higher speeds. Compared with other types of printers, most dot-matrix printers are fairly inexpensive.

Band Printers and Chain Printers

Band printers and chain printers are impact printers that operate on the same general principle. A **band printer** uses a rotating band or belt containing characters. A **chain printer**

FIGURE 7.5

A dot-matrix printer produces a character by forming it
from rows and columns of dots.

uses a rotating chain containing the characters. Both printers
have hammers which strike the characters against the paper. A
ribbon between the characters and the paper produces the
images. Figure 7.6 shows a band printer.

Band printers and chain printers are much faster than the
daisy wheel and dot-matrix printers described earlier. They can
print as fast as 2,000 to 3,000 lines per minute. They are also
much more expensive. Figure 7.7 shows a chain printer.

Nonimpact Printers

As a general rule, nonimpact printers are faster than impact
printers. This section discusses some commonly used nonimpact
printers. Two such printers are the ink-jet printer and the laser
printer.

Ink-Jet Printers

The **ink-jet printer** is a nonimpact printer which is
growing in popularity. As the name implies, liquid or dry ink is
squirted onto the paper. The exact technology used varies from
one manufacturer to another. Ink-jet printers produce nice-
looking print, and many of them can produce different sizes and
styles of characters on the same line. Some can print in several
colors. A typical ink-jet printer is shown in Figure 7.8.

BAND

FIGURE 7.6

The band printer uses a rotating band containing characters.

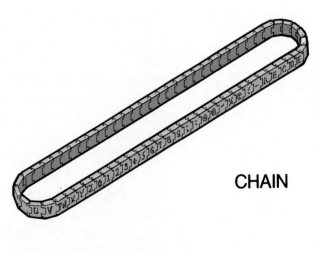

CHAIN

FIGURE 7.7

The chain printer uses a rotating chain containing characters.

FIGURE 7.8

The ink-jet printer forms characters by squirting ink onto the paper.

Laser Printers

The **laser printer** is the fastest and most expensive printer available. The fastest ones can print over 20,000 lines per minute. When printing 12 lines per inch, for example, the laser printer shown in Figure 7.9 can print approximately 167 11-inch pages per minute. Another advantage of the laser printer is that a business form can be printed on blank paper at the same time the output data is being printed. The laser printer can also produce different sizes and styles of printing.

A laser printer is a nonimpact printer that works somewhat like a copying machine. In a copying machine, light shines on an original copy. The light is reflected onto a drum which transfers toner (ink) to the copy. In a laser printer, a laser beam "writes" the character output from the computer onto a drum sensitive to photographic images. The drum then transfers the characters to paper. Figure 7.10 shows a drum.

The printers that have been discussed here are ones that are commonly used. There are other types, and manufacturers are constantly introducing new printer models, some of which use different types of technology.

FIGURE 7.9

The laser printer is a nonimpact printer that works somewhat like a copying machine. It can print over 20,000 lines per minute.

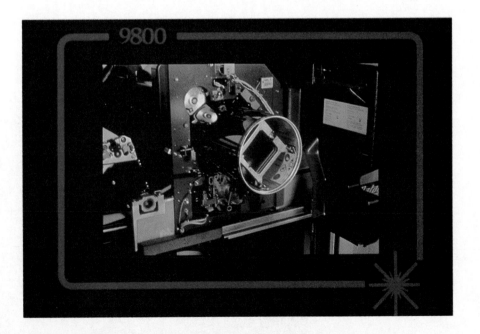

FIGURE 7.10

The drum inside a laser printer is sensitive to photographic images. After receiving impressions of the images, the drum transfers the characters to paper.

SPEECH SYNTHESIZERS

Speech synthesizers, output devices which imitate the human voice, are available for nearly every application. There are so many "talking" machines—talking games, talking cars, talking appliances, talking calculators, and music-reading singing computers—that it sometimes looks as if manufacturers want each item to have a voice, whether it needs one or not. Figure 7.11 shows an example of one of these talking machines.

Seriously, however, synthesized voices are properly used in many situations. Talking machines are giving phone numbers to persons who dial directory assistance. They enable electronic banking by allowing people to use the phone as a terminal. Talking typewriters, calculators, and reading machines are tremendous aids for the blind. In addition, computer-assisted learning in such areas as foreign languages can be much more effective when the computer can speak.

COMPUTER OUTPUT MICROFILM

Computer output microfilm, commonly referred to as COM, is used when large amounts of data must be printed and

FIGURE 7.11

Speech synthesizers are very popular in learning toys.

stored for future use. Under such conditions, output printed on paper may require too much storage space. Also, too much time may be needed to search through the paper output to find a given item.

Computer output microfilm uses a photographic process much like a camera. Computer output is recorded directly on photographic film as shown in Figure 7.12. The unit translates computer signals to written characters and exposes the film, which is similar to taking a picture. The image of each character is reduced greatly in size, making it possible to store many characters in a small space.

The microfilm produced may be in long rolls. It may also be in small rectangular sheets called **microfiche**. To read either type, a person must use a special reader. The microfilm reader shown in Figure 7.13 is a machine that magnifies the images to a size that can be read by the human eye.

COM provides a very fast way of recording output from a computer. The film itself is inexpensive and compact. However, complete COM systems can be very expensive. Government agencies, insurance companies, banks, utility companies, and other businesses that must store large volumes of computer-generated data are the most likely users of COM.

FIGURE 7.12

Computer output is recorded directly on photographic film.

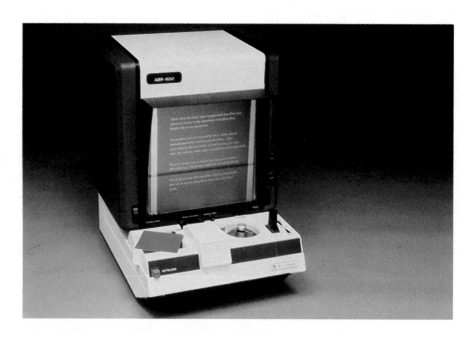

FIGURE 7.13

The microfilm reader magnifies the COM so that people can read it.

PLOTTERS

A **plotter** is generally used to print graphic output; that is, it can draw maps, produce art work, draw any shape line, and so on. A plotter draws output using one or more pens that are controlled by instructions from the processor. Since the pens can contain various colors of ink, multicolored output is easy to achieve. Some plotters are limited to printing on standard-sized sheets of paper; others can work on extremely large-sized paper. Mapping, weather forecasting, drafting, and engineering are just some of the areas in which plotters are used. In addition to producing graphic output, plotters can also perform some printing functions. Figure 7.14 shows a plotter in use.

REAL-TIME CONTROLLERS

A **real-time controller** is an output device that changes computer output to some kind of action that controls a process. Often, the action consists of a physical movement, such as turning a valve on or off. Sometimes the action is less obvious,

FIGURE 7.14

Plotters are used mainly for producing graphic output.

as in making changes in electrical circuits. In an automobile, the computer gives commands to controllers on the ignition and fuel systems. In an aircraft, computer commands go to controllers for the various flight-control commands as well as to the engines. When commanded by a computer, a real-time controller performs the function for which it was designed. Figure 7.15 shows one application of real-time controllers.

FIGURE 7.15

This airplane control panel uses many real-time controllers.

ROBOTS

In addition to being an input device, a robot can serve as a general-purpose output device. Under control of a computer, the robot produces output in the form of motion to perform work. If the instructions being given to the computer are changed, the robot's motions can change and it can do a different kind of work. Newer robots can also provide input to the computer through the use of televisionlike cameras and real-time sensors. The processor uses this input along with the programmed task instructions to produce output.

A WORKING COMPUTER SYSTEM

This chapter introduced several new output devices. Figure 7.16 highlights the discussion of these output devices.

A WORKING COMPUTER SYSTEM

I. HARDWARE

  A. Input devices
    1. Video display terminal
    2. Speech recognition device
    3. Optical-character reader
    4. Optical-mark reader
    5. Bar-code scanner
    6. Magnetic ink character reader
    7. Magnetic scanner
    8. Real-time sensor
    9. Light pen
    10. Mouse
    11. Digitizer

  B. Processing
    1. Processor
    2. Memory (RAM and ROM)

  C. Output devices
    1. Video display
    2. Printer
      a. Impact
      b. Nonimpact
    3. Speech synthesizer
    4. Computer output microfilm
    5. Plotter
    6. Real-time controller
    7. Robot

  D. Auxiliary storage

II. DATA

  A. Categories
    1. Character
    2. Field

FIGURE 7.16a

Partial outline of a working computer system with emphasis placed on output devices.

```
            3.  Record
            4.  File

        B.  Common coding systems
            1.  ASCII
            2.  EBCDIC

    III.  SOFTWARE
```

FIGURE 7.16b

Outline of a working computer system continued.

SUMMARY

Whatever the computer application, an appropriate output device is available. Video displays and printers are the most commonly used devices. Video displays are especially helpful for interactive applications and for showing graphic information. Full-color displays are especially good for graphics. Many different kinds of printers are available. Some of them can print graphics or print in different colors.

Speech synthesizers may be used in any application where voice output is appropriate. Plotters quickly draw complex designs, such as building plans. Real-time controllers enable computers to operate various kinds of machinery. Robots under computer control can produce useful work through their ability to perform movement.

REVIEW QUESTIONS

1. What output device is commonly used for interactive applications? Describe its characteristics. (Objs. 1, 2)

2. Discuss the differences between daisy wheel and dot-matrix printers. (Obj. 1)

3. Which kind of printer would you select to print letter-quality documents? huge numbers of telephone bills? Explain your reasoning. (Objs. 1, 2)

4. When would you consider using COM rather than a printer? Why? (Obj. 2)

5. What characteristics of a plotter make it an appropriate output device for outputting the plans of a large building? (Objs. 1, 2)

6. What is the main difference between a real-time controller and a robot? How are they alike? (Objs. 1, 2)

7. What is the fastest printer? (Obj. 1)

8. What does impact printing involve? (Obj. 1)

9. Give an example of a nonimpact output device. (Obj. 1)

10. Give two examples of applications for speech synthesizers. (Obj. 2)

VOCABULARY WORDS

The following terms were introduced in this chapter:

video display	band printer
monochrome	chain printer
graphic	ink-jet printer
impact printer	laser printer
printhead	speech synthesizer
nonimpact printer	computer output microfilm
daisy wheel printer	microfiche
letter quality	plotter
dot matrix	real-time controller

WORKBOOK EXERCISES

Complete all exercises in Chapter 7 of the workbook before proceeding to Chapter 8 in this text.

DISKETTE EXERCISE

Complete the diskette exercise for Chapter 7 before proceeding to Chapter 8 in this text.

Computers Keep Planes in the Sky

When one is considering the use of computers by various kinds of businesses, the airline industry quickly comes to mind. It is an industry in which the use of computers is extremely widespread. In fact, without the use of computers, the industry simply could not operate at its current level of activity. With this in mind, let's take an imaginary flight from Hartsfield Atlanta International Airport.

The planning for your trip starts several days before the actual scheduled departure. You call the airline's local reservation number. Through computer magic, you will be answered by the first available agent, regardless of the city in which the agent is located. The reservation agent has instant access through a computer terminal to information about every seat on every flight for the next several months. Instant recall of fare informa-

tion is also only a few keystrokes away. As you make your choice of flight, the agent keys in information which includes your name and phone numbers. The agent then asks whether you desire to be seated in a smoking or nonsmoking section of the plane, and the computer assigns a seat to you. With your ticket, you receive a boarding pass. Both the ticket and the boarding pass are needed to get you on the plane.

Now the day of your flight has come. Arriving at the airport terminal, you turn your luggage over to the curbside check-in attendant. Looking at your ticket for your flight number, the attendant places a bar-code sticker on the side of each suitcase. Then, placing your bags on a conveyor belt, he or she starts them on an automated journey toward your aircraft. Sensors connected to computers read the labels on the bags. The bags are thus shunted onto the correct conveyors to get them loaded onto the trucks headed for your flight.

Since you already have your computer-issued boarding pass, you don't need to check in with a ticket agent. Instead, you find your gate number on a computer-controlled monitor. Clearing security, you begin a long descent into a tunnel. As the esca-

137

lator takes you steadily downward, a voice floats from the public address system, telling you about the train system. A subway system that would be the envy of many a city, the Atlanta airport train system moves millions of passengers, with trains departing every two minutes. When the next operatorless, computer-driven train glides in and opens its door, you enter. You obey the computer-generated voice saying, "Please move toward the center of the vehicle and away from the doors." Just as the train's doors begin to close, a tardy passenger rushes between them. Rather than injure the passenger, the computer senses the obstruction and reopens the doors. As the doors reopen, a noise like a space-age gunshot rings out twice. As the second shot fades, the computerized voice explains, "This train is being delayed because someone has interfered with the closing of the doors." The computer's voice has proven very effective in aiding with the punctual operation of the trains.

Arriving at your station, you exit the train and board an escalator to go back up to ground level. Once there, you quickly walk to your gate and give your boarding pass to the flight attendant as you board the aircraft. The sleek craft, scheduled by computer and maintained according to computerized records, sits at the gate awaiting your boarding. The crew, likewise scheduled by computer, is making final preparations for departure. The food, also "scheduled" by computer to meet the needs of the flight, has been loaded aboard. Settling into your seat, you decide that the role of the computer in your flight is over. That is not the case, however. The captain checks the computerized weather reports and feeds a flight plan into the aircraft's computer. The craft you are in today is totally capable of flying itself under computer control. Indeed, after receiving instructions from the captain, it can fly to its destination and land by itself. Obviously, if the flight plan changes along the way, the crew will input updated information into the computer, thus altering the way the plane is flown. As the giant-sized craft pushes its way through the atmosphere toward its destination, computers in the air traffic control system are monitoring its location, as well as the locations of all other aircraft in the area at the moment. These computers, providing output to air traffic controllers working in centers and control towers around the country, help

prevent collisions between aircraft as well as ensuring that aircraft remain on their desired flight paths.

While your destiny is in the hands of computers as you rush into the night, other computers back at the airline headquarters are working on the more mundane tasks of accounting and providing information for management. And, as your aircraft lands and noses its way to a gate, yet one more entry goes into the computer at airline headquarters. The entry says that Flight 293 arrived on time. A few months later you are not surprised to see an advertising campaign trumpeting the fact that your airline is on time more frequently than any other—a fact documented by the data entered into the computer system.

CHAPTER 8

Storage Devices and Media

Objectives

1. Identify the way auxiliary storage is used by the computer.

2. Identify commonly used storage devices and media.

3. Describe appropriate applications for storage devices and media.

As we learned in Chapter 4, RAM, which stores data and instructions while processing, is a temporary storage location. Once the processing is finished or if the computer is powered down, then RAM is erased. For that reason, more permanent storage devices are needed to keep data and programs for later use.

THE MANUAL STORAGE PROCESS

The storage process used by computers is very much like the use of storage cabinets in an office. Imagine that you work in an office and have responsibility for customer records. For our imaginary office job, let's refer to the customer file used in Chapter 5. You may very well keep those customer records in a file cabinet, as shown in Figure 8.1.

Your boss tells you to process customer invoices at the end of the month. When the end of the month arrives and you are working on processing the invoices, the file with all the information should be on your desk as shown in Figure 8.2. You decide to begin the task by working on the first customer's record (in this case, Ernest Grover). When that processing is finished, you go on to the next customer's record and continue until you have completed the job. When the job is done, you place the file in the file cabinet so that you can use it at a later time. The task of storing the file is illustrated in Figure 8.3.

FIGURE 8.1

Meet Margie. Margie stores her customer records in this file cabinet.

FIGURE 8.2

Margie has pulled her customer file so that she can work on processing the invoices.

FIGURE 8.3

Now that Margie has finished her work with the customer file, she stores the file back in the file cabinet.

THE COMPUTER STORAGE PROCESS

The computer storage process is very similar to the manual storage process. The storage process is often referred to as auxiliary storage, meaning that it is used as extra storage. Auxiliary storage devices are on-line to the computer. Therefore, auxiliary storage is available to the processor and is under the processor's control. It may be separated from the other parts of the computer and connected by cables. Auxiliary storage will store or record data whenever instructed to do so by the processor. When instructed, it will also read or play back data to the processor.

In Chapter 5 we discussed the processing of information in the computer system. If we take that one step further, it is easy to understand how auxiliary storage works. Let us consider the same customer file that was used in the manual example.

In Chapter 5 we learned that this file would be processed one or more records at a time by the processor. Each record would be stored in RAM memory while processing was taking place. Once the processing for that record was completed, the RAM storage location would place the next record in the same storage location. Now continue the process one step further. What if we want to keep the customer file for later use, which is what most businesses would want? In that case, auxiliary storage is needed. When the processing of the customer file is completed, a command can be given by the program or the operator for the file to be saved in auxiliary storage for later use. An example of saving a file on computer is shown in Figure 8.4.

FIGURE 8.4

The command to save a file is entered on the keyboard and appears on the screen.

STORAGE DEVICES

Just as there are different devices to input and output data, there are different storage devices. In this chapter, we will discuss the different devices that can be used for storage. All auxiliary storage devices are either sequential-access or random-access devices. **Sequential access** is a term used to describe a device that records and reads back data only in a one-after-the-other sequence. **Random access** is a term used to describe a device that can go directly to the location of particular data without having to read through all the data in front of it. A sequential-access storage device is somewhat like a cassette tape player. The tape player cannot get to the fourth selection, for example, without actually winding the tape through the first three. It does not matter whether the tape is on play or fast forward, you still have to wait for it to move past the unwanted selections. A random-access storage device, on the other hand, is somewhat like a stereo record player; you can set the needle down exactly on the desired selection. It is not necessary to play through the unwanted selections.

Magnetic Disks

Data to be processed by a computer is often recorded on magnetic disks. Disks are especially useful for applications in which data must be accessed (retrieved) in random order. A good example of such an application is an airline reservation system. One caller may be interested in a flight to Los Angeles on February 4, the next may want to fly to London on January 5. The system must be able to read flight information quickly from auxiliary storage. Random access of these records is a necessity. The use of a disk is the easiest way to accomplish this.

Principles of Magnetic Disks

A **magnetic disk** is an input, output, and storage medium similar in appearance to a stereo record with a grooveless surface. Figure 8.5 shows a magnetic disk. It is coated on both sides with tiny particles of a substance that can be magnetized. Recording is done magnetically by a method similar to that used by a tape recorder. A **track** is a path on which data is recorded

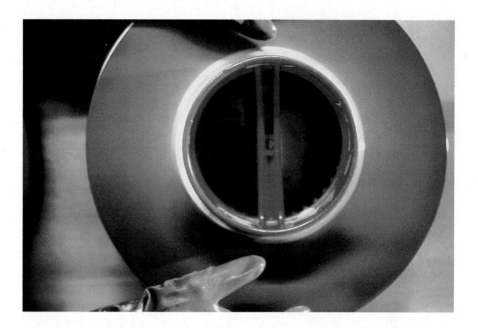

FIGURE 8.5

A magnetic disk is coated on both sides with a substance that can be magnetized.

on the disk. As the disk turns beneath a read/write head, the tiny particles are magnetized in the proper code for each character.

To make reading and writing easier, disks are divided into sections known as **sectors**. Imagine that a disk is marked into slices as if it were a pie already cut into servings. This cuts each track on the disk into small pieces, as shown in Figure 8.6. Each of these small pieces is a sector. One sector full of data is the smallest amount of data that can be read or written (recorded) at one time.

Each side of a disk has a recording surface. Therefore, data on a disk may be recorded on either one or two surfaces. The disk drive uses a movable read/write head for each surface on which recording may be done. Thus, if recording is to be done on one side of a disk, there is one head. If recording is to be done on both sides of a disk, there are two heads. The heads travel in or out to position themselves over the disk track that is to be used. When data is read from the disk into RAM, there is no change; the data remains on the disk. However, when new data is written on a disk, any data previously recorded on the same area of the disk is erased. This is similar to a tape recorder. You can play a tape many times without ever erasing it. But you erase a tape on a tape recorder by recording over it. The idea is the same.

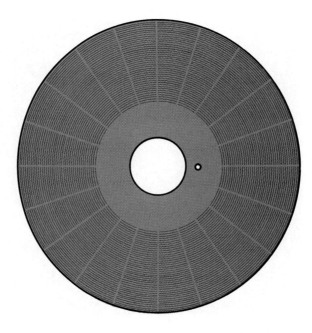

FIGURE 8.6

Disks are divided into sections known as sectors.

As mentioned earlier, data stored on a magnetic disk can be read randomly. Random access is sometimes referred to as **direct access**. In other words, the head can move directly to the desired track rather than sequentially moving through all other tracks before it. If you wish, however, a disk drive can also read data sequentially. The ability to act as either a sequential-access or a random-access device has made the disk drive the most popular auxiliary storage device. It can be used for practically all applications.

Disks can be divided into two categories: flexible disks and hard disks. Flexible disks and their drives cost much less than hard disks and their drives. However, flexible disks cannot hold as much data and are much slower.

Flexible Disks

A **flexible disk**, frequently referred to as a **floppy disk**, is a small, easily bent magnetic disk. The first floppy disks were 8 inches in diameter. However, disks 5 1/4 inches in diameter and 3 1/2 inches in diameter are now commonly used. Figure 8.7 illustrates a 5 1/4 inch disk and the drive into which it is inserted for writing and reading.

FIGURE 8.7

This 5 1/4 inch disk is being inserted into its drive.

The read/write heads actually contact the disks as the drives operate. The amount of data that can be stored on one disk depends upon the way the particular drive and disk are made. The amount ranges from about 120K to 2 megabytes (mega means million, so 2 million bytes) are common, and 10 megabytes of storage is possible. Floppy disks are frequently used in home computers.

Hard Disks

A **hard disk** gets its name from the fact that it is made of hard material; it does not bend like a floppy disk. While the read/write head on a floppy disk actually contacts the disk surface, the head of a hard disk floats a tiny distance above the disk surface (often less than a millionth of an inch). Since there is no physical contact, there is no wear of the disk surface. Hard disks can transfer data to and from the computer at a much faster rate than floppy disks.

Hard disks are usually 5 inches, 8 inches, or 14 inches in diameter, although other sizes are available. In a hard disk drive, there may be one disk, or there may be several disks stacked on top of one another on the same vertical bar, or **spindle**. When there are several disks, you may refer to the group of disks as a **disk pack**. Figure 8.8 shows a disk pack. There is just enough space between the disk surfaces to allow movement of the read/write heads. Figure 8.9 shows read/write heads. Many hard disk

FIGURE 8.8

A disk pack is a group of disks.

FIGURE 8.9

Read/write heads move in and out of the spaces between disk surfaces.

drives use disks that are sealed against dust and dirt; these drives are called Winchester drives, a nickname for the particular technology they use.

The use of many disks can increase the speed of reading and writing by reducing the amount of head travel time. For example, suppose the words of a rather long document are to be recorded on disk. If the entire document is recorded on one disk surface, the write head moves into position over a track and uses all available space on that track. The head then moves to another track and uses all space available on that one, and so on. This may require several moves from one track to another. Suppose, however, that the data to be written is divided among several disk surfaces. In this case, all the write heads can move into position over the different surfaces and the entire document can be written with no further head movement. This can greatly increase the speed of data reading and writing. You may refer to all the tracks of the same number on different disk surfaces as a **cylinder**. For example, all the third tracks put together make up a cylinder (Figure 8.10).

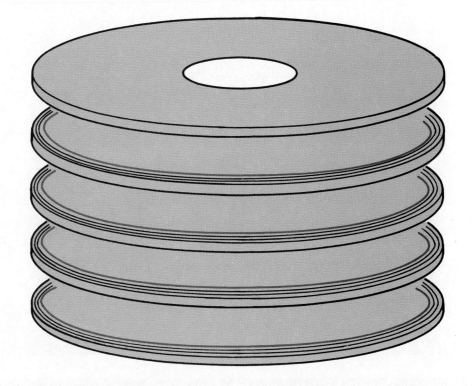

FIGURE 8.10

All the third tracks put together make up a cylinder.

Hard disks may be either fixed or removable. If a disk is removable, it may be taken out of the disk drive for storage and replaced by a different disk. A fixed disk cannot be removed from the disk drive. Figure 8.11 shows a picture of removable disks.

Because a hard disk does not bend, data can be packed much closer together than it can be on a floppy disk. Since many disk drives can be attached to the same computer system, the total amount of storage that can be on-line to the computer at any one time is almost unlimited.

Magnetic Tape

Magnetic tape is a long strip of flexible plastic like the tape used in an ordinary cassette tape recorder. The tape is coated with material that can be magnetized. Magnetic tape may be on reels or contained in one of several kinds of cartridges. Figure 8.12 shows a magnetic tape strip.

FIGURE 8.11

These fixed disks cannot be removed from their drives.

FIGURE 8.12

Magnetic tape is coated with material that can be magnetized.

Tape drives like the one in Figure 8.13 record data on the tape as magnetized spots in the proper pattern for each character. When the tape is read, the spots produce electronic impulses as they are moved past the read head of the tape drive. Figure 8.14 shows how the magnetic spots might appear if they were visible. Note that each character code is recorded across the tape in what is called a channel. A **channel** is a recording path along the tape. A read/write head is positioned over each channel on the tape. Tapes generally have nine channels, even though seven-channel tapes are available. The heads either read the data that is already on the tape and transfer it to the computer for processing, or they write the processed data coming from the computer onto the tape.

Many very inexpensive home computers use ordinary cassette tape recorders for data storage. Such a cassette tape contains only one channel where bits are recorded one after the other. In other words, a character that is written across a seven-channel or nine-channel tape is written lengthwise on a cassette tape. A cassette tape, therefore, is not capable of storing much data.

As with a disk, writing on tape erases data previously recorded on it. The new data erases the old data as the new data is recorded. However, reading data on tape does not erase the data.

FIGURE 8.13

Tape drives record data on the tape as magnetized spots in the proper pattern for each character.

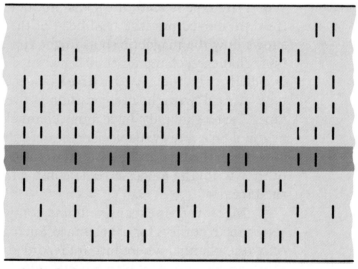

0 1 2 3 4 5 6 7 8 9 A B C M N O X Y Z

FIGURE 8.14

If the magnetized spots on a tape were enlarged, they might appear as shown above.

A tape drive is a sequential-access device. When a certain item of data is to be found on a tape, the computer reads all the items one after the other until it locates the desired one. The contents of the record (related data treated as a unit) can then be displayed on a video display, printed, or otherwise processed. For many applications where data needs to be stored or read in random order, the use of tape is not practical. For some jobs, however, it is very useful. For example, suppose wages are to be computed and paychecks prepared. A tape contains the name and other information about each employee. The tape can simply be read from start to finish, processing the information about each employee in order. Tapes are also good for making backups. A **backup** is a copy of all the data on an auxiliary storage medium. The copy is made so that the data will still exist if something should happen to the first copy.

Bubble Memory

Bubble memory consists of small magnetic "bubbles" that move on an endless "notched track" through the chip containing them. Figure 8.15 shows what bubble memory looks like.

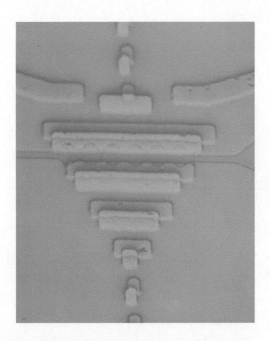

FIGURE 8.15

Bubble memory, as seen through an electron microscope.

The bubbles are arranged according to the binary code used by the computer; the presence of a bubble represents a 1, while the absence of a bubble represents a 0. For access, the bubbles move through the chip. Therefore, bubble memory is a sequential-access device. It is, however, very fast for a sequential-access device. Bubble memory is also valuable for applications where data needs to be recorded away from an office or plant; the data remains in the chips even when power is removed.

Laser Disks

A **laser disk**, shown in Figure 8.16, is one of the most exciting storage methods that has been developed. Laser disks are similar to disks used with video disk players and audio disk play-

FIGURE 8.16

Laser disks record data by the presence or absence of tiny holes.

ers. They record data by the presence or absence of tiny holes. The holes are burned in the disk by a laser beam and they are read back by a beam. The holes represent the codes for the recorded characters. A laser disk is a random-access medium. Most laser disks are not erasable and reusable, though a few are. Storage capacities for laser disks begin at about one billion characters per disk. This makes them very valuable for applications where huge quantities of data must be stored. For example, insurance companies with large files of customer data would find laser disks very attractive.

A WORKING COMPUTER SYSTEM

With the addition of storage devices and media, the hardware component of the working computer system is completed. Figure 8.17 adds the storage devices discussed in this chapter to the outline of the working computer system. Chapter 9 begins a discussion of the third component of the working computer system, that of software.

A WORKING COMPUTER SYSTEM

I. HARDWARE

    A. Input devices
        1. Video display terminal
        2. Speech recognition device
        3. Optical-character reader
        4. Optical-mark reader
        5. Bar-code scanner
        6. Magnetic ink character reader
        7. Magnetic scanner
        8. Real-time sensor
        9. Light pen
      10. Mouse
      11. Digitizer

FIGURE 8.17a

Partial outline for a working computer system.

B. Processing
    1. Processor
    2. Memory (RAM and ROM)

C. Output devices
    1. Video display
    2. Printer
        a. Impact
        b. Nonimpact
    3. Speech synthesizer
    4. Computer output microfilm
    5. Plotter
    6. Real-time controller
    7. Robot

D. Auxiliary storage
    1. Magnetic disk
        a. Floppy disk
        b. Hard disk
    2. Magnetic tape
    3. Bubble memory
    4. Laser disk

II. DATA

A. Categories
    1. Character
    2. Field
    3. Record
    4. File

B. Common coding systems
    1. ASCII
    2. EBCDIC

III. SOFTWARE

FIGURE 8.17b

Continuation of the outline for a working computer system with emphasis placed on auxiliary storage.

SUMMARY

Auxiliary storage operates much like a manual filing system. Almost all computers intended for general use have some form of auxiliary storage. The storage may be either random access or sequential access. If it is random access, the device can read or write a particular group of data without reading or writing everything that physically comes before it on the medium used. If it is sequential access, the device can read or write a particular group of data only by going through everything recorded before it on the medium.

The most commonly used random-access device is a disk drive. Some disk drives are designed to use floppy disks, while others use hard disks. Storage capacities and access speeds are higher with hard disk drives. The most commonly used sequential-access device is a tape drive. Bubble memory (which is sequential access) and laser disks (which are random access) are newer methods that are becoming more widely used.

REVIEW QUESTIONS

1. How is auxiliary storage used by the computer? (Obj. 1)
2. Compare auxiliary storage to a manual filing system. (Obj. 1)
3. Name two commonly used random-access media. (Obj. 2)
4. Name a commonly used sequential-access medium and a sequential-access device. (Obj. 2)
5. What is the main difference between floppy disks and hard disks? (Obj. 2)
6. What is the most important thing to consider in deciding whether to use random-access storage or sequential-access storage? (Obj. 3)
7. Name an application for which random-access storage is appropriate. (Obj. 3)
8. What are two applications for which sequential-access storage is appropriate? (Obj. 3)

9. How is data recorded with bubble memory? (Obj. 1)

10. How is data recorded with a laser disk? (Obj. 1)

VOCABULARY WORDS

The following terms were introduced in this chapter:

sequential access   spindle
random access   disk pack
magnetic disk   cylinder
track   magnetic tape
sector   channel
direct access   backup
flexible disk   bubble memory
floppy disk   laser disk
hard disk

WORKBOOK EXERCISES

Complete all exercises in Chapter 8 of the workbook before proceeding to Chapter 9 in this text.

DISKETTE EXERCISE

Complete the diskette exercise for Chapter 8 before proceeding to Chapter 9 in this text.

Using Electronic Mail Systems

In its simplest form, electronic mail means that one computer is used to send a message to another computer. In its most complex form, electronic mail is a network of thousands of computers or terminals, all of which may transmit messages to each other. Let's take a look at several different electronic mail systems. The persons and companies are fictitious, but the systems are very real.

It is 9:00 a.m. in New York. President Mary Hargood has just completed an extremely urgent business plan that must go to her company's office in San Francisco. Since the plan is needed for a meeting this afternoon, President Hargood uses the electronic service of one of the air couriers. She calls the courier's local number and they immediately send a truck to pick up the report. The report is then carried to the courier's local office and fed into an electronic scanner. The scanner converts the writing

on the document, as well as the charts and diagrams, to electronic signals. The signals are transmitted almost instantaneously by satellite to the courier company's San Francisco office. There they are received and converted into a printed copy of the original document. The printed copy is then taken by courier to the Hargood Company's local office, where it arrives in plenty of time for the meeting. In fact, it is in the San Francisco office about two hours after the call to the air courier to pick up the original copy.

In contrast to the Hargood Company, Braswell Jones's company in Seattle has purchased electronic mail services from an information utility. This service has both advantages and disadvantages in relation to the courier company's electronic mail

used by Hargood. Let's see how they compare. This morning, Jones's sales department has just finished work on a sales proposal that is needed by a salesperson in Peoria. To get the proposal to the salesperson as quickly as possible, the information utility's mail service is used. First, a word processing program is used to prepare the sales proposal. Therefore, the proposal is still stored on a computer diskette. The diskette can be used to electronically transmit the proposal to the information utility's local phone number. The utility then electronically transmits the message to Peoria. If the Peoria office has computer equipment, the message is transmitted to the computer there. Otherwise the document is printed out and delivered by mail the next day. From this example, it may be seen that the use of the information utility made it possible to send the message directly and electronically—no pickup courier was necessary. However, when the receiver of the message has no computer, the service is slower than the air courier's electronic service. Also, this type of service may not include the capability of sending graphs and charts, except for simple ones constructed of normal characters. In general, you can expect this kind of service to be less expensive than ones that require pickup and delivery by courier.

Hargood and Jones both rely on outside companies for occasionally used electronic mail. Increasing numbers of businesses, however, are finding it advantageous to have "full-time" electronic mail systems that connect most, if not all, of their business locations. In such a setting, each employee on the system has an electronic address, in much the same way that each building has a street address for the postal service.

Take a look at such a system. After a busy meeting, Janice Irwin returns to her office. A small icon (image) on the screen of her computer terminal tells her that mail is waiting. By pressing appropriate keys on the keyboard, she can scan a list showing the names of the persons who have sent mail. A couple of keystrokes later, the full text of an electronically stored memorandum (memo) appears on the screen. If she desires, Janice can compose and transmit a response directly from the keyboard. She can also "file" the memo and her response in permanent computer storage.

Many electronic mail systems used within companies provide the capability of transmitting messages to selected groups of

individuals. For example, a particular memo could be electronically sent to all sales managers. More advanced systems integrate the use of data, documents, and spoken messages. When it is desired to send a written message to one or more persons, written electronic mail is used. When a voice message is more appropriate, the system functions much like a standard telephone system. One advanced feature for the voice messages, however, is the digital recording of messages. If the intended person does not answer the phone, the system will record a message in computer storage. Then, when the intended receiver of the message returns, the computer system can play the message back from digital storage as many times as desired. The message is replayed in spoken form just as if it were being uttered by its sender.

The use of advanced electronic mail systems such as those described here is growing. Such systems have caused a permanent change in the way many businesses operate. Regardless of the level of sophistication of the communications system, however, the human qualities of the users of the system still determine the success or failure of the communications to accomplish their desired goals.

PART 4
Software

CHAPTER 9

Systems Software

Objectives

1. Define systems software.
2. Describe the functions of systems software.
3. Describe the differences between the operating system and other systems software.

Software is the third component required in a working computer system. Chapter 9 discusses systems software. Chapter 10 will discuss applications software, which is software that is written to solve particular problems. During the discussion in this chapter, remember that the terms *software* and *programs* mean the same thing.

SYSTEMS SOFTWARE

Systems software consists of programs designed to keep the computer running and programs to perform many everyday tasks related to the operation of the computer system. That is, systems software is concerned with keeping the computer system working. It also performs general operations rather than operations concerned with solving certain problems for the user. Some of the commonly used systems software is discussed in the following sections.

Operating Systems

The **operating system** is a series of programs that control the operation of the computer system. The primary responsibility of the operating system is control. To help you understand the role of the operating system, we will compare it to the role of a receptionist working in a large company.

The receptionist greets visitors and directs them to the people they need to see. Many times the visitors sign in upon arrival and sign out as they leave. All of these duties help the efficiency of the company, as shown in Figure 9.1.

Operating systems work in much the same way. The operating system can provide the needed resources to process a job. It can also check to see if the individual trying to use the computer has permission to use it. Figure 9.2 shows this function.

Additional Functions of the Operating System

Some of the other functions of the operating system are as follows:

FIGURE 9.1

The duties of an operating system are similar to the duties of a receptionist.

FIGURE 9.2

The computer asks the user for a password so that the user may gain access to the system.

1. It helps the processor, auxiliary storage, and the input and output devices communicate. The operating system helps all of the devices work together.

2. It provides a way of copying programs and data into memory from auxiliary storage.

3. It provides a way of saving programs and data from memory to auxiliary storage.

4. It provides commands for telling the processor what to do.

A computer system cannot do anything without an operating system. The operating system can be stored in ROM. The manufacturing company can build the operating system into ROM before it leaves the factory. An example of a popular ROM-based microcomputer is shown in Figure 9.3.

The operating system can also be stored in RAM. In many computer systems, you must load the operating system from a diskette before you can perform any task. When the operating system transfers from the diskette to RAM, a portion of available memory is reduced. If the operating system is on diskette or cartridge, you can replace it with a newer, more powerful operating system. Figure 9.4 shows a microcomputer that uses a cartridge to store an operating system.

FIGURE 9.3

ROM integrated circuits contain the operating system of this microcomputer.

FIGURE 9.4

Cartridge and diskette slots are used with this microcomputer.

Many different operating systems are on the market today. Although most of the operating systems can perform the tasks that have been mentioned, there are differences in their speeds and in their abilities to perform additional tasks. Some of the operating systems that have recently been developed make it very easy for a user to operate the computer. In fact, a user may not even be aware of the existence of the operating system.

Popular Operating Systems

There are several popular operating systems that are used with microcomputers. Here are some of the more popular operating systems, along with their developers:

The **UNIX** operating system was developed by Bell Laboratories. It is considered to be one of the most powerful operating systems on the market. It is used on microcomputers and minicomputers. One of the ways that the UNIX operating system is more powerful than some other operating systems is that it can perform more than one task at a time. For example, the UNIX operating system can print one program while you continue to work on another program. Figure 9.5 shows a single microcomputer having two input devices (keyboards) and two output devices (monitors).

FIGURE 9.5

Many microcomputers use the UNIX operating system.

The **XENIX** operating system is very much like the UNIX. In fact, it is called the UNIX work-alike operating system. It was developed by Microsoft Corporation. It, too, can work on more than one program at a time. The Microsoft Corporation also developed another operating system used on many popular microcomputers called **MS-DOS**.

PC-DOS is an operating system that was developed for International Business Machines Corporation (IBM) for use on IBM's Personal Computer. It is an operating system that is very similar to MS-DOS. Microsoft Corporation developed both operating systems.

One of the operating systems that has been used for a long time is **CP/M**. It was developed by Digital Research, Inc. and is used on many popular microcomputers. Figure 9.6 shows a microcomputer with a CP/M operating system.

Two other popular operating systems are **Apple DOS** (developed by Apple Computer, Inc.) and **TRSDOS** (developed by Radio Shack Division of Tandy Corporation).

FIGURE 9.6

The CP/M operating system is used by many popular microcomputers.

Utility Programs

Utility programs are another kind of systems software. A **utility program** is a program that will do routine jobs, such as copying data from one disk to another, making duplicate copies of disks, and putting data into a certain order.

As an example, suppose you are using a microcomputer with a hard disk drive and a floppy disk drive. Since the hard disk is so much faster and holds so much more data, all your data is stored on that disk. To prepare against the possibility of losing your data in case of computer failure, you decide to regularly copy your new data onto floppy disks. By having extra copies or backups, the data can be recovered if the disk drive fails. Instead of writing your own program to make the copies, you most likely use a utility program furnished by the supplier of your operating system. Your backup utility program probably will have enough decision-making power built in so that it copies only data that has been changed or added since the previous backup. This way, it does not take as many floppy disks.

Utility programs (often called utilities) are available from computer manufacturers, from those who sell operating systems, and from other companies. Other companies frequently "fill in the gaps" by supplying useful utilities that are not available from the manufacturer or operating system seller.

User-Interface Shells

Many operating systems and utilities that come with the computer use commands that are somewhat difficult to remember. This did not create a large problem when all computers were operated by specially trained operators who used the commands on a regular basis. As more and more persons began using their own computers, however, an easier way to use all the commands was needed. As an example, look at the following command line:

FORMAT B:/V/S/1

This is a command line that can be used by one of the most popular operating systems for microcomputers. The command will prepare a new floppy disk so that it can be used. The meaning of each part of the command is shown in Figure 9.7.

FORMAT	Record the necessary information on the disk so that it can be used.
B:	Use Disk Drive B (the second drive on the computer).
/V	Verify the disk. (Check the disk to see if there are bad spots on it. If there are, do not use them.)
/S	Place a copy of the operating system software on the disk.
/1	Prepare only one side of the disk.

FIGURE 9.7

The meaning of each part of the command *FORMAT B:/V/S/1* is shown above.

Since this command may have all, none, or any combination of the characters after the slash marks, the user of the command may not be able to remember it easily. Many other commands are just as difficult to remember. That is where user-interface shells come in.

A **user-interface shell** is simply a program that comes between the operating system and the user; it makes the use of operating system commands easier. It is loaded into memory and is there to help the user when the computer is **booted up** (started up). The shell uses a series of **menus** (lists of choices) to make operation of the system easier. An example of such a menu is shown in Figure 9.8.

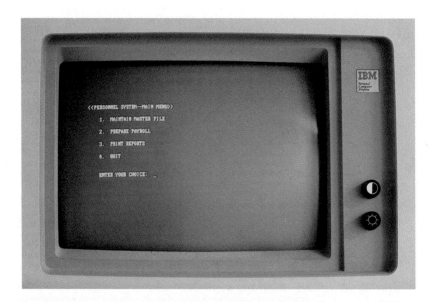

FIGURE 9.8

A video display with menu options.

The user-interface shell makes the computer system easier to use. It replaces confusing command lines with simple answers to questions. As with all computer software, there are a great deal of differences in the way these user-interface shells work.

The operating system software is the heart of the computer system. The utilities come with an operating system and perform other functions necessary to operate the computer. The user-interface shell makes it easy for the user to work with the operating system. The relationship of these three parts of systems software is shown in Figure 9.9.

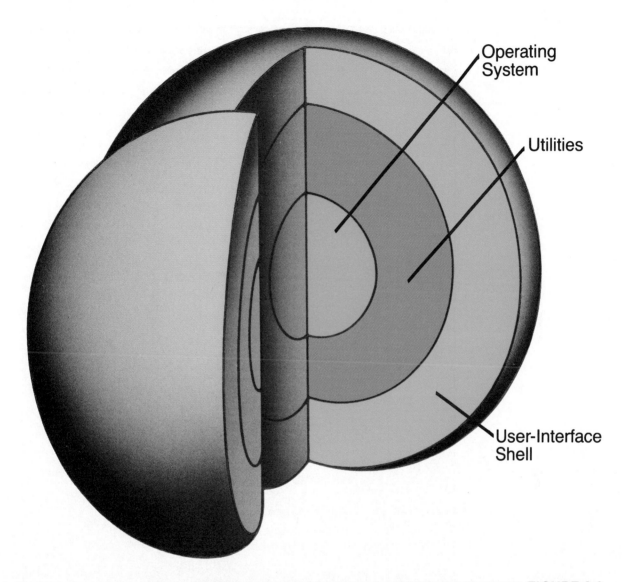

Operating
System

Utilities

User-Interface
Shell

FIGURE 9.9

The user-interface shell provides a menu-driven selection of utility programs, which in turn use the operating system routines. This illustration
shows the relationship of these three parts of systems software.

A WORKING COMPUTER SYSTEM

A working computer system requires software, as well as
hardware and data. The outline of the systems software component of the working computer system is shown in Figure 9.10.

A WORKING COMPUTER SYSTEM

I. HARDWARE

   A. Input devices
       1. Video display terminal
       2. Speech recognition device
       3. Optical-character reader
       4. Optical-mark reader
       5. Bar-code scanner
       6. Magnetic ink character reader
       7. Magnetic scanner
       8. Real-time sensor
       9. Light pen
     10. Mouse
     11. Digitizer

   B. Processing
       1. Processor
       2. Memory (RAM and ROM)

   C. Output devices
       1. Video display
       2. Printer
          a. Impact
          b. Nonimpact
       3. Speech synthesizer
       4. Computer output microfilm
       5. Plotter
       6. Real-time controller
       7. Robot

   D. Auxiliary storage
       1. Magnetic disk
          a. Floppy disk
          b. Hard disk
       2. Magnetic tape
       3. Bubble memory
       4. Laser disk

FIGURE 9.10a

Partial outline for a working computer system.

II. DATA

   A. Categories
      1. Character
      2. Field
      3. Record
      4. File

   B. Common coding systems
      1. ASCII
      2. EBCDIC

III. SOFTWARE

   A. Systems
      1. Operating system
      2. Utility program
      3. User-interface shell

FIGURE 9.10b

Continuation of outline for a working computer system with emphasis placed on systems software.

SUMMARY

Systems software operates and controls the computer system. It consists primarily of operating systems, utility programs, and user-interface shells. These are designed to keep the computer functioning and to perform many general operations. Operating systems perform duties, such as saving programs and data from memory into auxiliary storage and providing commands that tell the processor what to do. Utility programs do routine jobs, such as making backup copies and putting data into a certain order. Finally, user-interface shells make the use of operating system commands easier through the use of menus.

REVIEW QUESTIONS

1. What is systems software? What are its functions? (Objs. 1, 2)

2. What are some of the tasks performed by the operating system? (Obj. 2)

3. Name four commonly used operating systems. (Obj. 1)

4. What is one of the most powerful operating systems? (Obj. 1)

5. What can the UNIX operating system do that some of the older operating systems cannot do? (Objs. 1, 2)

6. Describe one specific task performed by a utility program. (Obj. 2)

7. What is a user-interface shell? (Obj. 1)

8. How does the user-interface shell assist the user? (Obj. 2)

9. What is one task performed by the user-interface shell? (Obj. 2)

10. Name three examples of systems software. (Objs. 1, 3)

VOCABULARY WORDS

The following terms were introduced in this chapter:

systems software	Apple DOS
operating system	TRS-DOS
UNIX	utility program
XENIX	user-interface shell
MS-DOS	boot up
PC-DOS	menu
CP/M	

WORKBOOK EXERCISES

Complete all exercises in Chapter 9 of the workbook before proceeding to Chapter 10 in this text.

DISKETTE EXERCISE

Complete the diskette exercise for Chapter 9 before proceeding to Chapter 10 in this text.

The Robots Are Here

We are being invaded by robots, and some of them slightly resemble humans in appearance. From atomic-inspection robots to guard robots to lawn-mowing robots to many other kinds, the force is growing.

In contaminated nuclear power plants, robots are sent into the dangerous areas to check conditions. In some businesses, armed guard robots patrol the buildings and lots after closing hours. Skillful enough to open unlocked doors and powerful enough to crash through locked doors, the guard robot comes

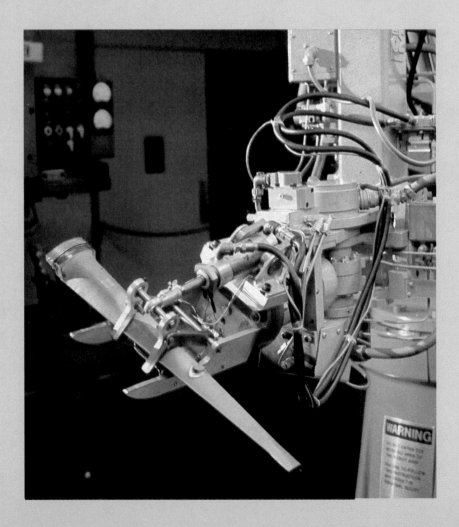

complete with voice to warn intruders and can withstand attacks from all commonly used weapons. Intruders can be cornered and held by the robot until police arrive. Lawn-mowing robots follow a predetermined path around the yard, relieving their owners of the chore of guiding a mower.

Many students who have visited an Atlanta bank have been impressed by a robot there. Affectionately named Hot Lips, the robot performs the job of tape librarian in the bank's computer center. The bank uses many hundreds of magnetic tapes for auxiliary storage in its computer system. Between uses, the tapes are stored on shelves very similar to library shelves. If the bank used old methods, a person would have to find each tape and mount it on a tape drive when it was needed. With the bank's new method, however, the computer sends a message to the small computer controlling Hot Lips. Upon receiving the message, Hot Lips cruises almost silently between shelves of tapes until it comes to the place where the needed tape is stored. There it extends a set of pneumatic lips against the desired tape. With a powerful smack, the tape reel is sucked against the lips. Holding the tape in its lips, the robot glides to a tape drive, inserts the tape, and releases its kiss. Task accomplished, it waits

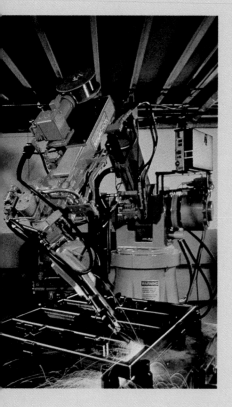

for its next assignment. Later, after the just-mounted tape is no longer being used, Hot Lips will remove it from the tape drive and replace it in its assigned storage location.

In an electronics manufacturing plant, a variation of the Hot Lips theme illustrates computerized warehousing. In this manufacturing plant, raw materials such as sheet metal, cabinets, wire, and electronic components are used for assembling electronic devices. Once the devices are assembled, the finished products must be stored temporarily until they are shipped to their buyers. In the olden days, people took all the incoming raw materials and placed them on shelves. When materials were needed, people searched for the correct materials, took them off the shelves, and delivered them to the assembly area. When the assembly of items was finished, people took the finished products and placed them on different shelves. Finally, when someone purchased a finished product, a person had to go to the shelf, remove the product, and take it to the shipping dock for loading onto a truck.

Now compare the current method with the old one. Assume that a shipment of integrated circuit chips has just come in. The chips are parts that will go into several models of computerized devices produced by the company. As the parts come off the delivery truck, they are checked in by a computer terminal operator. The operator verifies what the parts are, where they came from, and how many were received. She or he then places the parts in the possession of a robot. At the same time, information about the parts is keyed into the terminal. It is immediately available to the accounting system, so the personnel writing the checks to pay for the parts will know they have been received. The computer to which the terminal is attached also immediately looks in its record of warehouse space to find the location of enough empty space to hold the newly arrived circuit chips. Upon finding a large enough space, the computer directs the robot. The robot then whizzes down aisles and raises itself to the proper height to deposit the parts in precisely the instructed place. Now the robot's storage work is done. The computer, however, must remember where it placed the parts.

Now assume that several days have gone by and the circuit chips are needed on the assembly line for insertion into circuit cards being produced. The computer operator keys in the item

number of the desired chips. The computer looks up the location in which it stored the chips earlier, and it instructs the robot to go back to that spot and get them. The chips are then carried by conveyor to the proper point on the assembly line.

A little further along, finished products are coming off the assembly line. As one step in its assembly process, each product has had a label attached. This label, containing the stock number, is read by a scanner at the end of the assembly line. The information is fed into the computer, and the product is carried by the robot to a storage place designated by the computer. When the product is sold, the operation is similar to the retrieval of parts. A data entry person enters the item number being requested by a customer on the terminal. The computer looks up the location in which it has placed the product and instructs the robot to go get it. Once the robot has the product off the shelf, it is transported by conveyor to the shipping area. In the shipping area it is labeled and turned over to the transportation company that will deliver the product to its buyer.

CHAPTER 10

Applications Software

Objectives

1. Define applications software.
2. Describe some commonly used applications software.
3. Describe some commonly used programming languages.

In the last chapter, software that runs the computer was discussed. You learned that the operating system controls the different parts of a computer system. The operating system contains the instructions that are necessary for writing and reading, auxiliary storage, and printing. Utility programs are instructions for doing tasks such as copying disks. User-interface shells are programs that make the use of operating system commands easier. The main purpose of systems software is to operate the computer system. The main purpose of applications software is to perform jobs required by the user.

DEFINITION

Applications software consists of programs designed to solve specific problems for the user. Applications software does work such as accounting tasks, mailing lists, or helping a retail store keep up with sales and inventory. Applications software may be either canned or custom written. **Canned software** is software that has already been written by a programmer and can be purchased from a store. Figure 10.1 shows a display of some popular canned software. Some canned software can be

FIGURE 10.1

Canned software can be purchased from a store.

purchased and used like it is, or with a few changes it can perform a specific job. Other canned software may require major changes to perform the job you want done. In this case, it is usually better to buy what is known as custom-written software.

Custom-written software is software written exactly for the job that you want done. Custom-written software, therefore, is usually much more expensive than canned software. For many programming jobs, however, the use of custom-written programs is the only way to be certain that the job is done exactly as needed.

Data Processing Examples

There are many different software applications available. A couple of the more popular applications are included in the next section.

Spreadsheets

Spreadsheets are one of the fastest growing data processing applications. A **spreadsheet** is a program that uses a table (row and column arrangement) of numbers to perform calculations. Some of the numbers are calculated by performing arithmetic on other numbers in the table. Once the table is set up, all the calculations are done by the program. Since calculation of many of the numbers is automatic, spreadsheets are excellent "what if" tools to help make predictions. The example in Figure 10.2 shows a spreadsheet application.

If you wanted to calculate your budget for the next year, a spreadsheet could do the job for you. In fact, if you wanted to test several different possible budget combinations, a spreadsheet would be one of the fastest ways to perform the calculations. Since many spreadsheets are canned software, it is very easy to go to the store and purchase one of the many brands of spreadsheets available.

Accounting Applications

Accounting tasks were among the first tasks that businesses used the computer to perform. One of the best known accounting jobs is writing paychecks for a business. Other accounting tasks include billing customers, keeping records of the payments, and keeping up with what the business owes other people, as well as general record keeping. Figure 10.3 shows one accounting job completed by the computer.

FIGURE 10.2

Spreadsheets can be used for many different applications.

FIGURE 10.3

Writing paychecks for businesses is one of the best known accounting jobs performed by the computer.

Word Processing Examples

Word processing is the writing and storing of letters and reports on a computer. Once a report is written using the computer, it can be stored and changed again and again as desired. This makes it possible to make corrections easily. Word processing is one of the most popular purchases of canned software. If you purchased this canned software, it would allow you to write letters using your computer. There are several other application programs frequently used with word processors. The most common program is the spelling checker. Writing-style checkers are also becoming more popular.

Spelling Checkers

A **spelling checker** program goes through a keyed-in document one word at a time, looking up each word in a dictionary stored on auxiliary storage. Any word not found in the dictionary is called to the attention of the operator. The operator decides whether the word is wrong and needs correction, or whether the word is correct and is just not in the dictionary. Words that are not in the dictionary can be added. Some spelling checkers show the operator words whose spellings are close to that of the word not found; if one of them is the correct word, the program will automatically put it in.

Writing-Style Checkers

Writing-style checkers do even more for you than spelling checkers. For example, some of them check for overuse of particular words and suggest other words whose meaning is similar. Some of them check for sentences that are too long. Some even check for such errors as incomplete sentences.

PROGRAMMING LANGUAGES

All computer programs, whether they are systems software or applications software, are written in a computer language. In this section, we will take a look at different languages that have been written to make it easier to communicate with the computer.

Machine Language

Computers were first programmed in **machine language**, where the instructions were written in the binary number code that is directly understood by the processor. Computer instructions written in machine language, or binary numbers, are written as a series of 1's and 0's to represent on and off conditions to the computer. Machine language is the most difficult programming language. It is also very time-consuming. Not only must the instructions be in numbers, the programmer must keep up with the exact memory locations where the data items are to be stored. Programming is currently done in machine language only when nothing else will work or in rare instances.

Assembly Language

Assembly language is a step up from machine language. Instead of using numbers, the programmer can express instructions in alphabetic terms. For example, *ADD* might mean *add*, or *LAD* might mean *load accumulator direct* (take a number and put it in storage in the processor). Assembly language also allows storage locations in memory to be referred to by names rather than the actual numeric locations. Assembly language is much easier than machine language, but is still rather difficult and time-consuming. It is used when the high-level languages to be discussed in the next section are not suitable. Figure 10.4 shows an example of instructions written in assembly language.

ASSEMBLY LANGUAGE	EXPLANATION OF LANGUAGE
MVC Amount, NBR	Move NBR to Amount
AP Total, NBR	Add NBR to Total
SP NBR1, NBR2	Subtract NBR2 from NBR1

FIGURE 10.4

With assembly language, the programmer can express instructions in unique abbreviated form.

Before programs written in assembly language can be understood by the computer, they must be translated into machine language. The translation is done by a program called an **assembler**. The assembler is supplied by the computer manufacturer or a company that sells computer software.

High-Level Languages

Machine language and assembly language require that the programmer think in terms of the distinct processor being used and the instructions the processor requires. **High-level languages**, on the other hand, allow the programmer to think in terms of solving the problem rather than making the processor happy. The programmer is able to write instructions to the computer using English and English-like terms. Because of this ease of use, most application programs are written in high-level languages. Like assembly language programs, however, programs written in a high-level language must be translated into machine language before they can be understood by the processor. The translation is done by either an **interpreter program** or a **compiler program**. The interpreter or compiler is supplied by the computer manufacturer or a company that sells computer software.

The operation of an interpreter is somewhat like an English-speaking person talking to a Spanish-speaking person through a human interpreter. The English-speaking person says a sentence, then the interpreter repeats the sentence in Spanish. This process is repeated as long as the English-speaking person talks. In like fashion, an interpreter program for a computer looks at one instruction written in a high-level language, translates the instruction into machine language, and relays it to the processor. The processor then immediately carries out the instruction. Now the interpreter looks at the next instruction and translates it. The process is repeated until all instructions are carried out. Using an interpreter makes it easy for a programmer to debug the program. To **debug** a program means to find and correct the errors in it. Using an interpreter causes a program to operate more slowly than if a compiler is used because of the translations after each instruction.

Compilers also translate high-level languages into machine language. Their operation is similar to a person who translates a book from English to French. After the entire book is translated and written in French, a French-speaking person can read it. A compiler program similarly translates the entire high-level program into machine language and stores the machine-language version. The computer's processor then looks at the machine-language version as it follows the instructions. Programs translated with a compiler operate faster than those translated with an interpreter. Finding problems in the programs, however, is more difficult.

Three of the most commonly used high-level languages are introduced in the following paragraphs.

BASIC

The **BASIC** language was designed to make interactive programming less difficult. It is usually translated by an interpreter, which makes the identification and correction of programming problems easier. BASIC is considered an easy-to-learn language, partly because of its limited capability. More recent versions of the language, however, are very capable and are suitable for writing application programs in nearly every area. There are many different versions of the BASIC language. BASIC stands for Beginner's All-Purpose Symbolic Instruction Code. You will learn more about this language in Chapters 14 through 16.

Pascal

Pascal is a relatively new language. It is useful for writing programs for nearly every application. Pascal includes features that make program writing easier. These features are not available in some versions of BASIC. When you learn about structured programming concepts in Chapter 14, remember that Pascal is generally considered a well-suited language for doing structured programming. Pascal is generally translated with a compiler, which makes finding and correcting errors more difficult. The Pascal language was named in honor of the mathematician Blaise Pascal, who lived in the seventeenth century.

COBOL

COBOL was the first language written for use in business applications. It is still commonly used, especially with minicomputers and mainframes. Many businesses prefer COBOL to the other languages. Its strong point is the handling of large amounts of data stored on auxiliary storage. It is also one of the wordiest languages. While some programmers object to the large number of words required, the English-like sentences make COBOL programs easier to understand than those written in some other languages. COBOL is translated by a compiler. Its name is short for COmmon Business Oriented Language.

Natural Language

The ultimate computer language can be called a **natural language**. At present, natural-language processing is available in a very limited form. Research, however, is progressing. The existence of a complete natural language would mean that you could instruct the computer by using ordinary, everyday English (or Spanish, or whatever language the computer would be programmed to receive).

A WORKING COMPUTER SYSTEM

With this chapter, the outline of the working computer system is completed. The three main components of hardware, data, and software have been discussed. The final addition, applications software, has been added to our outline as shown in Figure 10.5.

SUMMARY

Applications software is used to solve specific problems for the user. It can be either custom-written or canned software. Some popular canned software are spreadsheets, spelling checkers, writing-style checkers, and word processing applications. Many data processing applications such as accounting and billing of customers can be either custom-written or canned software, depending on the exact requirements of the job.

Whether it is systems software or applications software, all instructions to the computer have to be written in a programming language. The programming languages briefly dis-

A WORKING COMPUTER SYSTEM

I. HARDWARE

  A. Input devices
    1. Video display terminal
    2. Speech recognition device
    3. Optical-character reader
    4. Optical-mark reader
    5. Bar-code scanner
    6. Magnetic ink character reader
    7. Magnetic scanner
    8. Real-time sensor
    9. Light pen
    10. Mouse
    11. Digitizer

  B. Processing
    1. Processor
    2. Memory (RAM and ROM)

  C. Output devices
    1. Video display
    2. Printer
      a. Impact
      b. Nonimpact
    3. Speech synthesizer
    4. Computer output microfilm
    5. Plotter
    6. Real-time controller
    7. Robot

  D. Auxiliary storage
    1. Magnetic disk
      a. Floppy disk
      b. Hard disk
    2. Magnetic tape
    3. Bubble memory
    4. Laser disk

II. DATA

  A. Categories
    1. Character
    2. Field
    3. Record
    4. File

  B. Common coding systems
    1. ASCII
    2. EBCDIC

III. SOFTWARE

  A. Systems
    1. Operating system
    2. Utility program
    3. User-interface shell

  B. Applications
    1. Canned software
    2. Custom-written software
    3. Data processing examples
      a. Spreadsheet
      b. Accounting applications
    4. Word processing examples
      a. Spelling checker
      b. Writing-style checker

FIGURE 10.5

Outline for a working computer system with emphasis placed on applications software.

cussed in this chapter were machine language, assembly language, BASIC, Pascal, and COBOL.

REVIEW QUESTIONS

1. What is applications software? How is it used? (Objs. 1, 2)
2. Describe the two forms of applications software. (Obj. 1)
3. Name three popular canned software applications. (Obj. 2)
4. Name two data processing applications. (Obj. 2)
5. Name the canned software that could be used to prepare a budget. (Obj. 2)
6. How is an interpreter used? (Obj. 3)
7. How is a compiler used? (Obj. 3)
8. What is the most difficult programming language? (Obj. 3)
9. What is the most commonly used language in business? (Obj. 3)
10. What language is considered an easy-to-learn language? (Obj. 3)

VOCABULARY WORDS

The following terms were introduced in this chapter:

applications software	assembler
canned software	high-level language
custom-written software	interpreter program
spreadsheet	compiler program
word processing	debug
spelling checker	BASIC
writing-style checker	Pascal
machine language	COBOL
assembly language	natural language

WORKBOOK EXERCISES

Complete all exercises in Chapter 10 of the workbook before proceeding to Chapter 11 in this text.

DISKETTE EXERCISE

Complete the diskette exercise for Chapter 10 before proceeding to Chapter 11 in this text.

Kids Write the Darndest Programs!

It's the week before Valentine's Day. In the cafeteria of Briarwood High School, two microcomputers have been set up. In front of each computer is a line of students, each student eagerly awaiting the chance to part with his or her cash. In exchange for the cash, each will receive a list of the most compatible students of the opposite sex.

Yes, this is a computer dating system in operation. During the previous week, most students in the school filled out a questionnaire. The questionnaire included questions about the student's preferred characteristics in a date, as well as questions about her or his own characteristics. Students involved in the

project then spent the greater part of a week keying the responses to the questionnaire into a computerized data base.

Now, as each student in the line says good-bye to his or her cash, the student operating the computer enters the student's name on the keyboard. In a matter of seconds, the names of the most compatible dates are displayed on the printer attached to the computer. Compatibility was computed by the computer's program on a point basis. For example, if a person had indicated on the questionnaire that a tall date was preferred, tall persons were given more points toward a match. By the same token, if a student said a younger date was preferred, younger persons were given more points toward the match. Adding together all the points for the different matching factors gave a summary total. The potential dates with the highest totals appeared on the printout.

For the grand sum of one dollar, each student received five names. Therefore, one dollar would buy the names of the five most compatible persons. Another dollar would buy the names of the next five persons, and so on. For Brad, a very persistent student, this scheme would cause the loss of much money. Brad

had been dating Lu for several months and considered that they were the perfect couple. Just out of curiosity, though, he wanted to see how compatibly the computer would rank them. Thus, when Brad reached the front of the line and paid his dollar, he fully expected to find Lu's name at the top of the list. However, when the list was torn from the printer and handed to him, Lu's name was nowhere to be found. Not one to give up easily, Brad pulled out another dollar and asked for the names of the five next most compatible girls. Again, no Lu. Exasperated, Brad paid again . . . and again . . . and again. Finally, the computer said "Sorry, there are no more names in the data base." Crestfallen, Brad made his way to his next class, only to find out from Lu that she had failed to fill out the questionnaire and her name was not in the data base.

The program used in this dating project was very sophisticated and extremely difficult to write, yet it was planned and written by three ninth grade students at Briarwood. Those three students are just a few of the many kids who are accomplishing great things in the computer business. Some of them work for school benefit, but many are in profit-making ventures for themselves.

One such student, while still in school, was employed as a contract programmer by a computer vendor. In this job, the student was exposed to a whole segment of society about which he knew nothing. You see, the computer vendor had just sold a new system to the county jail. It was the student's job to write the programs to be used in booking prisoners and collecting bail bond money. Bail is the amount of money that must be paid if the prisoner wants to be released from jail while awaiting trial. Bail is rather like insurance to help guarantee that the prisoner will show up for the trial. If the prisoner does not show up, the bail money is lost. If he or she does show up, the bail money is returned to the person who paid it. In the student's program, each time a person was arrested, his or her data was entered into the computer. Then, when a magistrate set bail for the prisoner, the amount of bail required was entered into the system. When the bail was paid, the computer issued a receipt to the person who put up the money.

Many whiz kids, such as the ones you have read about here, start very young. From writing newspaper columns about

computer games, to writing game software, to writing serious computer programs, young persons across the country have gotten into the act. Many kids in computer businesses got started by playing games, then decided to program some games of their own. They then hit on a money-making idea involving the computer. Making money from writing computer software, however, is not as easy as it once was. Once almost anybody with even a mediocre program could place an advertisement in a computer magazine and make some sales. Programs and their marketing are much more sophisticated now. Many companies have entered the business of writing and selling computer programs, and many have failed. There is always room for those with worthwhile new ideas, however. If nothing is ventured, nothing will succeed. Trying to make money with your computer can be a lot of fun, even if you don't make a fortune.

PART 5
Processing

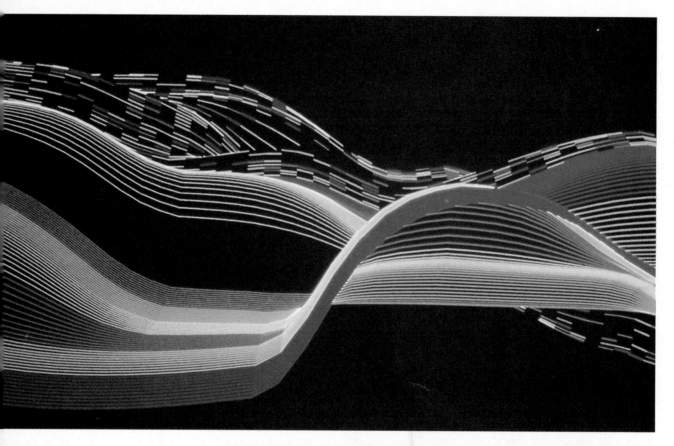

CHAPTER 11

Information Processing: How Data Flows Through the System

Objectives

1. Define data processing and word processing. Describe how they are alike and how they are different.

2. Describe the data processing functions.

3. Describe the word processing functions.

4. List the benefits of integrating data processing and word processing as information processing.

In the previous chapters you have looked at the three components of a working computer system. This chapter puts it all together.

INTEGRATION OF DATA PROCESSING AND WORD PROCESSING

The term **integration** is defined as the process of bringing together. When it is used to describe data processing and word processing functions, it means to bring them together to work on the same task.

History

Computers were first used in business mainly for data processing. **Data processing** is the job of putting facts into usable form. Most computer applications involved arithmetic calculations or the storage and changing of various facts. Computer use in accounting and engineering became widespread. Later, typewriters were connected to special computers and word processing was born. Word processing is the writing, revising, printing, and storing of documents such as letters and reports.

As time went on, programs were developed to allow computers to do word processing. Then newer word processors such as shown in Figure 11.1 were made to do arithmetic. In fact, word

FIGURE 11.1

Newer word processors were made to do all kinds of jobs previously left to computers.

processing machines could be programmed to do all kinds of jobs previously left to computers. After all, a word processor was nothing but a computer specially programmed for writing text. Thus, data processing and word processing began to be integrated and known as information processing. It makes a lot of sense, for example, to be able to take figures calculated by data processing and place them in documents being created by word processing. As an example of this, data processing might compute which students made the honor roll based on their final grades. Letters of congratulation could then be sent to these students by using word processing. The word processing operation could take the names, addresses, and grades of each student and insert them into a form letter. Figure 11.2 shows an example of this process.

Another example of the integration of data processing and word processing can be found in the input of data. Frequently, the same input needs to be included in a letter and also used in further processing. For example, a sales manager may use a program to estimate predicted sales and expense figures for the following year. The numbers from this estimate can then be input into the word processing system to produce a report for the marketing department. The numbers may also be input into the accounting system. Comparisons can then be made between the estimates and the actual figures that will be computed as the year progresses. This comparison report can then be sent to top management. See Figure 11.3 for an illustration of this process.

Benefits of Integration

The benefits of integrating data processing and word processing into information processing include the following:

1. Data already in the computer can be used for more than one job. Thus, data may be input only once instead of two or more times.

2. Records are more accurate. In the past, large offices often duplicated the same information several times so that the same information would be available to many workers. However, the more times information is recorded, the greater the possibility that the information on one record will be changed and the information on another record will not. With the integration of

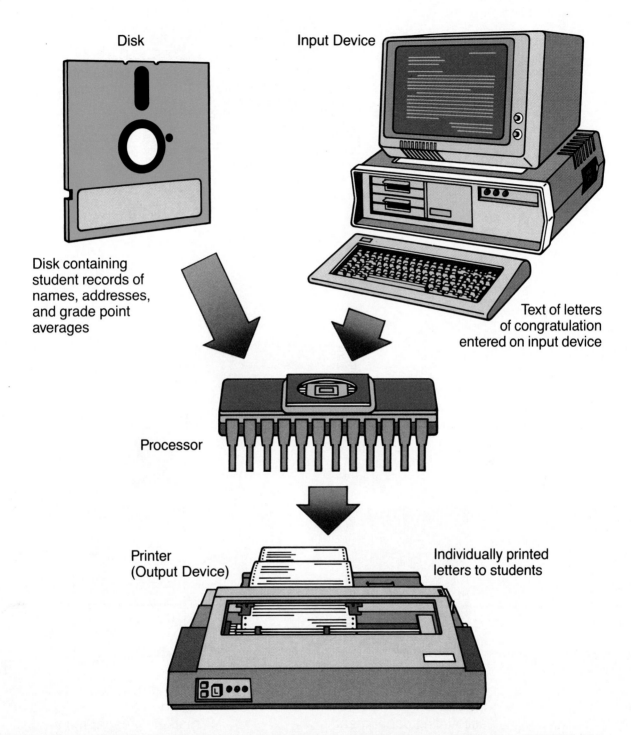

Disk

Input Device

Disk containing
student records of
names, addresses,
and grade point
averages

Text of letters
of congratulation
entered on input device

Processor

Printer
(Output Device)

Individually printed
letters to students

FIGURE 11.2

Data processing and word processing can be integrated into information
processing. In this example, the input from two different sources is used to
create output (letters).

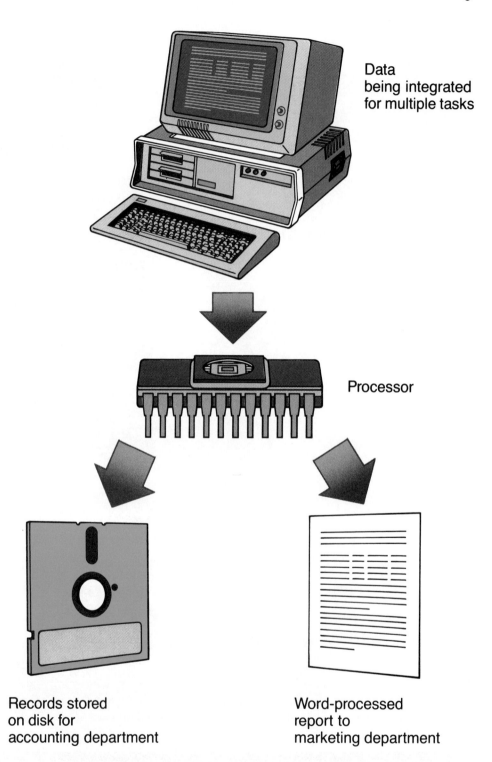

Data
being integrated
for multiple tasks

Processor

Records stored
on disk for
accounting department

Word-processed
report to
marketing department

FIGURE 11.3

Frequently the same input needs to be included in a letter and also used in
further processing.

data processing and word processing, the necessity of having more than one record with the same information is reduced.

3. It reduces waste. Trends in office work indicate that computer equipment, such as terminals and microcomputers, is being used more and more by managers, accountants, and secretaries. It is not being operated all day by specialized data entry personnel. As a result of this, expensive equipment often stands idle without much use. For example, one study has shown that the average microcomputer in a business office is actually in use about 30 minutes a day. By combining both word processing and data processing functions on one machine, the machine is used more of the time and is, therefore, more economical.

In the remainder of this chapter, we will take a more detailed look at the functions of information processing. We will break the functions into two areas: those typically thought of as data processing functions and those typically thought of as word processing functions. Keep in mind, however, that some of the functions are common to both areas, and that all of the functions are frequently integrated with each other and performed on the same equipment.

DATA PROCESSING FUNCTIONS

Data processing includes one or more of the following operations: recording, coding, sorting, calculating, summarizing, communicating, storing, and retrieving.

Recording

Recording is the process of writing, rewriting, or reproducing data by hand or electronically. Recording includes many different operations. Some of the operations are handwriting, typewriting, duplicating, microfilming, entering data on a terminal, and recording data on magnetic tape or disk. For example, the employees in Figure 11.4 are recording work hours with a time clock.

FIGURE 11.4

Time clocks record work hours.

Coding

Coding is the process of assigning certain symbols to stand for something else. It is used as a shortcut, much like using your initials instead of writing your complete name. You probably use codes when you register for classes at your school. For example, *1* might stand for seventh grade, *2* for eighth grade, and so forth. Similar codes may be assigned to major programs of study, names of courses, and students' career preferences.

Stores identify stock items by codes in order to keep accurate sales and inventory records. Items appearing in catalogs have codes or stock numbers. ZIP codes on letters are used to sort the letters by cities and various locations in the cities. The names of states have two-letter abbreviations as shown in Figure 11.5. A single sales slip may contain several codes. One code may be for the salesperson and another may be for the department. One code may be the customer's account number, and another code may be the stock number identifying the article sold. A telephone number is a code in which some of the numbers stand for a part of the country (area code), some for a city or part of a city, and some for a particular telephone.

FIGURE 11.5

One example of the use of codes.

Codes speed up data entry time and processing. They help in selecting the data needed to solve a given problem. They also save space in a computer. Note the codes used in the enrollment page in Figure 11.6. These are codes for: (1) students in each class, (2) female students, (3) male students, (4) age of female students, and (5) age of male students.

Sorting

Sorting is the process of arranging information according to a logical system. Sorting includes (1) the *sequencing* of names or other data in alphabetic or numeric order; (2) the *grouping* of data by date, product, department, state, or some other classification; and (3) the *selecting* of a certain record from a group of similar records. Sorting may be done on the computer by actually

NAME				BIRTHDATE			
LAST	FIRST	CLASS	SEX	MO	DAY	YEAR	NUMBER
--------------------	--------	-----	---	----------------			-------
Salomon	Kathy	1	F	1	9	74	744
Santana	Ruben	2	M	12	24	73	313
Sayers	Don	1	M	3	12	74	495
Shaw	Becky	3	F	5	6	72	484
Smith	Ray	1	M	10	11	73	749
Sumio	Linda	3	F	9	7	71	751

CODES

FIGURE 11.6

Codes speed up data entry time and processing.

rearranging the data in memory or on an auxiliary storage medium such as a disk. Sorting the data in this manner is one of the most time-consuming operations performed on most computers. For many applications, therefore, programs have been developed that provide sorting functions.

Sometimes the only task that you would want to do would be to arrange a list of names in alphabetic order or to group records into separate categories. For other applications, however, sorting speeds up further processing. Before course grades are recorded on student record forms, for example, the grade reports for each student might be grouped together to make the process easier. Figure 11.7 shows part of a mailing list that might be sorted before processing.

Calculating

Calculating is the process of computing in order to arrive at a mathematical result. It includes adding, subtracting, multiplying, dividing, and other mathematical operations. There are many calculations needed to arrive at the wages earned by an employee, for example. Note the results of these calculations in the paycheck shown in Figure 11.8. Regular hours worked were added and multiplied by the hourly rate to get the regular earn-

ORIGINAL LIST OF NAMES	NAMES SORTED BY STATE	NAMES SORTED ALPHABETICALLY WITHIN EACH STATE
Mr. Tom Martin-Smith 999 Forestry Dr. Santa Ana, CA 92707-3942	Mr. Tom Martin-Smith 999 Forestry Dr. Santa Ana, CA 92707-3942	Mrs. Connie Conway 1020 Crossway Blvd. San Diego, CA 92128-5029
Miss Karen Wilson 5209 Wonder Lane Plainfield, NJ 07060-5556	Mrs. Connie Conway 1020 Crossway Blvd. San Diego, CA 92128-5029	Mr. Tom Martin-Smith 999 Forestry Dr. Santa Ana, CA 92707-3942
Ms. R. J. Morgan 40 Hopewell Place Newark, NJ 07110-6777	Mr. Shandon White 8001 East 3rd Street Wheaton, IL 60187-4433	Mr. Shandon White 8001 East 3rd Street Wheaton, IL 60187-4433
Mrs. Connie Conway 1020 Crossway Blvd. San Diego, CA 92128-5029	Miss Karen Wilson 5209 Wonder Lane Plainfield, NJ 07060-5556	Ms. R. J. Morgan 40 Hopewell Place Newark, NJ 07110-6777
Mr. Shandon White 8001 East 3rd Street Wheaton, IL 60187-4433	Ms. R. J. Morgan 40 Hopewell Place Newark, NJ 07110-6777	Miss Karen Wilson 5209 Wonder Lane Plainfield, NJ 07060-5556

FIGURE 11.7

This partial mailing list is sorted first by state (grouping), then alphabetically by each person's last name (sequencing).

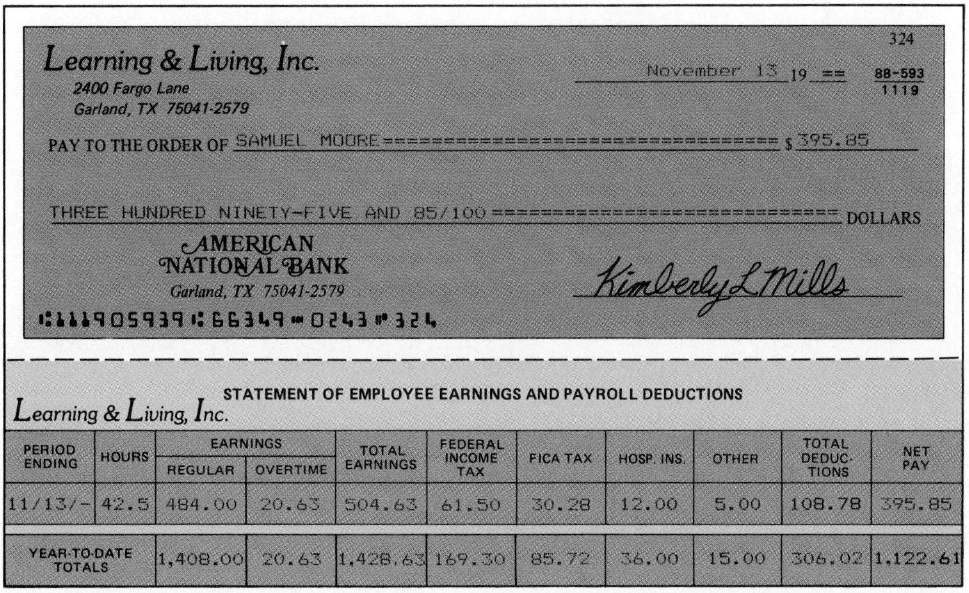
Learning & Living, Inc.
2400 Fargo Lane
Garland, TX 75041-2579

324

November 13 19 ==

88-593
1119

PAY TO THE ORDER OF SAMUEL MOORE ================================ $ 395.85

THREE HUNDRED NINETY-FIVE AND 85/100 ========================== DOLLARS

AMERICAN NATIONAL BANK
Garland, TX 75041-2579

Kimberly L Mills

⑆111905939⑆ 66349⑈ 0243⑈ 324

STATEMENT OF EMPLOYEE EARNINGS AND PAYROLL DEDUCTIONS

Learning & Living, Inc.

PERIOD ENDING	HOURS	EARNINGS		TOTAL EARNINGS	FEDERAL INCOME TAX	FICA TAX	HOSP. INS.	OTHER	TOTAL DEDUC-TIONS	NET PAY
		REGULAR	OVERTIME							
11/13/-	42.5	484.00	20.63	504.63	61.50	30.28	12.00	5.00	108.78	395.85
YEAR-TO-DATE TOTALS		1,408.00	20.63	1,428.63	169.30	85.72	36.00	15.00	306.02	1,122.61

FIGURE 11.8

This paycheck shows typical calculations performed by the computer.

ings. Deductions were then subtracted from the regular earnings to arrive at the amount of the paycheck.

Summarizing

Summarizing is the process of changing processed data into brief, meaningful form. Summaries of information help managers because they contain only the most necessary information. Printed reports usually involve summaries. As already explained, many calculations must be made to prepare paychecks for employees of a company. The data from the calculations of all the paychecks can be summarized to make it useful to a business. For example, summaries can list some of the following: (1) total wages paid, (2) total deductions for social security taxes, and (3) total number of employees on the payroll. Figure 11.9 shows an example of a business financial summary.

Communicating

Communicating is the process of sending information from one point to another point. Communicating may consist of nothing more than the transfer of reports from one desk to another. Frequently, however, it includes such activities as the sending of electronic information by telephone, microwave, satellite, and television. A microwave that is used to send information is shown in Figure 11.10.

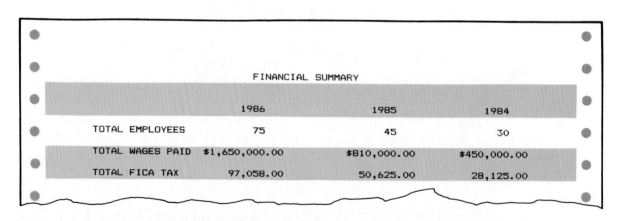

FIGURE 11.9

A partial business financial summary.

FIGURE 11.10

Microwaves are used to send electronic information.

Storing

Storing is the saving of information so that it may be used later. The operation should allow for prompt storage of data, for strict following of rules about the use of stored materials, and for destruction of records when they are no longer needed. With a computerized data processing system, storage is done by use of the auxiliary storage devices you learned about in Chapter 8.

Retrieving

Retrieving is the process of making stored information available when needed. Records stored in a computer or on magnetic tape, disks, or COM can be easily retrieved only if the information is properly coded. When it is properly coded, retrieval is accomplished very quickly.

WORD PROCESSING FUNCTIONS

Word processing includes those functions necessary for producing, revising, printing, and storing text in the form of documents. These functions include entering text, revising text, assembling text, merging text and data, communicating the text in the form of a document, and storing and retrieving the document.

Entering Text

Text entry is the process of getting words from the mind of the writer or from a written document into the computer system. Text is usually entered into the system by using a keyboard and video display, as the operator is doing in Figure 11.11. Any errors made while entering the text are quickly and easily corrected by rekeying. If desired, changes can also be made during the entry process. Eventually the entry of text may be done with speech recognition devices. The entry of text is similar to data processing's recording function.

Revising Text

Once text is entered, any change made to it is known as a **revision**. Words or characters may be added or deleted, misspellings may be corrected, or sentences may be changed or moved. In making revisions, any text that is already correct does not need to be rekeyed. Figure 11.12 gives an example of corrections that could be made.

FIGURE 11.11

Text is usually entered into a system by using a keyboard and video display.

```
This is an example of text that needs to be revised.

The first sampel contanes mispelings and other errrors?

the second smple shows the same text with all all the

corrections corrections made.
```

```
    This is an example of text that needs to be revised.

The first sample contains misspellings and other errors.

The second sample shows the same text with all the

necessary corrections made, including words that have

been added as well as deleted.
```

FIGURE 11.12

With word processing, text can be easily revised.

Assembling Text

Assembly is putting together different parts of text to form a new document. For example, hundreds of paragraphs may be stored on disk. To reply to a letter, the writer could choose paragraphs from the disk and combine them as shown in Figure 11.13. Once the paragraphs are combined, any changes that are desired can be made.

Merging Text and Data

Merging is the process of combining text and data into the same document. Merging is useful in many applications. For example, you may want to send letters to a particular group of people. All the names and addresses you need may already be stored on a disk as data. You can compose the letter with the word processing functions, then have the computer merge together the names, addresses, and letter text. This process works as shown in Figure 11.14.

January 9, 19--

Mr. Michael Bishop
428 Meadowlark Way   ⎤
Greensboro, NC 27410-8888 ⎬ Name and address from keyboard

Dear Mr. Bishop: ⎦

Thank you for your letter of inquiry concerning any ⎤ Paragraph
job openings with our agency.   ⎦ from disk

Your letter and resume were very impressive. You ⎤
obviously have had much experience working in the   ⎪
social service community. The many volunteer hours ⎪
you have spent working in the various agencies are ⎬ Paragraph
evidence of a strong and sincere commitment to a   ⎪ from keyboard
higher quality of life for all the residents of our ⎪
community.   ⎦

However, I am sorry to inform you that you do not yet ⎤
meet the educational requirements of our agency. When ⎪
you have completed your studies, please contact us   ⎪
again.   ⎬ Paragraphs
                                                     ⎪ from disk
We will keep your resume on file, and we wish you the ⎪
best in all of your future undertakings.   ⎦

Sincerely,

Ron Jackson

Ron Jackson
Social Service Director

IT/RJ

FIGURE 11.13

Text from the disk and the keyboard is assembled to form a letter.

Communicating Documents

Once a document has been created, it must be communicated to the intended user. Usually this means the document is printed, and mailed or delivered. Frequently, however, finished documents are now sent to the user in the form of electronic mail. Figure 11.15 shows electronic mail being received on the screen.

Ms. Sarah Adams
77 Hamilton Drive
Seattle, WA 98103-4977

D. Pat Malloy
936 Venus Place
Seattle, WA 98115-5936

Kenneth Tass
108 West Westshire Blvd.
Seattle, WA 98106-8330

List of names and
addresses stored
on disk

LIGHTHOUSE ART CENTER

30 Echo Lake Place

Seattle , Washington 98126-8677

February 1, 19--

As a loyal patron of the arts, you are invited to
our annual Spring Showing, where the best works of
30 local artists will be proudly displayed.

As you may know, the trends of expression in the
art world have drastically changed in the past
year. I think I can promise that you will be very
impressed and inspired by the beauty and idealism
that many of our artists represent.

We look forward to seeing you at our showing in
May.

Best regards,

L. B. Gordon

L. B. Gordon
Art Director

acz/LBG

Body of letter composed with
word processing functions

FIGURE 11.14

Merging data into a letter.

Storing and Retrieving Documents

The word processing storage and retrieval functions are similar to the data processing storage and retrieval functions. Entire documents or parts of documents may be stored. The storing of documents such as letters and reports has historically been done by keeping the paper on which they were written.

FIGURE 11.15

Electronic mail has become a popular way of sending and receiving up-to-date messages.

However, growing numbers of these documents are being stored on computer media such as disks and COM. As you learned in Chapter 8, these media can store much more information in a smaller space.

SUMMARY

When computers were first used in business, they were used for data processing applications—applications dealing with numbers and facts. Functions carried out by data processing included recording, coding, sorting, calculating, summarizing, communicating, and storing. Later, specialized equipment was developed for processing words. Functions supported by word processors included text entry, revision, assembly of text, merging of data and text, communicating of documents, and storage of documents.

As technology progressed, these two areas of application began to be combined. Computers were equipped with word processing software, while word processors were equipped with programs to allow them to do data processing applications. It became possible for the data processing and word processing applications to share text and data with each other. The combining of data processing and word processing is known as information processing. There are many benefits from information processing, including less wasted effort, greater accuracy of records, and better use of equipment.

REVIEW QUESTIONS

1. What is data processing? (Obj. 1)
2. What is word processing? (Obj. 1)
3. Briefly state how data processing and word processing are alike. How are they different? (Obj. 1)
4. List three benefits to be gained by integrating data processing and word processing into information processing. (Obj. 4)
5. Name and describe the eight functions of data processing. (Obj. 2)
6. Name and describe the six functions of word processing. (Obj. 3)
7. Define the sequencing aspect of sorting. (Obj. 2)
8. What is retrieving and how is it used? (Obj. 2)
9. How is merging useful to a business? (Obj. 3)
10. Why is summarizing useful to managers? (Obj. 2)

VOCABULARY WORDS

The following terms were introduced in this chapter:

integration
data processing
recording

communicating
storing
retrieving

coding   text entry
sorting   revision
calculating   assembly
summarizing   merging

WORKBOOK EXERCISES

Complete all exercises in Chapter 11 of the workbook before proceeding to Chapter 12 in this text.

DISKETTE EXERCISE

Complete the diskette exercise for Chapter 11 before proceeding to Chapter 12 in this text.

A Brief Guide to Telecommunicating with Computers

For students, their parents, and just about anyone else, telecommunication can open up new worlds of use for microcomputers. Telecommunication allows the microcomputer user to access other computers to do such things as obtain information, share information, or order merchandise.

To get started with telecommunicating, you will need a microcomputer or terminal, a modem, appropriate computer software, and a phone line. The modem (MODulator-DEModulator) is the electronic circuit required to connect the computer or terminal to the phone line. The modem you use may be built into your computer or terminal. Or it may be a separate

box connected by a cable. More sophisticated modems can automatically make phone calls to the remote computer. Less expensive ones require the operator to manually dial the phone number.

Regardless of the kind of modem you are using, by calling an information utility you have access through your computer to a wealth of information. Depending on where you live and the arrangements made by the particular information utility, your phone call may be either local or long distance. Several utilities, for example, have local phone numbers in just about all major cities. Once the phone call is made, you enter your account number and password.

The cost of accessing an information utility varies tremendously. Some of the general-use utilities such as CompuServe Information Service and The Source are quite inexpensive, with low hourly rates. Others, such as specialized services for particular professions, can be very expensive. For some services there may be additional fees above the normal rates. The data you can access and the actions you can perform vary somewhat from one service to another. Look at some of the more common services that are available:

Electronic Bulletin Boards. Messages may be posted by callers for reading by other callers. The messages may be posted as part of a large group, or they may be posted as part of a smaller special-interest group. For example, there may be an area for messages between users of particular brands of computers. Some of the special-interest group bulletin boards may be provided as part of the basic service of the utility. Others may require the payment of a separate subscription fee.

Electronic Mail Service. Similar to the electronic bulletin board, the electronic mail services provided by some utilities make messages available only to the designated individuals to whom they are addressed. Since not everyone calls the information utility every day, some utilities will (for an extra fee) phone the persons who have messages waiting and alert them.

General Information Lookup. Some utilities can provide all kinds of obscure or hard-to-find information. This information is accessed by entering words descriptive of the kind of information desired.

News. The kinds of news that can be accessed through an information utility range from the news provided by wire services such as Associated Press and United Press to specialized news such as the financial news provided by Dow-Jones. There is an extra charge for some news services, while some may be included as part of a utility's basic service.

Banking. Some utilities have made arrangements with certain banks to provide banking services by computer. Funds may be transferred from one account to another, or payments may be ordered. There may be extra charges for this service.

Travel Planning. For those planning trips, complete airline schedules as well as other travel information are available. Some

services even allow the user to make reservations directly from the computer. There may be an extra charge for this service.

Shopping. Several information utilities provide for varying amounts of shopping to be done by computer. By entering your major credit card number and the stock numbers of the items you want to buy, a purchase is made. The merchandise is shipped directly to you from the distributor. The range of merchandise that can be purchased is varied. However, it tends to be either computer-oriented or high-tech consumer merchandise. Some services advertise their prices as being lower than those available in most stores.

Telecommunications using microcomputers is a fairly new area. Many microcomputer users do not yet have the necessary modems and software for doing telecommunicating. The number of persons using such services is rapidly increasing, however. Some persons predict that within a few years telecommunicating with your computer will be as common as making a routine telephone call.

CHAPTER 12
Personal Productivity Tools

In a previous chapter, you learned some of the ways in which applications software enables computers to improve the operations of businesses. Word processing, data processing, and real-time applications of the computer are a few of the ways computers help businesses. In this chapter, you will learn how the computer can increase the productivity of individuals.

DEFINITION OF PERSONAL PRODUCTIVITY TOOLS

Increasing the productivity of a person means that the person can produce work in less time than previously required. The computer can help do this by taking over many of the tasks that otherwise would have to be done by hand. Therefore, a **personal productivity tool** is any program that helps a person do work with less effort or time than would be required without the computer.

COMMONLY USED PERSONAL PRODUCTIVITY TOOLS

Personal productivity tools can be divided into four main groups based on the work to be done. These groups include word processors, spreadsheets, data bases, and graphics programs. These programs will be explained in the following sections.

Word Processors

As you learned in Chapter 10, word processors are programs that simplify the process of writing. The three main functions of word processors are text entry, revision (editing), and printing. A word processor allows the user to enter text on a keyboard, then print it out whenever desired. By making it easier to correct errors and eliminating the need for retyping, word processors reduce the amount of time required for composing documents. For example, by using a word processor, the author of this chapter was able to complete the work in about one fifth of the time that would have been required with a typewriter. Word processors can also lead to more accurate spelling and make the creation of multiple documents easier. As you study the following detailed explanations of the different things word processors can do, try to think about a school or club assignment that could be made easier by using the program.

Text Entry

In entering text with a word processor, the words appear on a video display as they are keyed in. The process is started with a command from the keyboard. For example, depending on the program, you might enter the letter *D* for document or the letter *I* for insert. At some point, the word processor will ask you for a name under which to store the document.

If an error is made in entering text, the error can be corrected immediately simply by backing up and rekeying it. The ease with which errors are corrected results in much "cleaner" original text (text with fewer errors). Once the text is entered, it is saved on a disk for future use.

Text Editing

Editing is the process of making changes in text. Several kinds of changes can be made, including those in the following paragraphs.

Insertions An **insertion** is new text that is added to existing text. It may be a single letter, a word, a group of words, or even whole paragraphs, sections, or chapters. Suppose you had entered the text for a school assignment. In the assignment, you mentioned George Washington and something he did when he was a general. In reviewing the assignment before handing it in, you decide that your paper is not clear on whether Washington was a general or a president at the time he took the action. The easiest way to improve the paper is to insert the title *General* in front of the name. Figure 12.1 shows you how to make an insertion with a typical word processor.

After the insertion is made, it is possible to print out only the page with the correction on it. You can then replace the old page with the new page of hard copy. The ability to go back and insert the new word prevents you from having to retype the entire page or rewrite it in longhand.

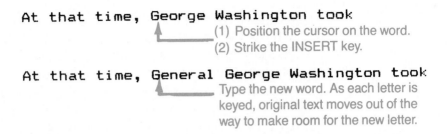

FIGURE 12.1

Follow the steps above when making an insertion with a typical word processor.

Deletions The ability to delete is exactly the opposite of the ability to insert. The amount of text to be deleted may be a character, a word, a sentence, a paragraph, or an entire section or chapter. In the previous example, suppose you decide that *General Washington* would sound better than *General George Washington*. The name *George* could be deleted with the steps shown in Figure 12.2.

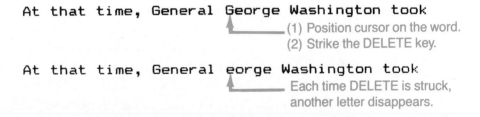

FIGURE 12.2

Follow the steps above when making a deletion with a typical word processor.

In addition to the letter-by-letter deletion shown here, many word processors have commands for deleting an entire word, line, or paragraph at the same time.

Replacement The **replacement** function of most word processors enables you to change one word to another, either in one place or throughout a document you have written. Suppose you have written another paper for school and referred to the name *Ralph Smith* in several places. After completing the paper, you find out that Smith is spelled *Smythe*. A single command can make the change in all places. The process is started by striking the key or key combination that means *find and replace*. This key might be a separately labeled key, it might be Control-A for *alter*, Control-F for *find*, or some other combination. Once the command is given, the word processor usually will respond with a series of questions to be answered by the user. The conversation between word processor and user might go as presented in Figure 12.3. The word processor's questions are shown in blue, while possible responses you might make are shown in red.

```
FIND? Smith

REPLACE WITH? Smythe

GLOBAL (Y/N)? Y

CONFIRM EACH OCCURRENCE (Y/N)? N
```

FIGURE 12.3

When the replacement command is given, the word processor usually responds with a series of questions to be answered by the user.

The *GLOBAL(Y/N)?* question is asking whether to replace the word every time it occurs in the document. If you had answered *N* for no, the name *Smith* would be replaced with *Smythe* only the first time it occurs. The *CONFIRM EACH OCCURRENCE(Y/N)?* question gives you the chance to tell the word processor whether to pause for your approval before making the change at each occurrence. Frequently, it is a safer idea to have the word processor stop for confirmation. Suppose you enter the replace command, telling the word processor to change each occurrence of *ham* to *pork*. That seems straightforward enough, so you tell the program not to stop for confirmation: in other words, to change each occurrence automatically. Though that sounds logical, think for a moment. Your paper may include the words *shame* and *hammer* in addition to *ham*. With a global change without confirmation, *shame* would have been turned into *sporke* and *hammer* would have been changed to *porkmer*. Obviously, these were changes you didn't want to make. The lesson to be learned from this is that usually you don't want to do a global replacement without confirmation. Confirmation is always the safe route to travel.

Moves Moves allow text to be moved from its present location and placed in a new location. You may, for example, want to move a paragraph from one location to another. The steps are typically as follows:

1. Mark the text to be moved with the following steps:

   a. Move the cursor to the beginning of the text to be moved.
   b. Enter a command generally called BLOCK BEGIN.
   c. Move the cursor to the end of the text to be moved.
   d. Enter a command generally called BLOCK END. When this command is given, the marked text usually changes to reverse video (highlighted) or to a different color to make it easy to see. Figure 12.4 shows a paragraph of text marked and ready to be moved.

2. Move the cursor to the location to which the text should be moved.

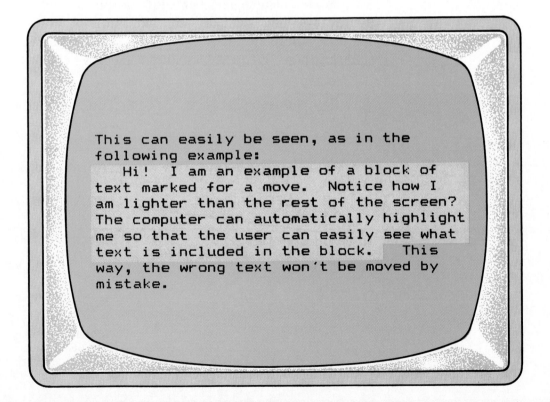

FIGURE 12.4

A block of text marked for moving.

3. Enter a command generally called BLOCK MOVE. The block should now be in its new location.

Just about all word processors can do the functions just described. Most word processors can also follow many other commands. In selecting a word processing program, you should look at all the commands various programs can carry out. Then select the one whose commands most nearly match your needs for the kind of writing you do. For example, if your writing frequently requires the entry of long, difficult-to-spell medical or legal words, it is important to obtain a word processor with a glossary feature. Such a program allows you to enter a long word only once. After that, every time you want to use the word, all you need to do is strike a certain key and the word will be inserted at the desired location.

Spreadsheets

A spreadsheet is a row and column arrangement of data. Some of the data is usually calculated from other data entered by the user. There are many examples of spreadsheets. Let's look at some of them. Figure 12.5 shows a grocery receipt. While most

```
Qty   Description        Price        Ext

  2   ST GREEN BEANS        .75       1.50

  1   HZ CATSUP            1.80       1.80

  3   LBS SAUSAGE          1.90       5.70

                       SUBTOTAL       9.00

                       TAX            .45

                       TOTAL         9.45
```

Numeric data entered by the user or Universal Product Code.

Numeric data calculated from data entered by the user or Universal Product Code.

FIGURE 12.5

A grocery receipt is an example of a spreadsheet.

persons may not think of grocery receipts as spreadsheets, they are just that. The receipt shown consists of four columns: quantity, description, price, and extension. The extension is computed by multiplying the quantity by the price. Once all the items are entered, the subtotal is found by adding together the extensions. The sales tax is computed by multiplying the subtotal by the tax rate. The total is found by summing the subtotal and the tax.

The next example of a spreadsheet, shown in Figure 12.6, is one you are more likely to find being calculated with a computer's spreadsheet program. This spreadsheet keeps records of the stock owned by an individual. The figures entered by the user are shown in red. Those automatically calculated by the program are shown in blue. Note that some of the stocks have increased in price, resulting in a profit. Others have decreased, resulting in a loss.

Name of Stock	Price Paid	Current Price	Number of Shares	Calculated Profit	Total Value of Stock
ARNCO	12.50	14.75	100	225.00	1475.00
BARGE	8.50	6.50	100	200.00-	650.00
BLAND	55.00	32.00	200	4600.00-	6400.00
ZORCO	15.00	25.00	100	1000.00	2500.00
				------------	------------
			TOTALS	3575.00-	11025.00

FIGURE 12.6

An example of the type of spreadsheet generally calculated with a computer's spreadsheet program.

Now let's see how the spreadsheet would be entered into the computer. When the program is run, the computer display might appear as shown in Figure 12.7.

In the entry screen, notice that the columns are identified with letters of the alphabet, while the rows are identified with row numbers. The rectangle at Location A1 (the A column and the first row) is known as the cell pointer. It appears in inverse video and indicates the position at which any keyed value will be entered.

Once the entry screen is displayed, as shown in Figure 12.7, values are entered. To do this, the cell pointer is first moved by using the cursor control keys on the keyboard. Once the desired

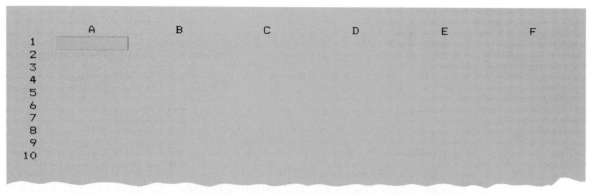

■ **FIGURE 12.7**

The entry screen of a computerized spreadsheet program.

cell is highlighted, the value is keyed on the keyboard. For example, when Cell A1 is highlighted, you might key in the heading *Name of*. Then the pointer might be moved to Cell A2 and the heading *Stock* can be entered. Look now at Figure 12.8. It shows the example values that are entered as constants from the keyboard.

```
              A             B          C          D          E           F
 1    NAME OF        PRICE      CURRENT    NUMBER OF  CALCULATED  TOTAL VAL
 2    STOCK          PAID       PRICE      SHARES     PROFIT      OF STOCK
 3
 4    ARNCO          12.50      14.75        100
 5    BARGE           8.50       6.50        100
 6    BLAND          55.00      32.00        200
 7    ZORCO          15.00      25.00        100
 8                                                   ----------  ----------
 9                                          TOTALS
10
```

■ **FIGURE 12.8**

The example values from Figure 12.6 have been entered from the keyboard into the spreadsheet program.

Since the computer is to calculate the remaining values, it must be told how to do so. The first value to be calculated is the "Calculated Profit" for the ARNCO stock. This is to be found by subtracting the price paid from the current price, then multiplying by the number of shares. In terms of the spreadsheet, the program subtracts the amount in Cell B4 from the amount in Cell C4. Then it multiplies the result by the number in Cell D4 to arrive at E4. The exact manner in which the formula is entered varies from one brand of spreadsheet to another. However, the first step is almost always to move the cell pointer to the location at which the calculated result should be placed. Once the cell pointer is placed, the following commonly used method of entering the formula can be completed. Let the first thing you key be an arithmetic symbol. This will be the signal to the spreadsheet that you are about to enter a formula rather than a value. Following is the line you might enter for the example. The asterisk (*) means multiplication:

$$+ (C4 - B4) * D4$$

The parentheses are necessary to tell the program to do the subtraction before it does the multiplication. As soon as the formula is entered, the calculated amount is placed in its position on the spreadsheet. Formulas can be copied from one cell to another if desired, reducing the amount of keying required. Once all formulas are in place in the example, the data on the screen appears as shown in Figure 12.9. The spreadsheet can be printed and/or saved to disk for future use.

The best thing about a spreadsheet is that once it has been set up, any change in data automatically changes everything else calculated from that figure. In the example, suppose another day has gone by and the current stock prices have changed. Simply by moving the cell pointer back to that column and changing the current values, everything in the calculated cells is recomputed to show the correct current values. Figure 12.10 shows how these changes appear. Compare this spreadsheet with the original in Figure 12.9.

	A	B	C	D	E	F
1	NAME OF	PRICE	CURRENT	NUMBER OF	CALCULATED	TOTAL VAL
2	STOCK	PAID	PRICE	SHARES	PROFIT	OF STOCK
3						
4	ARNCO	12.50	14.75	100	225.00	1475.00
5	BARGE	8.50	6.50	100	200.00-	650.00
6	BLAND	55.00	32.00	200	4600.00-	6400.00
7	ZORCO	15.00	25.00	100	1000.00	2500.00
8					----------	----------
9				TOTALS	3575.00-	11025.00
10						

FIGURE 12.9

Once all the formulas are in place, the calculations can be made.

	A	B	C	D	E	F
1	NAME OF	PRICE	CURRENT	NUMBER OF	CALCULATED	TOTAL VAL
2	STOCK	PAID	PRICE	SHARES	PROFIT	OF STOCK
3						
4	ARNCO	12.50	14.00	100	150.00	1400.00
5	BARGE	8.50	7.00	100	150.00-	700.00
6	BLAND	55.00	40.00	200	3000.00-	8000.00
7	ZORCO	15.00	25.25	100	1025.00	2525.00
8					----------	----------
9				TOTALS	1975.00-	12625.00
10						

If you change these figures, fields E and F will also be changed.

FIGURE 12.10

Simply by changing current values, everything in the calculated cells is recomputed to show the correct current values.

Data Base Programs

A **data base program** is a program for entering, saving, and retrieving information with the computer. For example, the stock names, prices, and other information in Figure 12.10 can be thought of as a data base. A list of names and addresses is also a data base. Most data base programs use a "fill in the blank" form on the screen for the entry of data. Examine Figure 12.11, which shows a typical screen for entering data into a name and address data base. The form is simply "filled in" by entering the data on the keyboard. Once one entry has been completed, another blank form appears on the screen for the next person.

```
Name    _____

Street  _____

City    _____

State   _____    ZIP  _____
```

FIGURE 12.11

Most data base programs use a "fill in the blank" approach.

Some data base programs are very simple, some are very complex. Even the most simple programs let you enter information, save the information, make changes or corrections in the information, retrieve the information, and display it in the same form in which it was entered. For example, you could ask such a program to show you any information about Susan Jones (address, phone number, etc.).

More capable data base programs allow the use of more than one set of information at once and allow more complex questions to be asked. For example, you might ask for an alphabetic listing showing the names of all football players who have an A average and who have taken ballet lessons.

Graphics

A **graphics program** represents data in the form of a graphic, or picture. For many applications, presenting data in graphic form is much more effective and easier to understand than in text or table form. Sales by product, percents of students taking certain courses, and load factors on aircraft are all examples of results that can be grasped much more easily when they are in graphic form.

Graphics generally are done in one of several forms. Some of the more common forms are bar graphs, line graphs, and pie charts. Bar graphs, such as the one in Figure 12.12, are good for showing comparisons between different items. Line graphs indicate changes in data over a period of time as illustrated in Figure 12.13. Pie charts like the one in Figure 12.14 are excellent for showing the division of data into parts. The whole circle generally represents 100 percent. Each wedge represents a portion of the whole. Good graphics programs can take input from the keyboard or from a data file and produce the desired type of graph. When color is available, graphs can be in color on both the screen and printouts.

INTEGRATION OF PRODUCTIVITY TOOLS

While each of the productivity tools we have discussed is useful by itself, the tools are much more valuable when they are integrated. Integration means that the different program func-

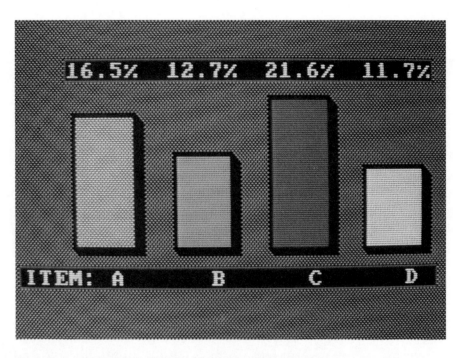

FIGURE 12.12

Bar graphs show comparisons between different items.

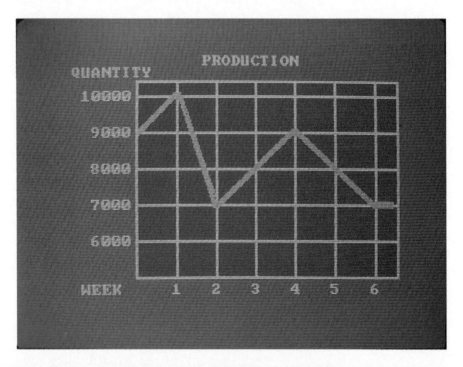

FIGURE 12.13

Line graphs indicate changes in data over a period of time.

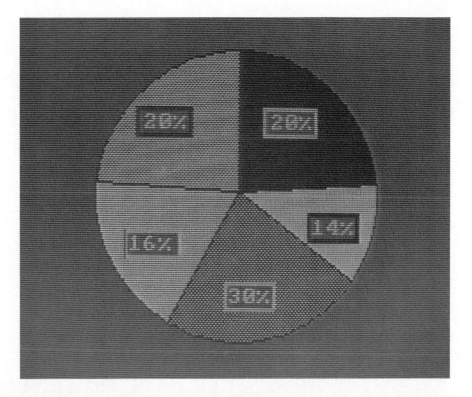

FIGURE 12.14

Pie charts are excellent for showing the division of data into parts. The whole circle generally represents 100 percent. Each wedge represents a portion of the whole.

tions can be used together with the same data. The greatest benefit obtained by integrating productivity tools is that the same data can be used by several programs without being reentered. Software is available that provides all kinds of combinations of the functions of word processing, data base programs, spreadsheets, and graphics programs. Some of them add other capabilities such as providing for communication with other computers or maintaining an appointment calendar. Many integrated systems use **windowing**, which is a process that allows the user to have different applications in use in different areas of the display at the same time. For example, part of a document might be on the screen at the same time as a graphic, as shown in Figure 12.15.

As an example of integration, data can be maintained by the data base portion of a program. The spreadsheet portion can be used to summarize the data and make various calculations. The graphics part can produce pictorial representations of the results, and the word processor can be used to send personalized

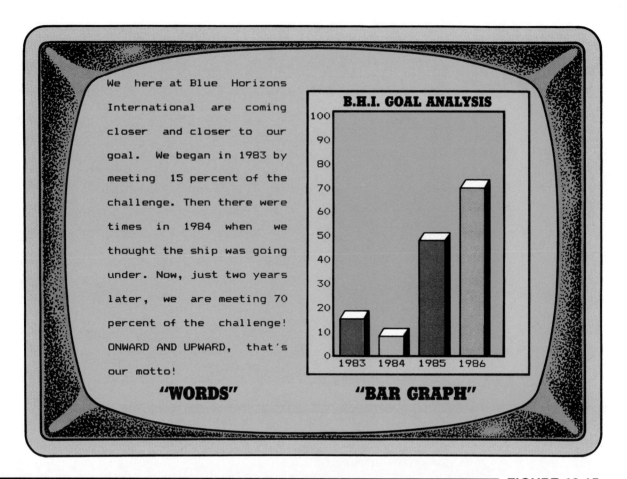

FIGURE 12.15

The use of windowing enables the user to see different applications on the screen at the same time.

letters to the stockholders in the business telling them of the results for the year. Figure 12.16 illustrates how this integration might work.

SUMMARY

Personal productivity tools are computer programs that enable an individual to be able to do work in less time and with less effort. Commonly used productivity tools include word processors, spreadsheets, data bases, and graphics programs. Frequently, several of these applications are combined into an integrated package of programs that work

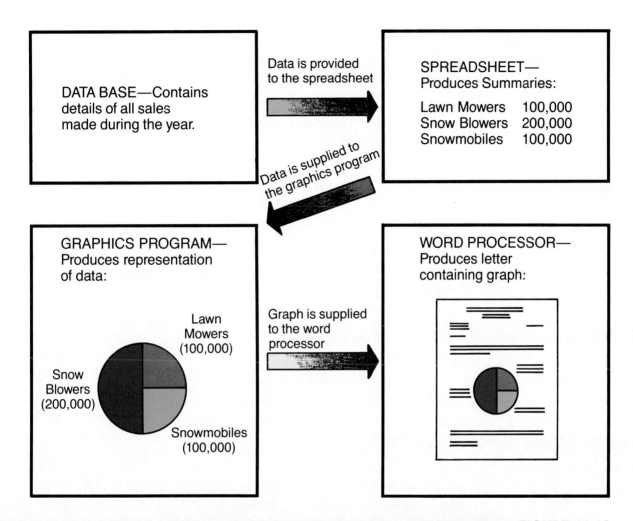

An example of how the integration of productivity tools might work.

together. Integrated packages frequently provide for different applications to be running in different windows on the screen at the same time. By using the same data for different purposes, integrated packages make work still more efficient.

REVIEW QUESTIONS

1. What are personal productivity tools? (Obj. 1)

2. Name four types of text changes involved in text editing. (Obj. 2)

3. Define a spreadsheet program and how it is used. (Obj. 2)

4. Define a data base program. (Obj. 2)

5. Define a graphics program. (Obj. 2)

6. What is the greatest benefit of the integration of personal productivity tools? (Obj. 3)

7. What is the value of having windows when using integrated programs? (Obj. 3)

VOCABULARY WORDS

The following terms were introduced in this chapter:

personal productivity tool	data base program
insertion	graphics program
replacement	windowing

WORKBOOK EXERCISES

Complete all exercises in Chapter 12 of the workbook before proceeding to Chapter 13 in this text.

DISKETTE EXERCISE

Complete the diskette exercise in Chapter 12 before proceeding to Chapter 13 in this text.

Microcomputers in Sports

For Biff Barden it is a typical Friday night. As he wheels his sleek new 300ZX into the dusty, unpaved parking area, he thinks about other Friday nights--Friday nights six and seven years ago, Friday nights when he was the center of attention as the starting quarterback for the Adel Argonauts. The roar of the crowd was music to his ears back then, and the roar was all for him. The roar will be here tonight, too, but not for Biff. Tonight, Biff will be just one of many crowded into the steamy press box overlooking Grant Garfield stadium. At least he will be warm and toasty, unlike the thousands who are fighting a fierce winter wind from their open stadium seats.

Far below, the teams for tonight's massacre burst onto the field to the accompaniment of cheerleader yells and the thunderous applause of the expectant crowd. The Riverside Bears and the Westwood Wildcats will give it their all tonight. The Wildcats are seeking revenge for the defeat they received last year at the hands of the Bears. Next week the Bears will play the Troyland Blue Devils for the regional championship, and they would love to go into the championship game with an unblemished record.

Beginning with the kickoff, Biff notices every move of the opposing players. With no rest for the weary, other than a quick halftime break, Biff labors through the game. After each play, he makes secretive marks on the top card of a deck of cards he carries. After being marked, each card takes its new place on the bottom of the deck, exposing a fresh card to be marked on the next play. At the end of the game, Biff's cards are quickly pocketed, and he disappears as quickly as he came. Maybe Mary Lou will still be waiting.

Biff is the first computerized scout for the Troyland Blue Devils. The first thing Monday morning, the information from Biff's cards will be read into a microcomputer in his office. At the office this new data will join data gathered from other games played this year by the Riverside Bears. Films of other Bears games will be watched, and the team's actions in those games will also be entered into the computer.

Once the data is entered into the computer, the computer's program begins its work. The program was written by Biff, who had taken a BASIC programming course in college. Quickly and methodically, the program summarizes and analyzes the data. The program is designed to analyze each play of an opponent in several games. The items examined include down, type of play, and yards gained or lost. The program attempts to spot tendencies in the opponent's play. For example, what do the Bears tend to do when it is fourth down and six to go? How do they tend to defend against particular offenses? Add to these tendencies such things as the performance of kickers in various situations, and the Blue Devil's coach has a potent weapon to use in planning the strategy for the championship war against the Bears. The only catch is that the Bear's coach, too, is using the microcomputer to aid in his scheme for the defeat of the Blue Devils. Since the Bear's coach had money to burn, he purchased the program he is using rather than writing it himself. Oh well, may the best program win!

While Biff and his school are not an actual person or place, they are quite representative of what is going on at many schools. Whether at numerous high schools, universities, or in the pros, the computer has joined the football team--as well as the baseball team, the basketball team, and the soccer team. The computer has become an extension of the coaching staff. At many schools coaches, or other faculty members or students, have written their own programs to look at scouting report data and spot tendencies. By writing their own programs, they have saved money and have also been able to tailor the programs to their exact needs and desires.

At Big City University, Coach Hulk Grizzly has used the computer to analyze scouting reports for about ten years. He has developed a tremendous football program, complete with cham-

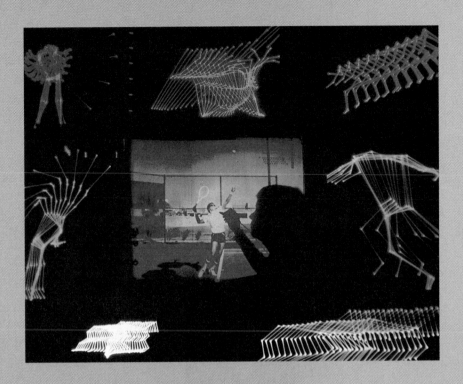

pionship teams and Coach of the Year Awards. At first, Grizzly used the university's mainframe computer to analyze his scouting reports. When microcomputers became available, however, Coach Grizzly developed software to run on the microcomputer instead of the mainframe. Since the microcomputer is located in the coach's office and is available whenever he needs it, the entry and analysis of the data has become much more convenient. The data is quickly entered, the analysis is made, and Coach Grizzly tailors his game plan accordingly. Under the old mainframe system, results were sometimes not available until too late to be of any value in preparing for a game. Now results are produced on a very timely basis. Added to its duties in analyzing opponents' plays, Big City's microcomputer is also used to keep up with team statistics, recruiting information, and financial information.

With the coming of computers to sports, life under the old stadium lights will never again be the same. From animated scoreboards controlled by computers to scouting report analysis, statistical analysis, and record keeping for the home team, it's a new ball game.

CHAPTER 13

Computer Uses in Industry

Objectives

1. Describe how the computer benefits businesses.

2. Describe how CAD/CAM is used in industry.

3. Explain how decision support systems and information centers are used in industry.

BENEFITS TO BUSINESS

Computers are needed to perform business operations requiring the handling of much data. Computers have made it possible for businesses to serve more customers and to earn profits by doing so. Many people believe that business in developed countries could not operate today without the computer. The services and goods needed by the public require many companies to supply them. Millions of people living in our communities are served by numerous companies that produce or sell cars, food, and other merchandise. Goods and services, such as banking, telephones, gas, and electricity, are supplied by many other companies. These items could not be provided to so many people without the use of the computer. The following paragraphs present several of the benefits of computers to business.

Speed and Availability of Information

Information can be quickly obtained about business operations. How many payments are due from customers? How much money is owed to other businesses? Is inventory low? What is the current profit or loss of the company? These are important questions to any business, with or without a computer to help obtain the answers. A computer makes information about what is happening in the business available immediately, allowing timely response to both problems and opportunities. Figure 13.1 shows one service provided by the computer.

Forecasts and Predicting Future Trends

One of the most important benefits of the computer for businesses is that it enables them to accomplish tasks that were previously considered impossible. With its great computation speed, the computer can perform analyses and estimate future trends in time for them to be of value in making decisions. The computer also enables the manager of a business to do a lot of "what if" testing, which compares the results of different actions. For example, what should happen to the company's profits if it could produce 300 products an hour instead of 290? What about 310 products an hour? Figure 13.2 shows a manager using the output of a computer to help make a decision.

FIGURE 13.1

Billing of customers by computers is prompt and efficient.

FIGURE 13.2

The computer can help managers make decisions.

Better Control of Expenses

The computer can help control expenses in many ways. One way is in the control of inventory, the merchandise on hand. To serve its customers, a business needs to have on hand the merchandise a customer wants to purchase. Yet, tying money up in items that people aren't buying generally reduces profit. The computer can be of great value in keeping up-to-date records of all stock purchased, tracking all completed sales, and showing when reorders should be made. A small computer can be located in a warehouse for keeping up with inventory; it can "talk to" a larger computer at company headquarters. The computer can help produce savings in many other areas as well. For example, manufactured items can be made to meet higher quality standards, resulting in less waste. Figure 13.3 shows a computer being used in a warehouse to keep up with inventory.

FIGURE 13.3

Warehouses often use computers to help keep up with inventory.

Improved Image

Computers can help a business provide much better service to its customers. In such cases, the customer thinks more highly of the business and is likely to speak of it favorably to friends. In Figure 13.4, customers are pleased with the fast service provided by the business. Keep in mind, however, that this can also work the other way. A business can, through poor management, use computers in such a way that customers become upset and take their business somewhere else.

FIGURE 13.4

Customers are more satisfied when the computer is used properly.

CAD/CAM

CAD/CAM stands for computer-aided design/computer-aided manufacturing. Although CAD/CAM is fairly new, it is having a great impact in manufacturing businesses.

CAD

One of the most exciting developments in industry is the use of CAD. With the use of CAD, an object can be displayed on the screen of a VDT for inspection. This object can be moved, magnified, and reduced. It can also be changed with the use of a light pen. This change can be temporary or permanent. All changes are figured by the computer. The light pen is used exactly like a pencil would be to make drawings on paper. Figure 13.5 shows a light pen being used for CAD.

Engineers also use CAD to design new products more easily than ever before. Computers can do all the necessary mathematical calculations such as the calculations to determine the size of a certain part and the materials required to build it. The computer can produce a drawing of the product and even demonstrate how it would work. Changes in design desired by the engineer can be immediately displayed on the computer, complete with new drawings. With CAD, a product can be perfected on the screen before the decision is made to actually manufacture it. Figure 13.6 shows an engineer using CAD to plan a new product.

Another way that CAD is being used is in the design of buildings. Planning and designing buildings requires many drawings before the details are completely worked out. CAD eliminates much of the paperwork that would otherwise be required to get a clear idea concerning the way a building should look. Figure 13.7 shows an architect using CAD to plan an office layout.

FIGURE 13.5

Light pens can be used for CAD.

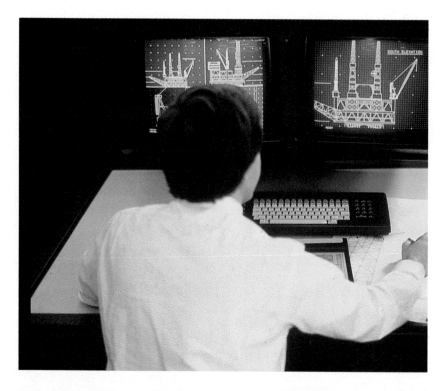

FIGURE 13.6

Engineers use CAD to plan new products.

FIGURE 13.7

Architects use CAD to plan new buildings and office layouts.

Businesses may use CAD to help them decide where to put new work stations in addition to what new furniture needs to be purchased. All drawings about how the new office furniture will fit with the existing furniture can be done with the use of CAD. If someone wants to move the office furniture around, several different arrangements can be tried using CAD without ever moving a piece of furniture. You can also make sure that the electrical outlets are in the proper location so that all equipment can be used.

CAM

The operations described in the previous paragraphs are the CAD part of CAD/CAM. The ideal is that CAD is used to design parts, then tools under the control of CAM actually produce the parts as designed. Computer-aided manufacturing (CAM) is the use of computers to control the activities of machinery. The machinery could be one device or an entire factory complex.

Numerical Control

Early development of this process relied heavily upon strips of paper tape, as shown in Figure 13.8. Because the holes in the tape represent numeric information, this technology is known as numerical control (NC). Each row of holes across the tape represents a specific function that controls the machinery. Examples of some of these functions might be the turning speed, work direction, starting, stopping, rotation, timing functions, and cutting depth. Because the machine's motions are stored on a paper

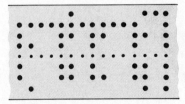

FIGURE 13.8

The holes in this paper tape represent numeric information.

tape that can be used over and over, the products can be expected to be of very high quality. This is because the paper tape is controlling the machine, eliminating any flaws caused by human error. Therefore, if the quality of the first part manufactured is good, the quality of all other parts should be good, since they would be identical to the first.

Numerical control tapes can store the design information used to produce a product without an actual drawing. Instead, as the designer develops the sizes and shapes of the product, the "points of reference" are punched into the tape. These are holes punched into paper tape which take the place of the drawn lines of the design. This is done with an NC typewriter. An NC typewriter is very similar to a normal typewriter except it punches tape instead of printing on paper. Because the tape contains hundreds of codes, it is very easy to create an error on the tape. Figure 13.9 shows a block of steel (dotted line) to be machined into an object (solid line). The red spots indicate the "points of reference."

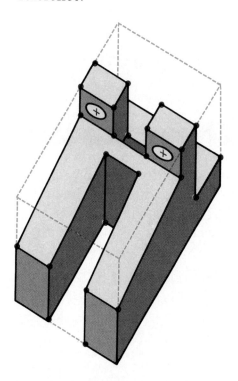

FIGURE 13.9

A block of steel (dotted line) to be machined into an object (solid line). The red spots indicate the "points of reference."

Machine Control

Numerical control is slowly giving way to a direct machine control which does away with the need for paper tape. In this technique, the CAD draftsperson draws and tests the design on a VDT. Once the design meets all the expectations the engineers require, the design data can be sent electronically to the memory of another computer which is directly attached to the required machinery. This method eliminates the human interpretation of the "point-of-reference" method and eliminates the typing errors associated with making an NC tape.

The receiving computer processes the design data into machinery-motion data (data that operates the machine). This computer can analyze the design and make thousands of decisions related to the operation of the machine. The data may also be stored on magnetic disks for later use. Let's take a look at a typical design problem shown in Figure 13.10.

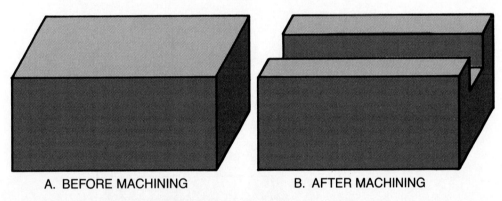

A. BEFORE MACHINING   B. AFTER MACHINING

FIGURE 13.10

A typical design problem: A block of aluminum (Block A) needs to have a groove cut into it (Block B).

In Figure 13.10 we see a block of aluminum (Block A) which our engineers want to cut a groove into (Block B). The machine that would normally be used to accomplish this is known as a milling machine. Let's assume our very simple milling machine can be controlled by the computer for only four motions: (a) the rotation speed of the cutting bit, (b) the depth of cut (up-and-down motion of the cutting bit), (c) bed travel left and right, and (d) bed travel forward and back. To see these actions more clearly, refer to Figure 13.11.

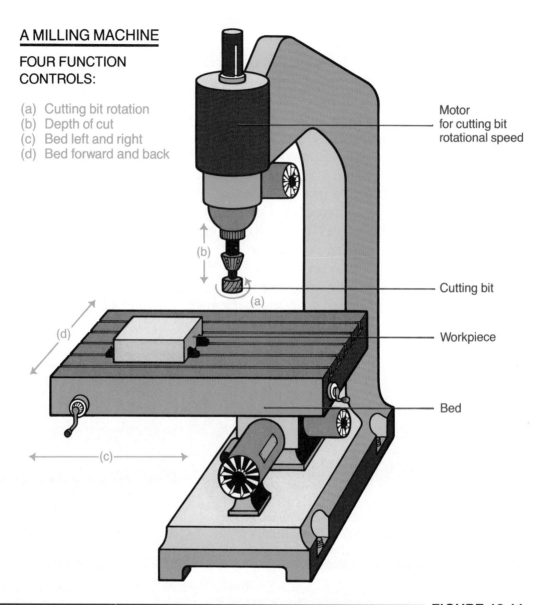

A MILLING MACHINE

FOUR FUNCTION CONTROLS:

(a) Cutting bit rotation
(b) Depth of cut
(c) Bed left and right
(d) Bed forward and back

Motor
for cutting bit
rotational speed

Cutting bit

Workpiece

Bed

FIGURE 13.11

A simple milling machine.

Assume that the cutting bit in Figure 13.11 is the same size as the groove we want to cut. The machine can be commanded to: (1) set the correct cutter rotation speed to cut aluminum, (2) set the bed far left, (3) lower the cutting bit to the correct depth, and (4) move the bed forward to the correct position. We are now ready to accomplish cutting the groove. Just by commanding the machine to move the bed slowly to the right, the groove can be cut into the block.

Our example milling machine only had four motions, but some real milling machines have many more motions and features. Some milling machines, for instance, have cutting tools of various sizes and shapes which can be automatically changed during the machining operation. The cutting tools are changed to allow for different types of cuts. By making all the cuts that use one particular cutting tool first, time is saved in tool changeover time. On the other hand, it might be faster to change cutting tools than to rotate the workpiece. The computer helps to make these and hundreds of other decisions related to the selection of the fastest and most accurate way of producing manufactured parts.

These computers can select the speed of each operation once the material to be machined is input. The final results of using computer-aided manufacturing are an increase in quality due to the elimination of human error, and an increase in speed because the computer controls most phases of the operation by making the best selections possible.

When CAD and CAM are combined together, they represent an extremely fast, accurate, and cost-effective way of producing materials for today's world. Rather than turn the drawings over to a model maker who would spend weeks engineering the first prototype part, it is now possible for the designer to see how the final product will look just moments after the idea is transferred onto the VDT. Production of the part could start just moments after the first part is inspected and tested. The CAD/CAM process is illustrated in Figure 13.12.

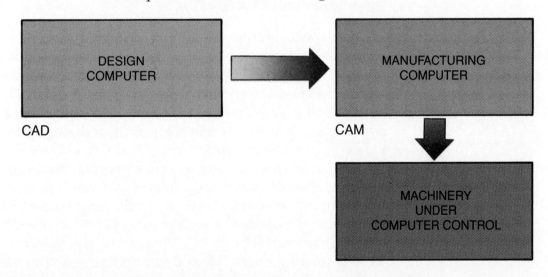

FIGURE 13.12

The CAD/CAM process.

Feedback

Another interesting aspect of computer use in the industrial setting is the ability of the computer to sense change. This ability is known as feedback. Let's take a look at an industrial problem that the computer can adjust for by having feedback. If the milling machine's cutting tool should break or get dull, the machine and the part being manufactured might be ruined if there were no feedback to the computer. However, if there is a circuit attached to the machine which can sense the motor slowing down (cutting bit getting dull) or speeding up (broken cutting bit), the circuit can send a signal back to the computer to change bits or to ring an alarm and stop the operation. The diagram in Figure 13.13 shows how feedback works.

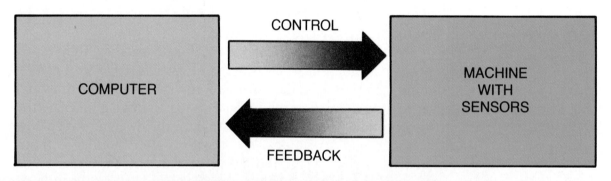

FIGURE 13.13

The process of feedback.

As robots become more sophisticated, this same feedback technology will become an important part of how the robots are used. By having a variety of sensors, the more sophisticated robot could react to a changing environment, much the same way as people do. If a person walked too close to a moving robot arm, the arm could sense the person's presence and stop, rather than knocking the person down. If a part had a flaw, the robot would be able to reject the part, just as a person would. With very sophisticated sensing devices, the computerized robot may even be able to accomplish some tasks better than any person could. The robot could detect variations in weight, size, and structure that a person would be unable to notice. The robot arm shown in Figure 13.14 is welding a very fine seam in a metal golf club head. The welding rod feed rate, arc temperature, and positioning of the welding tip are under computer control.

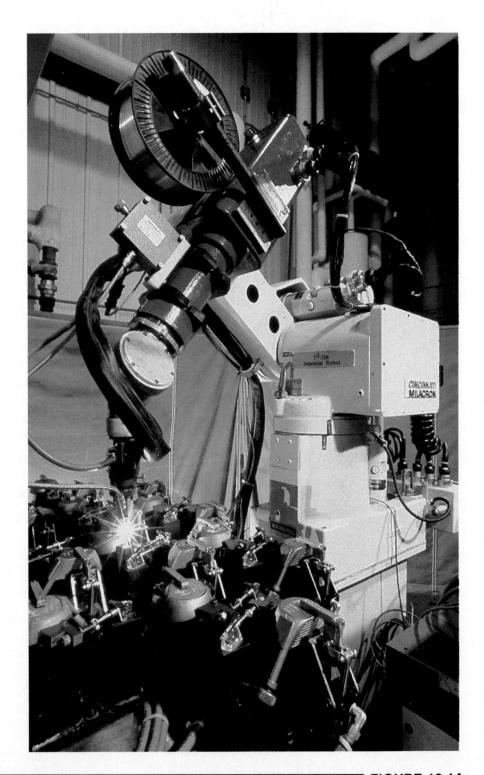

FIGURE 13.14

A robot at work.

DECISION SUPPORT SYSTEMS

A **decision support system** is a data processing system that helps managers make decisions. Although the term has been used by companies trying to sell software, a true decision support system has the following characteristics:

1. It is able to obtain information from many different departments within a company. For example, a marketing manager might want to know how many of a certain product were sold last year. With the help of a decision support system, that information could be provided from the accounting department. A data processing manager might want to know which department used the computer the most during a certain month. That information could also be provided.

2. It is capable of providing information while you wait. In other words, the information must be available in a very short time so that it can help managers make decisions. Before the computer was used, there was often a delay of days or even weeks before certain information could be available. Many decisions require a quick response, and using the computer makes it possible to make much faster and better decisions.

3. It can be used to determine the best of several possible decisions. The decision support system is good to use when a manager must invest the company's money and has several investment possibilities. Information can be input into the computer to provide calculations that help a manager predict the best investment.

4. It is very easy to use. Many managers did not learn about computers while they were in school. It is, therefore, important that the use of the computer be made as easy as possible so that managers can easily obtain needed information. In fact, you can think of a decision support system as user friendly (easy to use).

Managers at all levels of business are using the computer to help in decision making. With the aid of decision support systems, the computer provides needed information and helps managers compare different alternatives. The managers are then able to make decisions based upon the best possible information.

INFORMATION CENTERS

Another way of helping business is through **information centers**. These centers provide information and assistance to people other than data processing personnel and managers. The centers are usually staffed with data processing personnel who offer users help with using the computer. They also provide lessons on how to use existing software. The information center personnel do not write programs for the users; they help them use the computer to perform the work that they want to do.

Many companies provide trainers that teach classes on how to use the computer. As more and more companies use microcomputers and word processors, there are few people who could not profit from knowing how to use the computer in some way. As discussed in Chapter 3, it is important that the trainers know how to work with people who have little experience in using the computer. In Figure 13.15, a trainer is helping workers use the computer.

FIGURE 13.15

Trainers in information centers help workers use the computer.

SUMMARY

It is very hard to imagine running the businesses in our country without the use of the computer. The computer provides needed information quickly and accurately so that decisions can be made rapidly and customers can be served. It also assists in forecasting what a business should do in the future. With the use of the computer, a business also has better control of expenses and inventory.

One of the most exciting developments in industry is CAD/CAM. The use of CAD allows engineers and designers to look at an object on a VDT and perfect it before deciding to build or make the product. Once the decision has been made, then the computer can help in the actual manufacturing of the product (CAM).

Another exciting use of the computer is with decision support systems. Managers can use the computer to help them make better and faster decisions. Information centers are also a way of helping business. They provide information and assistance to users other than data processing personnel and managers.

REVIEW QUESTIONS

1. How have businesses benefitted from the use of the computer? (Obj. 1)

2. What is one way that the computer helps businesses control expenses? (Obj. 1)

3. Does the computer always improve the image of a business? Explain your answer. (Obj. 1)

4. Define computer-aided design. (Obj. 2)

5. Name one use of CAD. (Obj. 2)

6. Define computer-aided manufacturing. (Obj. 2)

7. Name a way that CAM is used. (Obj. 2)

8. Define a decision support system. (Obj. 3)

9. What are four characteristics of a decision support system? (Obj. 3)

10. How is an information center used by a business? (Obj. 3)

11. What types of people usually work in the information center of a business? (Obj. 3)

12. What characteristic must trainers have when working with users? (Obj. 3)

VOCABULARY WORDS

The following terms were introduced in this chapter:

CAD/CAM   decision support system
feedback   information center

WORKBOOK EXERCISES

Complete all exercises in Chapter 13 of the workbook before proceeding to Chapter 14 in this text.

DISKETTE EXERCISE

Complete the diskette exercise for Chapter 13 before proceeding to Chapter 14 in this text.

Computers in the
Auto Assembly Plant

In an earlier chapter you learned how computers are used to aid in the design of automobiles. You also learned that computers are used to help design and build the tools for making the cars. In this section you will learn some of the ways in which computers are used during the actual assembly process to produce automobiles.

First, all the special tools and equipment whose design and manufacture were aided by computers are put into place. Then the vehicles are ready to move down the assembly line. All along the assembly line, computers come into play. The first application may well be in the scheduling of the vehicle. Each assembly line may produce several brands of vehicles. For example, a plant may produce both Fords and Mercuries. Another

may produce Pontiacs, Oldsmobiles, and Buicks. Within each of these brands, there are multiple models. As an example, a Chrysler minivan may be available in three general models. There are multitudes of equipment that may be either standard or optional, depending on which model is being assembled. All this means that there may be thousands of different combinations of parts that might be assembled into a finished product. The computer can do a very efficient job of scheduling the proper part to arrive at the proper place at the proper time. Just imagine one example. You have ordered a bright red sports sedan with a red leather interior. Suppose that things get a little tangled up. The body of your car is painted pink. When the body and the seats come together on the assembly line, the seats happen to be blue cloth. This hardly produces the car you desire. Computer scheduling helps prevent this kind of problem by

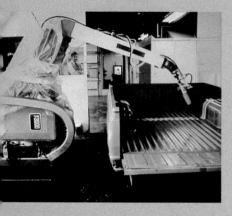

making sure that the proper sequence of parts and operations are done to produce the vehicle correctly.

While the output of the scheduling process is partially on paper or video displays for employees, some of it is in the form of instructions to robots, telling them which actions to take. Computer-controlled robots are found in growing numbers on assembly lines. These robots usually don't have two legs, two arms, and a head, and they don't usually run around talking with people as do many entertainment robots. Two examples will show the different kinds of duties given to these electronically controlled mechanical beings.

In old-style factories, workers who painted car bodies wore much protective clothing as they applied the paint to the automobile bodies. In spite of the high level of expertise of these workers, variations in spray movement and the lack of stretchable arms on the workers could lead to slight imperfections in the paint finish of the vehicles. With computer-controlled robot arms in new or newly remodeled factories, the paint sprayers can be perfectly positioned for every spot on the auto body. Different painting patterns are stored for each body style. For example, painting movements are different for two-door cars and four-door cars. In addition to providing a more consistent and higher quality paint finish, the robot spray arms offer another advantage. They are not affected by the breathing of paint fumes; therefore, they do not require protective clothing (or clothing of any kind, for that matter), and they are never made ill by their work environment.

The second example involves the assembly of the body components. This shows that even robots can work in teams. In this particular application, two robots are working with each other to fasten together two pieces of the rear body of an automobile. The parts are to be fastened by welding them together. This means that the steel of the two parts will be melted together using heat produced by an electric arc. The two robots work with each other in a fenced-in area. The fence is to keep people out. Since these particular robots have no sense of touch and have not been programmed to avoid people, they could hurt anyone who accidentally gets in their way.

Two parts bins, each of them containing the pieces to be welded, supply the robots with the parts they need to do their

work. As work proceeds, the first robot takes a piece from one of the parts bins and positions it on a special holding table. It then takes a part from the second parts bin and firmly holds it in position against the first part. While the first robot holds the parts in this steel embrace, the second robot starts welding a path from one end of the parts to the other. A weld is made every few inches. In a matter of seconds, the welding robot is done. The first robot quickly removes the welded part from the table and places it on a conveyor to go to the next processing step. As soon as the part is removed, the robot quickly picks up the next part to be welded and places it on the holding table, thus repeating the process for the next automobile.

The use of robots to help assemble automobiles (and other items, too) can result in higher quality products, as well as the elimination of many of the more dangerous jobs that it was once necessary for people to do.

PART 6
Programming

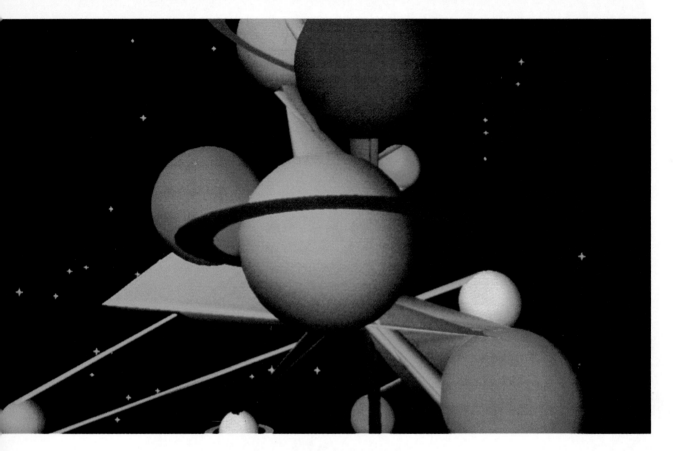

CHAPTER 14

Design of Computer Programs

Objectives

1. Describe what is meant by top-down design.
2. Define and explain the use of hierarchy charts in planning programs.
3. Describe how output is designed.
4. Define and explain the use of program designs.
5. Explain the procedure for coding and testing programs.

272

Just about everything that is done well is planned ahead of time. A football team plans its strategy for defeating an opponent. A painter plans a job before beginning to paint. A cook plans a menu before preparing a meal. In similar fashion, a programmer should plan a program before beginning to write it. This chapter explains how to plan a program and then proceed to write it.

STRUCTURED PROGRAMMING CONCEPTS

The recommended approach to writing programs is known as structured programming. **Structured programming** is simply defined as a sequence of steps designed to make programming as easy and effective as possible. Each of those steps is discussed in the following sections.

Top-Down Design

Top-down design means that you begin with the "big picture" and gradually refine the design, adding more and more detail at each step. This kind of thinking can be applied to many other undertakings as well as programming. "Big picture" thinking might include a statement such as "I want to write a program to draw a house." The process then continues in greater detail, such as "I want to draw an A-frame house." This process of adding detail continues as far as necessary.

Output Design

Once the top-down planning has gone far enough to allow for the entire picture, the output of a program is planned in detail. In the case of our house drawing example, the exact way the house will look is planned. In making the plan, a sheet known as a report spacing chart is used. A **report spacing chart** shows all the possible display positions that are on a screen or other output device. The way the output should look is planned by writing on the chart. The chart may be labeled with rows and columns for alphabet characters and numerals, or it may be labeled with X and Y coordinates for **pixels** (dots) of graphics. The size of the chart may vary, but it should be at least large enough to hold the design of the proposed output. Study Figure 14.1 to see how a report spacing chart using rows and columns looks. An A-frame house has been designed on the form by using standard keyboard characters (X's) to do the drawing. Note that the form shows 25 rows and 80 columns. If the computer you are using has a screen smaller than this, some of the rows and/or columns on the form may be left unused. On the form in Figure 14.1, note that the lower left corner of the house is on Row 11 and Column 1; the top center of the roof is on Row 1 and Column 11. The lower right corner of the house is on Row 11 and Column 21.

Figure 14.2 shows a report spacing chart arranged by pixels and containing the design for our house done with lines rather than keyboard characters. (The house is drawn with lines on the form, but it will be drawn with pixels on the screen.) Note that there are 320 locations across and 200 locations up and down. Again, portions of the chart may be left unused if necessary. Note that the lower left corner of the house is at Location 0,90. This means 0 pixels across the screen (the X coordinate) and 90 pixels down the screen (the Y coordinate). The center of the roof line is

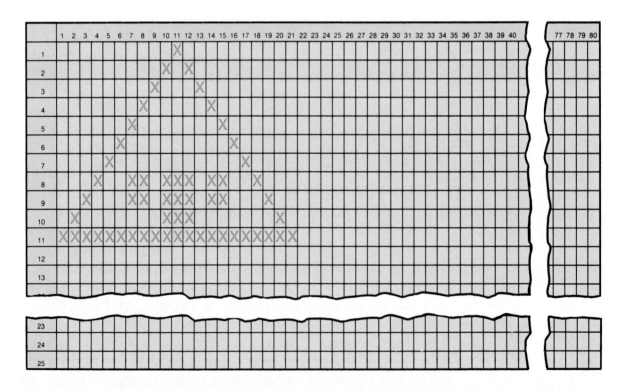

FIGURE 14.1

Output is planned by writing on the report spacing chart.

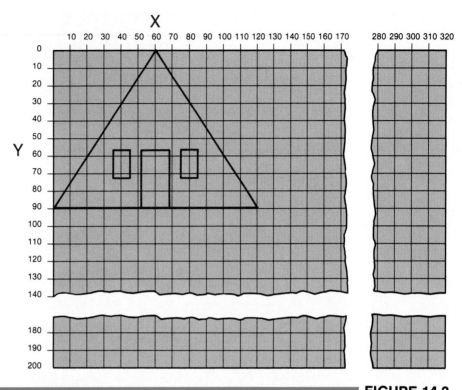

FIGURE 14.2

This report spacing chart is arranged by pixels (10 per line). Although the A-frame house is drawn with lines on the form, it will appear as pixels, or dots, on the screen.

at Location 60,0. This means 60 pixels across and 0 pixels down. The lower right corner of the house is at Location 120,90. This means 120 pixels across and 90 pixels down.

Hierarchy Chart

Once the output of a program is designed, a hierarchy chart is prepared. A **hierarchy chart** is a diagram showing the relationship of the different functions to be performed by the program. It is used to write down the results of the thinking that is done as more detail is added during the top-down design process. Suppose you have decided to write a program to draw the house discussed in the previous paragraph. This decision to write a program to draw the house is the "big picture" you have decided on. Show this by drawing a box and writing the title of the big picture inside it. This is shown in Figure 14.3.

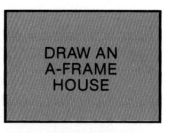

FIGURE 14.3

The Main Module is the first step in planning a
hierarchy chart.

Once the first box of the hierarchy chart has been drawn
and labeled with the "big picture" of the entire project, details are
added. Think about what must be done to draw an A-frame
house. The program must be able to draw the triangular shape of
the A-frame itself. It must be able to draw a door, and it must be
able to draw windows. Therefore, there are three processes that
the program must be able to carry out to complete the drawing of
the house. For each of these three processes, a box is added to the
hierarchy chart. Study the growing chart as shown in Figure 14.4.

Each of the boxes, or parts of the program, may be referred
to as a **module**. Each of the modules performs its particular
work whenever instructed to do so by the module above it. This
is somewhat like a building contractor employing various skilled

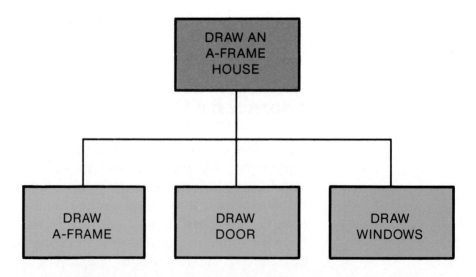

FIGURE 14.4

A hierarchy chart showing the three major processes of the Draw an A-
Frame House program.

workers such as carpenters and bricklayers. Each of the skilled workers performs work when instructed to do so by the contractor.

Program Design

Once the design of a program has been completed by preparation of the hierarchy chart, additional refinement is made by planning each of the modules in detail. This additional detail is known as **program design** or **pseudocode** and is written in plain, everyday English. Program design, therefore, involves writing down the necessary steps to solve a problem. The program design may be written on plain paper or on special forms. We will use a form called the Module Documentation form to write the program design. Each form includes space for the name of the program, the name of the module, and the program design.

The first module for which the program design is prepared is the original module, known as the **Main Module**. Study Figure 14.5 to see how the work of the Main Module of our example program can be designed. Note that the figure shows a sequence of steps to be taken by the program module. It is always

MODULE DOCUMENTATION	Program: DRAW AN A-FRAME HOUSE	Module: MAIN

Module Function (Program Design):

1. Prepare the computer for doing graphics.
2. Clear the screen.
3. Perform the Draw A-Frame Module.
4. Perform the Draw Door Module.
5. Perform the Draw Windows Module.
6. End.

FIGURE 14.5

Program design for the Main Module of the Draw an A-Frame House program.

important to clear the screen as one of your first steps. This is done so that any data that may already be on the display won't disrupt your program's output.

When the program design for the Main Module is complete, work proceeds to the other modules. Designs are made for each of them. Study Figures 14.6, 14.7, and 14.8 to see how the steps for these other modules are written.

The program designs should be checked by several persons other than their writer. This will frequently uncover cases of faulty logic (incorrect thinking) on the part of the writer. Any errors found in the logic are corrected at this time in the program designs. Later, each of the English steps from the program designs will be converted into a computer language.

Coding and Testing

Coding refers to the process of converting program designs into computer language. Testing refers to trying out the program to see that it is working properly. It has been determined that following a particular sequence of coding steps results in

MODULE DOCUMENTATION	Program: DRAW AN A-FRAME HOUSE	Module: DRAW A-FRAME

Module Function (Program Design):

1. Draw the left side of the roof.
2. Draw the right side of the roof.
3. Draw the base of the house.

FIGURE 14.6

Program design for the Draw A-Frame Module.

MODULE DOCUMENTATION	Program: DRAW AN A-FRAME HOUSE	Module: DRAW DOOR

Module Function (Program Design):

1. Draw the left side of the door.
2. Draw the top of the door.
3. Draw the right side of the door.

FIGURE 14.7

Program design for the Draw Door Module.

MODULE DOCUMENTATION	Program: DRAW AN A-FRAME HOUSE	Module: DRAW WINDOWS

Module Function (Program Design):

1. Draw the left side of the first window.
2. Draw the top of the first window.
3. Draw the right side of the first window.
4. Draw the bottom of the first window.
5. Draw the left side of the second window.
6. Draw the top of the second window.
7. Draw the right side of the second window.
8. Draw the bottom of the second window.

FIGURE 14.8

Program design for the Draw Windows Module.

programs being completed with less effort and fewer problems. Those steps are:

1. Convert the Main Module into computer language.

2. "Stub in" each of the other modules. This means to write just enough computer language to have the module print its name on the screen when the program is run. For example, in stubbing in the Draw A-Frame Module, the module would not draw an A-frame but would print the words *DRAW A-FRAME* on the screen.

3. Enter the Main Module and the stubbed-in modules into the computer.

4. Run the program to see whether the messages from the stubbed-in modules appear in the correct sequence.

5. If the messages appear in the correct sequence, it can be assumed that the Main Module is working correctly. If any of the messages are missing or are in the wrong order, the Main Module has a problem and must be fixed before proceeding.

6. One module at a time, convert the other modules to computer language and enter them into the computer. Run the program again after each module to see if it does what it is supposed to do. For example, enter the Draw A-Frame Module and then run the program. The A-frame should appear on the screen. If it does not, then fix it. Since that is the only module that has been keyed in to do any drawing up to this point, it is obvious that if any lines are drawn in the wrong place, then there is something wrong with that module. If all the drawing modules were in before testing the program, it would be difficult to determine which of the modules created any lines that appear in the wrong places.

EXAMPLE OF THE PROGRAM PLANNING PROCESS

Now that you have learned about the different parts of the program planning process as applied to drawing a picture with the computer, look at an example using a more practical application.

What the Program Is To Do

Remember that the first step in the top-down procedure is to decide in general what the program is supposed to do. In this case, we want a program that will tell us how much interest we will earn by depositing money in a bank account. By thinking about the problem in more detail, we decide on the following characteristics for the program:

1. The program will tell us how much interest we will earn and how much money we will have over a one-year period of time.
2. The program can handle any amount of money entered from the keyboard.
3. The program can handle any interest rate entered from the keyboard.

Planning the Program Output

Once we have decided on the general behavior of the program as listed in the previous section, the output is designed on a report spacing chart. Study Figure 14.9 to see how the output will

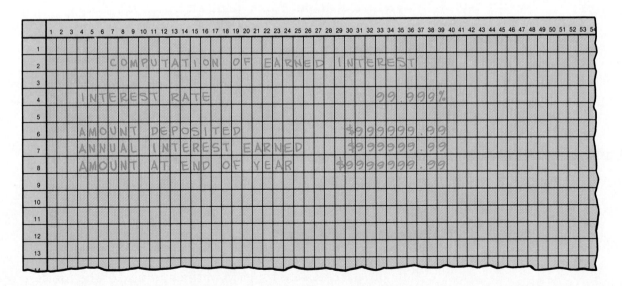

FIGURE 14.9

This report spacing chart shows how the output of the Compute Interest program would appear.

be arranged. Note that 9's have been used to indicate where numbers will appear in the output. This is a common practice. As an alternative, it is possible to use a number sign (#) in each place a number is to appear. When the program is ultimately written and used, the actual numbers will appear in these places.

Hierarchy Chart

Give some thought to what must happen in our program, and you will probably decide that there are three functions or processes the program must perform: (1) get all the information from the user, (2) calculate the amount of interest to be earned, and (3) print the report. These functions can be represented in a hierarchy chart as shown in Figure 14.10. Study the chart to see how it was prepared.

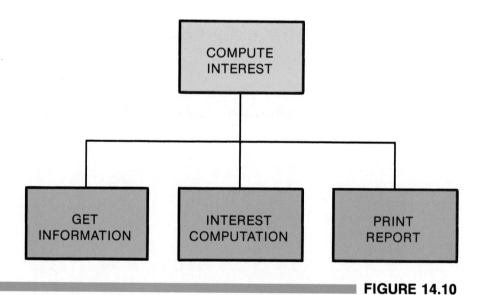

FIGURE 14.10

Hierarchy chart for the Compute Interest program.

Program Design

The program designs for each of the modules of the interest program are shown in Figures 14.11, 14.12, 14.13, and 14.14. Remember that the design for the Main Module is done first, followed by the designs for the other modules.

MODULE DOCUMENTATION	Program: COMPUTE INTEREST	Module: MAIN

Module Function (Program Design):

1. Clear the screen.
2. Perform the Get Information Module.
3. Perform the Interest Computation Module.
4. Perform the Print Report Module.
5. End.

FIGURE 14.11

Program design for the Main Module of the Compute Interest program.

MODULE DOCUMENTATION	Program: COMPUTE INTEREST	Module: GET INFORMATION

Module Function (Program Design):

1. Get interest rate from user and store it.
2. Get amount of money deposited from user and store it.

FIGURE 14.12

Program design for the Get Information Module.

MODULE DOCUMENTATION	Program: COMPUTE INTEREST	Module: INTEREST COMPUTATION

Module Function (Program Design):

1. Compute the interest and store the result.
2. Compute the amount of money on hand at the end of one year and store the result.

FIGURE 14.13

Program design for the Interest Computation Module.

MODULE DOCUMENTATION	Program: COMPUTE INTEREST	Module: PRINT REPORT

Module Function (Program Design):

1. Print the report heading.
2. Using the report spacing chart as a guide, print the following data:
    a. Interest rate
    b. Amount deposited
    c. Annual interest earned
    d. Amount at end of year

FIGURE 14.14

Program design for the Print Report Module.

The translation of these program designs into computer language, as well as the program testing process, will be covered in the next chapter of the text.

SUMMARY

The first step in writing any computer program is planning it. The planning process works best when a structured, top-down procedure is used. Planning the output, preparing a hierarchy chart, and writing program designs for each module complete the planning process. Then each line of the program design is translated to a computer language. Testing is involved along each step of the way.

REVIEW QUESTIONS

1. What is structured programming? (Obj. 1)
2. Describe the process of top-down design. (Obj. 1)
3. What is a hierarchy chart? (Obj. 2)
4. Describe the relationship of different modules in a hierarchy chart. (Obj. 2)
5. What is a report spacing chart? (Obj. 3)
6. What is the purpose of a program design? How is it related to a hierarchy chart? (Obj. 4)
7. What is meant by "stubbing in" a module? (Obj. 5)
8. What is the correct order for coding and testing the modules of a program? (Obj. 5)

VOCABULARY WORDS

The following terms were introduced in this chapter:

structured programming	module
top-down design	program design
report spacing chart	pseudocode
pixel	Main Module
hierarchy chart	coding

WORKBOOK EXERCISES

Complete all exercises in Chapter 14 of the workbook before proceeding to Chapter 15 in this text.

DISKETTE EXERCISE

Complete the diskette exercise for Chapter 14 before proceeding to Chapter 15 in this text.

Computers Make the
Space Program Possible

Without computers, the space program would be impossible. In fact, some advances in computer science are the direct result of designing computer equipment that is suited to the needs of the space program. These needs include small size, light weight, and incredible durability. It takes a tremendous amount of energy to get a spacecraft off the earth and into space. The lighter the computer equipment is, the less energy required to get it into space. This can allow larger payloads to be carried aboard the craft, or a less powerful, less expensive spacecraft. Also, computers on spacecraft are subjected to tremendous G forces and

vibration as the craft accelerates. Many computers not designed to take the strain would be ripped apart. Tremendous temperature changes during the voyage of a spacecraft are also normal. Temperature protection devices had to be developed to enable computers to withstand these changes. Many developments originally produced to help meet the needs of the space program for small, light, durable computers have found widespread use on earth.

The involvement of computers in the space program starts with the planning of spacecraft and missions and proceeds throughout actual flights. In the initial phases of planning space flights, computers are used to simulate the flight of the spacecraft. By computing the amount of engine thrust required to control the craft, the computer can help engineers determine which existing propulsion systems are capable of particular flights. If a totally new spacecraft is necessary, the computer can help in all phases of its design and manufacture. The computer can also simulate such things as the temperatures and forces to

be encountered along the way. It can compute the quantity of various supplies that must be on board and can generally make planning for the flight a much easier, more productive activity.

Once an actual flight is under way, many mathematical computations are required to navigate and control the spacecraft. In this application, computers both on the ground and in the spacecraft are used. Computations such as when to fire rockets, at what power, and for how long are necessary. If any factor is different from the way it was planned, many additional calculations must take place. For example, if a rocket burn was slightly shorter than it should have been, what must be done to correct for the problem? These computations would require much time if done by hand or with calculators. By the time the calculations were completed, it would be too late to make the required changes in power.

In addition to making all the necessary computations during space flights, computers can simulate on earth what the spacecraft is doing in space. This enables persons on earth to better follow the action of the flight and better aid in the solution of any problems that may arise. Computers are also used to keep check on each other during a flight to make sure that computer malfunctions are not occurring. Undetected computer malfunctions obviously could have disastrous consequences. If navigation of the spacecraft were erroneous, for example, it could mean death in space for all the crew members on a manned flight.

Another computer application in the space program is the area of photography. The fantastic full-color pictures you have seen of other planets which were made on board spacecraft are not made on photographic film. After all, if a spacecraft is one that is never to come back to earth, it is impossible to get such photographic film back for development. Instead, cameras with a computer assist are used. Basically similar to television cameras (some are more similar than others), these cameras convert the scene to a numeric representation. In other words, they visualize the picture as a computer screen with pixels making up the surface. Each pixel can be represented by a number indicating its shade or color. In the case of spacecraft, these numbers are sent back to earth by radio signals. The numbers are then converted back to pictures by a computer on earth.

Frequently the pictures can be enhanced by computer to make them even better. Enhancement means that a computer is used to highlight some things more than others, for example. By doing this, different versions of the same picture can be made, each of them highlighting certain features and making them easier to see. For example, all areas that are a particular color may be displayed in a higher contrast color to make them easier to see.

In addition to sending photographic images back to earth, digital signals are used to transmit much other information as well. Instrument readings of all kinds are sent this way. On manned spacecraft, the readings may include data about the condition of the crew on board, as well as data about the condition and location of the spacecraft itself. On both manned and unmanned craft, readings taken by scientific instruments are transmitted to earth in digital form. These readings may be anything from the temperature surrounding the spacecraft to data about the density of the gases on some other planet.

CHAPTER 15

Simple BASIC Programs

Objectives

1. List the advantages and disadvantages of BASIC.

2. Explain the difference between immediate execution mode and deferred execution mode.

3. Describe the different kinds of data with which BASIC works.

4. Explain how keywords are used to code programs.

5. Describe how input is obtained from the keyboard.

6. Code simple programs.

In the last chapter you learned about planning programs. Those same methods of planning apply no matter what language the programs are written in. In this chapter you will learn how to translate the program designs learned about in the previous chapter to the BASIC computer language.

OVERVIEW OF BASIC

BASIC is the most commonly used computer language. It is a standard feature on millions of microcomputers. Several items have led to BASIC's popularity. The most important one is that BASIC is generally an interpreted language. Therefore, you can enter a program from the keyboard, enter the command to run the program, and watch the program do whatever it does. Each line of the program is converted to the machine language required by the processor as it is executed (run). This is in contrast to a compiled language, where the entire program is converted to machine language before execution can begin. Interpreted programs are also easier to debug. This is because the program can be stopped and data values examined at any point during the program run.

The very same interpreted nature that makes BASIC so attractive also leads to one of its disadvantages. When programs must do involved computations, they may run too slowly to be acceptable. With some versions of the language, however, programs may be debugged using the interpreted language, then speeded up by compiling them with a compiler version of the language.

BASIC is a free-form language. This means that you may enter program instructions in just about any order you wish. There is no required structure to the language. While this appeals to many persons and makes simple programming much easier, many advanced programmers believe it leads to sloppy programming. Therefore, although structured programming techniques are not required with BASIC, it is in the programmer's best interest to use them. They make programs easier to debug. They also make it easier for other programmers looking at the programs to follow the logic.

BASIC MODES

The interpreted nature of most versions of BASIC allows the existence of two different **modes** or ways of operating. One of these modes is known as immediate execution mode, while the other is known as deferred execution or program mode.

In **immediate execution mode**, an instruction is keyed in and is immediately carried out by the computer. In **deferred execution mode** or **program mode**, an entire set of instructions is keyed in and is not executed (carried out) until the command is given telling the computer to run the program.

KINDS OF DATA WITH WHICH BASIC WORKS

Any fact is considered to be data. Therefore, all facts with which BASIC works are known as data. BASIC may work with unchanging data that is written into a program, or it may work with changeable data supplied by the user or computed during execution of the program. These kinds of data are discussed in the following paragraphs.

Literals and Constants

Data that does not change is known as either a literal or a constant. The word *HELLO* written inside quotation marks is a literal. It is easy to see from this example that a **literal** is anything written between quotation marks. Literals generally consist of alphabet letters and symbols, but numbers can also be written between quotation marks as literals. For example, "8321" is a literal. Literals may consist of any characters that can be represented by the computer being used. For example, if your computer can print a smiley face by striking a key on the keyboard, the smiley face can be part of a literal.

The other kind of unchanging data is known as a constant. A **constant** is any number not written in quotes. For example, the number 49 is a constant. Literals and constants are written into program instructions so that they are available when a program is executed.

Remember that literals consist of character data (anything that can be represented by your computer), while constants consist of numeric data only. Literals cannot be used to do mathematical operations. Constants can be used to do math.

Variables

Frequently the user of a program is requested to enter data from the keyboard, or data is computed during program execution. Data obtained in this manner is known as **variable data** since it may be different each time the program is run. In the computer, variable data is stored in specially named memory locations known as **variables**. For example, a place in memory may become known as *PHONE* and contain a phone number entered by the user. Likewise, a place known as *GRADE1* might contain a grade on a test.

Variable Names

The words that can be used as variable names vary from one version of the BASIC language to another. In general, however, variable names must begin with a letter of the alphabet and can consist of only letters and numerals. Examples of common variable names are *NUMBER1*, *NUMBER2*, and *TOTAL*. With some versions of BASIC, a few symbols or punctuation marks can be used within variable names. The length of name allowed also varies. For example, on the IBM PC, TRS-80 Model 4, and many others, variable names may be up to 40 characters long. On the Apple, Commodore, and some other machines, variable names should be only two characters; you can enter more, but the ones beyond the second character will be ignored by the computer. If using one of these computers, the variables *NUMBER1* and *NUMBER2* might be changed to *N1* and *N2*, while *TOTAL* might be changed simply to *T*.

Variables that are to hold nonnumeric data must be specified as **character variables** (also known as **string variables**) by placing a dollar sign at the end of the name. For example, *ADDRESS$* or *AD$* might be used as the variable name for a person's street address. No arithmetic operations may be done with character variables.

KEYWORDS

The BASIC language uses words that are "understood" by the computer. These words are known as **keywords**. Some keywords are used only as statements in programs, some are used only as commands in immediate execution mode, and still others may be used in either program or immediate execution mode. A **statement** is a keyword preceded by a line number. The line number enables the program to execute in deferred mode. A **command** is a keyword that is not preceded by a line number. The absence of a line number enables the computer to take immediate action. Before beginning to look at some simple BASIC programs, it would be good to know some of the keywords. Study the following keywords. They are the first ones with which we will become familiar.

Keywords Generally Used in Immediate Execution Mode as Commands

The following keywords are generally used as commands in immediate execution mode:

NEW: A command that erases any program that may have been in the computer's RAM (temporary) memory. This command should be used before entering any new program.

LIST: A command' that causes the entire program in memory to be displayed on the screen.

RUN: A command that causes the computer to execute the program that is in the computer's memory.

Keywords That May Be Used in Immediate Execution or Program Mode

The following keywords may be used as commands in either immediate execution or program mode:

CLS: A command used to clear the screen. Some computers use **HOME** instead of CLS.

PRINT: A keyword that causes data to be displayed on the screen.

LET: A keyword used to assign a value into a variable storage location. For example, the statement LET AVERAGE = (G1 + G2)/2 will do the arithmetic of averaging two grades and will store the average in a storage location known to the program as *AVERAGE*.

Keywords That Are Used in Program Mode Only

The following keywords are used in program mode only:

REM: A statement used to write comments or remarks in a program as part of the program's documentation.

GOSUB: A statement used to tell the computer to leave what it is doing and go perform another module, or subroutine. Lower level modules are often referred to as **subroutines**.

RETURN: A statement used at the end of a subroutine or module to tell the computer that the end of that module has been reached. The program should now return to the statement following the GOSUB statement.

INPUT: A statement used to accept data entered on the keyboard and store it in a variable.

IMMEDIATE EXECUTION EXAMPLES

As an example of immediate execution mode, suppose that you enter PRINT 3 + 2 and strike the ENTER or RETURN key. Immediately, the computer follows your instruction and prints 5, which is the answer to the problem you keyed in. Many things can be done in immediate execution mode by using different keywords. For example, such mathematical functions as square roots can be done. The square root of 36 could be printed, for example, by entering PRINT SQR(36). SQR is known as a math function. The BASIC language supports several built-in math functions.

PROGRAM MODE EXAMPLES

With most versions of BASIC, program mode is indicated to the computer by entering a line number in front of each step. Before keying in any instructions in program mode, you should make sure there is no "garbage" from the previous program left in the computer's memory. Do this by entering the word NEW and pressing ENTER or RETURN. Once the NEW command has been entered, the statements of the next program can be keyed in. For example, the two statements from the above example could be combined into a program by numbering the steps as follows:

```
1 PRINT 3+2

2 PRINT SQR(36)
```

The 1 in front of the first statement tells the computer that when the word RUN is keyed in and ENTER or RETURN is pressed, that statement will be executed first. The 2 in front of the second statement says that the statement is to be executed second. Therefore, if after entering the two lines as shown, you key in RUN and press ENTER or RETURN, the computer will print:

```
5
6
```

Most programmers don't number steps as 1, 2, 3, and so on, as we have done in the above example. Instead, they use numbers ten digits apart, such as 10, 20, 30, and so on. By leaving space between numbers, new steps can easily be added at a later date.

Let's suppose we have reentered our first program as follows, changing the line numbers to 10 and 20:

```
10 PRINT 3+2

20 PRINT SQR(36)
```

Now we decide to add a new line between the two existing lines. It is an easy matter to give the new line the number 15 and enter:

```
15 PRINT "HELLO"
```

When the program is run, the computer will automatically execute the step numbered 15 between the steps numbered 10 and 20, even though you may not have entered the new step until the end of the program. Also, if you command the computer to show you the entire program, line 15 will be in its proper place. To do this, key the command LIST and press ENTER or RETURN. The program will be printed on the screen as:

```
10 PRINT 3+2

15 PRINT "HELLO"

20 PRINT SQR(36)
```

If the program is executed, the result will be:

```
5
HELLO
6
```

To eliminate an instruction from a program, simply key the line number by itself and press ENTER or RETURN. For example, to eliminate line 10 from the example program, key the number 10 and press ENTER or RETURN. Then if you LIST the program, you will get:

If you RUN the program, you will now get only:

To make changes in a program after it has been entered, you may add lines or delete lines as you have learned to do in the previous paragraphs. You can also make changes in existing lines. The simplest way to make a change is to rekey a line using the same line number as the line you want to change. Then the new line will automatically replace the old one. With many computers, however, it is possible to move the cursor back to any line and type over characters, insert characters, or delete characters. For example, this may be done on the IBM and Commodore. Special programs available from companies that sell computer software can also make it easy to change programs when the computer does not normally have an easy-to-use method of editing.

CODING SIMPLE PROGRAMS

In the following sections, three simple example programs will be presented. Two of them are for drawing the house designed in Chapter 14. The other is a simple interactive program.

A Simple Graphics Program

When coding a program, you should use documentation inside the program. This means putting comments (REM statements) in the program to help you and others understand it. These comments are especially helpful in refreshing your memory if it has been a while since you have looked at the program. It is suggested that the first three lines of each program always be comments. The first line should contain a name you make up for the program. The second line should contain the name of the author. The third line should contain a brief description of the program. As many additional lines as desired may also be used for comments, either at the beginning of the program or in the middle of the program. Each comment line is known as a remark line and is indicated by the keyword REM at the beginning of the line.

Remember from Chapter 14 that the planning of a program precedes the writing of a computer language. Remember also that in Chapter 14 you saw the output plans for a program to draw a simple house on the screen. The house can be done with characters from the keyboard by using the keyword PRINT to print literals on the screen. This is so simple that the entire program design can consist of one statement:

1. Print literals for each line of the house.

Doing this, we can write the short program shown in Figure 15.1. Note that we have not used equally spaced line numbers (the line numbers skip from 40 to 110); this is perfectly acceptable to BASIC. The computer will perform the statement on the lowest numbered line first, followed by the next higher number, and so on.

Note that a literal is printed for each line of the house; each line contains the spaces necessary to place the characters in the proper position. When the program has been keyed in and the RUN command given, the output will appear as shown in Figure 15.2.

In Chapter 14, we developed a plan for the house drawing using computers that can do pixel graphics. This program was complex enough to require the preparation of a Main Module plus three other modules. To make it simple, the Draw Windows Module will now be taken out. Look now at how that program design can be turned into a coded program. Remember that when

```
10 REM AFRAME1
20 REM HODGES AND WATSON
30 REM PRINTS A-FRAME HOUSE WITH LITERALS
40 CLS    :REM (CHANGE CLS TO HOME ON APPLE, ?"SHIFT-CLR-HOME" ON COMMODORE)
110 PRINT "          X"
120 PRINT "         X X"
130 PRINT "        X   X"
140 PRINT "       X     X"
150 PRINT "      X       X"
160 PRINT "     X         X"
170 PRINT "    X           X"
180 PRINT "   X  XX XXX XX  X"
190 PRINT "  X   XX XXX XX   X"
200 PRINT " X        XXX      X"
210 PRINT "XXXXXXXXXXXXXXXXXXXX"
```

Note: In line 110 there are ten spaces after the opening quotation mark, in line 120 there are nine spaces, etc.

FIGURE 15.1

An example of a simple graphics program to draw an A-frame house.

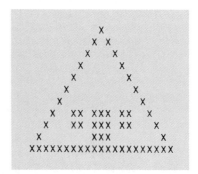

FIGURE 15.2

The output from the AFRAME1 program.

you have a program with different modules, the Main Module is turned into program code first. We will reproduce the program design for the Main Module on the left of the page, then show the computer language for that statement at the right of the page. Remember that the other modules should be stubbed in at this time, so they will be shown that way.

Since the program consists of three different modules, we will decide to use the numbers 10-999 for the Main Module, numbers 1000-1999 for the module that draws the A-frame, and numbers 2000-2999 for the module that draws the door. These numbers are entered on the appropriate lines on the Module Documentation forms previously filled out.

Figure 15.3 shows the program for the IBM, while Figure 15.4 shows the same program for the Apple.

PROGRAM DESIGN STEP—
                    MAIN MODULE

1. Prepare the computer for graphics.
2. Clear the screen.
3. Perform the Draw A-Frame Module.
4. Perform the Draw Door Module.
5. End.

BASIC LANGUAGE FOR IBM

```
10  REM AFRAME2
20  REM HODGES AND WATSON
30  REM DRAWS A-FRAME HOUSE ON IBM
40  SCREEN 1
50  CLS
60  GOSUB 1000
70  GOSUB 2000
999 END
1000 REM PERFORM DRAW A-FRAME MODULE
1010 PRINT "A-FRAME"
1999 RETURN
2000 REM PERFORM DRAW DOOR MODULE
2010 PRINT "DOOR"
2999 RETURN
```

FIGURE 15.3

The Main Module program design translated into the BASIC used with IBM.

PROGRAM DESIGN STEP—
                    MAIN MODULE

1. Prepare the computer for graphics.
   (HCOLOR sets color to white.)
2. Clear the screen.
3. Perform the Draw A-Frame Module.
4. Perform the Draw Door Module.
5. End.

BASIC LANGUAGE FOR APPLE

```
10  REM AFRAME2
20  REM HODGES AND WATSON
30  REM DRAWS A-FRAME HOUSE ON APPLE
40  HGR
45  HCOLOR=7
50  HOME
60  GOSUB 1000
70  GOSUB 2000
999 END
1000 REM PERFORM DRAW A-FRAME MODULE
1010 PRINT "A-FRAME"
1999 RETURN
2000 REM PERFORM DRAW DOOR MODULE
2010 PRINT "DOOR"
2999 RETURN
```

FIGURE 15.4

The Main Module program design translated into the BASIC used with Apple.

Notice that the keyword GOSUB was used to tell the program to execute the lines beginning at 1000 and at 2000. This stands for "go to subroutine." At the end of each of the modules (lines 1999 and 2999), note that the keyword RETURN was used to tell the program to "go back where you came from and execute the next step."

When the Main Module and stubbed-in submodules are entered into the computer as shown and executed, the output should be as follows:

```
A-FRAME
DOOR
```

If this output is obtained, it means the Main Module is calling on the submodules in the correct order and work can proceed to the coding of the next module. We will now code the module to draw the A-frame. Figure 15.5 is for the IBM, while Figure 15.6 is for the Apple. The keyword LINE is used on the IBM and HPLOT is used on the Apple to tell the computer to draw a line. The numbers indicate the X and Y coordinates of the points for beginning and/or ending the line. When no beginning point is given, the line begins where the previous line left off.

When this code is entered into the computer and run, the statements to draw the lines on lines 1010 through 1030 of the module are replaced with the actual drawn lines. Therefore,

PROGRAM DESIGN STEP— DRAW A-FRAME

1. Draw the left side of the roof.
2. Draw the right side of the roof.
3. Draw the base of the house.
4. Return to Main Module.

BASIC LANGUAGE FOR IBM

```
1000 REM DRAW A-FRAME MODULE
1010 LINE(0,90)-(60,0)
1020 LINE-(120,90)
1030 LINE-(0,90)
1999 RETURN
```

FIGURE 15.5

The Draw A-Frame program design translated into the BASIC used with IBM.

PROGRAM DESIGN STEP—
                DRAW A-FRAME

1. Draw the left side of the roof.
2. Draw the right side of the roof.
3. Draw the base of the house.
4. Return to Main Module.

BASIC LANGUAGE FOR APPLE

```
1000 REM DRAW A-FRAME MODULE
1010 HPLOT 0,90 TO 60,0
1020 HPLOT TO 120,90
1030 HPLOT TO 0,90
1999 RETURN
```

FIGURE 15.6

The Draw A-Frame program design translated into the BASIC used with Apple.

when the program is run after this module is entered, the A-frame should be drawn, followed by the word DOOR. DOOR will be printed by the Draw Door Module, which is still in its stubbed-in condition.

If the A-frame is not drawn properly when the program is run, make any necessary corrections to the code and try it again. When the A-frame is being drawn correctly, proceed to code the Draw Door Module in full as shown in Figure 15.7 for the IBM or Figure 15.8 for the Apple.

Entry of this last module into the computer should result in a complete program that runs properly. If the door does not appear to be correct, make any necessary changes in the code of the Draw Door Module and run the program again.

PROGRAM DESIGN STEP—
                DRAW DOOR

1. Draw the left side of the door.
2. Draw the top of the door.
3. Draw the right side of the door.
4. Return to Main Module.

BASIC LANGUAGE FOR IBM

```
2000 REM DRAW DOOR MODULE
2010 LINE(51,90)-(51,56)
2020 LINE-(69,56)
2030 LINE-(69,90)
2999 RETURN
```

FIGURE 15.7

The Draw Door program design translated into the BASIC used with IBM.

PROGRAM DESIGN STEP—
                DRAW DOOR

1. Draw the left side of the door.
2. Draw the top of the door.
3. Draw the right side of the door.
4. Return to Main Module.

BASIC LANGUAGE FOR APPLE

```
2000 REM DRAW DOOR MODULE
2010 HPLOT 51,90 TO 51,56
2020 HPLOT TO 69,56
2030 HPLOT TO 69,90
2999 RETURN
```

FIGURE 15.8

The Draw Door program design translated into the BASIC used with Apple.

A Simple Interactive Program

The keyword INPUT is used to get data from the keyboard and assign it to a variable. Consider the simple program shown in Figure 15.9. It asks for two numbers by using a PRINT statement in line 40. The semicolon at the end of the PRINT statement makes the cursor stay on the same line on the screen to wait for the user's response. The program then accepts the numbers from the keyboard with the INPUT statement in line 50 and places them into variables known as $N1$ and $N2$. It then prints the total of the numbers with the PRINT statement in line 60. Note that the PRINT statement prints both a literal and the answer to the computation.

```
40 PRINT "ENTER TWO NUMBERS (SEPARATED BY A COMMA) ON THE KEYBOARD: ";
50 INPUT N1,N2
60 PRINT "THE TOTAL OF THE TWO NUMBERS IS ";N1+N2
```

FIGURE 15.9

The statement INPUT is used to get data from the keyboard and assign it to a variable.

In addition to being entered from the keyboard, data may be assigned to a variable by the program as it executes instructions. The previous program can be modified, for example, to place the total into a new variable when the calculation takes place. The amount from that variable can then be printed. The keyword LET is used to assign a value to a variable as the program executes. This is done in line 60 of the changed program shown in Figure 15.10.

```
40 PRINT "ENTER TWO NUMBERS (SEPARATED BY A COMMA) ON THE KEYBOARD: ";
50 INPUT N1,N2
60 LET SUM = N1+N2
70 PRINT "THE TOTAL OF THE TWO NUMBERS IS ";SUM
```

FIGURE 15.10

The statement LET is used to assign a value to a variable as the program executes. Note also that the variable name *SUM* can now be used on line 70.

In the previous examples, a PRINT statement was used before the INPUT statement. The PRINT statement displayed a message to the user telling the user what kind of data to key in. That statement, known as a **prompt**, may be produced directly by the INPUT statement rather than with a separate PRINT statement. Study the following version of the program in Figure 15.11 to see how this can be done. Note that, in effect, lines 40 and 50 from the previous program have been combined.

```
40 INPUT "ENTER TWO NUMBERS (SEPARATED BY A COMMA) ON THE KEYBOARD: ";N1,N2
50 LET SUM = N1+N2
60 PRINT "THE TOTAL OF THE TWO NUMBERS IS ";SUM
```

FIGURE 15.11

The prompt can be easily combined with the request for input, eliminating the need for the first PRINT statement that was in the two previous examples.

This version of the program will run exactly as the version in Figure 15.10. The program has merely been made a little simpler by the combination of the two statements.

SUMMARY

BASIC is an easy-to-learn computer language that is usually interpreted, thereby making it easier to debug. Instruction statements may be given in either immediate execution mode or deferred execution mode. Line numbers indicate the deferred execution mode. Each program step consists of one or more keywords, usually combined with one or more pieces of data. If unchanging, the data may be either a literal or a constant. Changing data may be entered from the keyboard or computed by the program as it executes. Such changing data is stored in named memory locations known as variables. The same keywords may be used to work with changing and unchanging data.

REVIEW QUESTIONS

1. Name two advantages and two disadvantages of the BASIC language. (Obj. 1)
2. What is the difference between immediate execution mode and deferred execution mode? How does BASIC usually know the difference? (Obj. 2)
3. What is a keyword? (Obj. 4)
4. What is the difference between a literal and a constant? (Obj. 3)
5. Compare literals and constants to variable data. (Obj. 3)
6. What keyword is used to obtain input from the keyboard? (Obj. 5)
7. What are the rules concerning variable names? (Obj. 5)
8. How is each line of a program in deferred execution mode constructed? (Obj. 4)

VOCABULARY WORDS

The following terms were introduced in this chapter:

mode	CLS
immediate execution mode	HOME
deferred execution mode	LIST

program mode	NEW
literal	RUN
constant	PRINT
variable data	LET
variable	REM
character variable	GOSUB
string variable	subroutine
keyword	RETURN
statement	INPUT
command	prompt

WORKBOOK EXERCISES

Complete all exercises in Chapter 15 of the workbook before proceeding to Chapter 16 in this text.

DISKETTE EXERCISE

Complete the diskette exercise for Chapter 15 before proceeding to Chapter 16 in this text.

Expert Systems—"Smart" Programs

One of the most exciting new developments in computing is the emergence of expert systems. Frequently referred to as artificial intelligence, an expert system is a computer program that is capable of performing work normally left to human experts. In other words, expert system programs can simulate the thinking process of humans to at least some degree.

Let us look at several examples of the use of expert systems. For several years, expert system programs have been under development in the field of medicine. Given the patient's symptoms, these programs can make a diagnosis of what is probably wrong. One of the first of these programs was called Mycin. It was designed to diagnose and treat blood diseases. If asked to do so, it could explain why it reached its conclusions or why it asked a particular question. It was the first program that could do this.

Another medical program is known as Internist. It can handle almost 100,000 different relationships between symptoms and diseases. It has now achieved a skill level beyond that of most specialists in the field; that is, it tends to be right more frequently than doctors are in making diagnoses.

Another example of an expert system is in the area of equipment repair. Various symptoms and measurements on the broken equipment are fed into the program. The program then

makes a recommendation as to what part needs repairing or replacement to solve the problem.

A third example seems almost too simple in what it does to be called an expert system. However, it performs an extremely valuable service. In drilling for oil, there is a great chance that the drill will get stuck in the mud unless special precautions are taken. The expert system receives as input all kinds of data about the situation in which the drilling is taking place. It then makes recommendations on the actions to take in order to keep the drill from getting stuck.

All these expert systems are based on the behavior of human experts. The steps likely to be followed, as well as the knowledge of the humans, is written into the programs and their data. Many expert system programs have been put together only after untold hours of work with people who were recognized as experts in their fields. In effect, the expert system programs try to mimic the performance of knowledgeable people. This means that the programs don't do a mathematical analysis of every single possibility. Rather, they follow a set of rules put down by the developers. These rules, based on the logic of people, are frequently referred to as heuristic rules. Some persons refer to them as "seat of the pants" rules since they may be based on intuition gained from experience.

In developing an expert system, engineers generally follow four steps. First, they gather the heuristic rules from experts in the field. Second, they determine a way the knowledge can be represented for the computer. Once a representation is determined, the assembly of the knowledge into an expert system is accomplished. In this third step, a preexisting computer program is frequently used. Such programs, sometimes called inference engines, are specially designed to infer answers from rules. The fourth step is then undertaken. In this step, the knowledge and rules of the system are refined or improved. The performance of the system is tested and changes are made to enhance the performance.

An expert system interacts with the user in the same way other programs might. For example, a "conversation" might take place between the system and the user by using a display terminal. On the other hand, some data may be fed to the system

by on-line sensors or instruments of various types. The conversation between a user and an expert system, however, would seem somewhat different from a conversation between a user and a typical computer system. In a conversation between the expert system and a user, the user would note that the system seems intelligent; that is, its line of questioning would vary depending on previous answers. In other words, each time you would use the system, the questions would be different. Each question would be asked only if there were a reason to ask it. Additionally, the system would be able to explain why it was asking a particular question or how it arrived at particular conclusions.

Expert systems, while gaining in ability and usefulness, are still mainly subject specific. In other words, an expert system developed for medical purposes can handle only medical applications. One developed for mining can handle only mining problems, and so on. The computer system that can function in a "thinking" manner across a broad range of subject matters is still an object of research only. However, it may well be only a matter of time before such a general-purpose intelligent system is available.

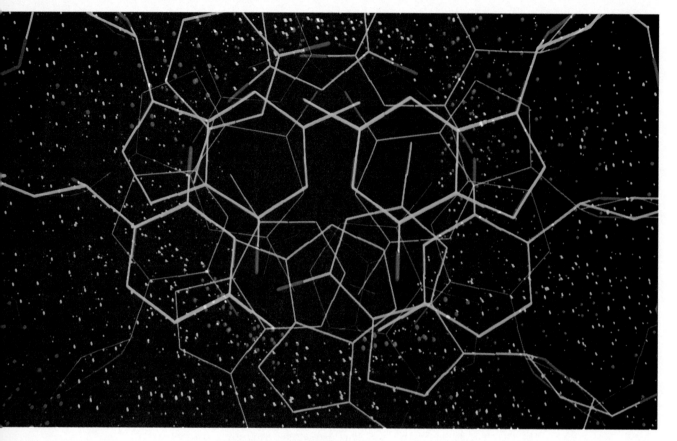

CHAPTER 16

Expanded BASIC Programs

Objectives

1. Explain how alternative actions are taken by BASIC.

2. Describe how data may be stored in variables for use by the program.

3. Describe how BASIC can repeat certain operations.

4. Plan and code programs using alternative actions and stored data.

In Chapter 15 you learned some of the actions that can be taken in the BASIC language by using sequential steps. Sequential steps are one of the kinds of building blocks from which programs are made. Other kinds of building blocks are ones for alternative actions and for repeating an action over and over. An alternative action is an action that is taken under one circumstance, but not under others. In repeated actions, the program performs the same steps repeatedly. In this chapter, you will learn how to use these two building blocks with the BASIC language. You will also learn how to store data in variables for use by the program.

MAKING DECISIONS IN BASIC

First, we will look at how decisions are made with BASIC. Then we will plan and code a simple program that makes a decision.

How BASIC Makes Decisions

The simplest way of making decisions in BASIC is to use the **IF . . . THEN . . . ELSE** statement. This statement allows BASIC to select one of two actions based on a logical relationship. This concept is easy to grasp because it is so similar to everyday logical thinking. Look at the following everyday examples, which have nothing to do with computers:

IF the light is green, THEN drive through, ELSE stop.

IF the bread is done, THEN take it out of the oven, ELSE let it continue to bake.

IF road conditions are good, THEN drive at the speed limit, ELSE slow down.

When such decision-making logic is applied to the BASIC language and computer programs, the relationship after the IF part of the statement is expressed with a relational operator. A **relational operator** is a symbol used to tell BASIC what relationship should exist between two data items in order for some action to be taken. Look at the list of commonly used operators in Figure 16.1.

SYMBOL	MEANING	EXAMPLE
=	Equal to	IF DEPT = 7 THEN...
<>	Not equal to	IF CHOICE$ <> "Y" THEN...
<	Less than	IF PAY < 5.00 THEN...
<=	Less than or equal to	IF YRBORN <= 1974 THEN...
>	Greater than	IF AGE > 13 THEN...
>=	Greater than or equal to	IF HEIGHT >= 54 THEN...

FIGURE 16.1

Commonly used relational operators and examples of how they are used.

Any BASIC statement or statements may be used after the word THEN. Frequently this will be an instruction to go to a subroutine (GOSUB). This action will be taken by the computer whenever the specified relationship is true. When the relationship is not true, on the other hand, the action given after the word ELSE will be taken. Again, any BASIC statement or statements may be used after the word ELSE. As with THEN, the statement will frequently be a reference to go to a subroutine. The example below shows how this works. If the department number is equal to 7 (true relationship), then the program will go to Subroutine 1000. If the department number is anything other than 7 (relationship that is not true), then the program will go to Subroutine 2000.

```
40 IF DEPT = 7 THEN GOSUB 1000 ELSE GOSUB 2000
```
         or (for units that do not use ELSE)
```
40 IF DEPT = 7 THEN GOSUB 1000
45 IF DEPT <> 7 THEN GOSUB 2000
```

A Simple Program That Makes a Decision

To try out a program that makes a decision, consider the case of computing sales tax. Assume that a particular automobile dealer delivers cars in various counties. For cars delivered in all but Bart County, the sales tax rate is 4 percent. In Bart County, however, it is 5 percent. Therefore, a program designed to calculate the sales tax must make a decision as to which rate to use. Because of the simplicity of such a program, there will be only one module. Writing a program design in English yields the steps shown in Figure 16.2. Study these steps.

1. Clear the screen.
2. Get the price of the car from the user.
3. Get the name of the county from the user.
4. If the county is Bart,

   Then set the sales tax rate to 5 percent

   Else, set the sales tax rate to 4 percent.
5. Calculate the tax.
6. Print the tax.

FIGURE 16.2

A program design for a simple program that makes a decision.

Converting the program design to BASIC instructions yields the result shown in Figure 16.3. In that figure, the step numbers from the program design are printed at the ends of the program lines to help you see the relationship. This version of the program works on the IBM PC and PCjr, TRS-80 Models III and 4, and similar computers.

Note that the step on line 70 makes the decision as to which tax rate to use. The way that line is written, with the ELSE statement on the following line, is easy to read. With many computers, to enter the line in this manner requires the user to space past the end of the first line to get the cursor to go to the second line. In other words, you cannot hit ENTER/RETURN to go to

```
                    10 REM AUTOTAX FOR IBM, ETC.
                    20 REM BARTLETT AND SIMPSON
                    30 REM COMPUTES SALES TAX ON AUTOS
Step 1 ──▶          40 CLS
Step 2 ──▶          50 INPUT "PRICE OF CAR";PRICE
Step 3 ──▶          60 INPUT "COUNTY NAME";COUNTY$
Step 4 ──▶ {        70 IF COUNTY$ = "BART" THEN TAX = .05
                                          ELSE TAX = .04
Step 5 ──▶          80 LET FINAL = PRICE * TAX
Step 6 ──▶          90 PRINT "TAX IS ";FINAL
Step 7 ──▶          100 END
```

FIGURE 16.3

This BASIC program introduces the ELSE keyword. The ELSE keyword works on the IBM PC, PCjr, TRS-80 Models III and 4, and similar computers.

the second line. Many other BASICs will not allow the use of two lines in this manner at all. For those, one line is sufficient as follows:

```
70 IF COUNTY$ = "BART" THEN TAX = .05 ELSE TAX = .04
```

Now look at Figure 16.4 for those computers that do not allow the keyword ELSE at the end of the IF . . . THEN statement. When there is no ELSE statement in the version of BASIC being used, then another IF . . . THEN statement can be added to take care of the false condition, as on line 75. In other words, the logical relationships on lines 70 and 75 are exactly opposite. Therefore, one line takes care of one situation and the other line takes care of the other situation.

As mentioned earlier, IF . . . THEN statements are frequently used with GOSUB instructions. Let us look at an example of such a use. We will modify the previous program so that it is written in modules, or subroutines. One subroutine will compute Bart County tax, the other subroutine will compute the tax for all other counties. By taking this approach, we will not set the tax rate based on the IF . . . THEN statement. Instead, the computation will be performed within each module. Study the code in Figure 16.5.

```
                10 REM AUTOTAX FOR APPLE, ETC.
                20 REM BARTLETT AND SIMPSON
                30 REM COMPUTES SALES TAX ON AUTOS
Step 1 ——→      40 HOME   :REM (?"SHIFT-CLR-HOME" ON COMMODORE)
Step 2 ——→      50 INPUT "PRICE OF CAR";PRICE
Step 3 ——→      60 INPUT "COUNTY NAME";COUNTY$
Step 4 ——→      70 IF COUNTY$ = "BART" THEN TAX = .05
                75 IF COUNTY$ <> "BART" THEN TAX = .04
Step 5 ——→      80 LET FINAL = PRICE * TAX
Step 6 ——→      90 PRINT "TAX IS ";FINAL
Step 7 ——→      100 END
```

FIGURE 16.4

Decisions can also be made in programs without the use of ELSE. This program can be used with the Apple and Commodore.

```
10 REM AUTOTAX FOR NEARLY ALL MICROCOMPUTERS
20 REM BARLETT AND SIMPSON
30 REM COMPUTES SALES TAX ON AUTOS, USING MODULES
40 CLS  :REM (HOME ON APPLE, ?"SHIFT-CLR-HOME" ON COMMODORE)
50 INPUT "PRICE OF CAR ";PRICE
60 INPUT "COUNTY NAME ";COUNTY$
70 IF COUNTY$ = "BART" THEN GOSUB 1000
80 IF COUNTY$ <> "BART" THEN GOSUB 2000
999 END

1000 REM BART COUNTY TAX MODULE
1010 PRINT "TAX = ";PRICE * .05
1999 RETURN

2000 REM ALL OTHER COUNTIES TAX MODULE
2010 PRINT "TAX = ";PRICE * .04
2999 RETURN
```

FIGURE 16.5

IF . . . THEN statements are often used with GOSUB instructions.

Taking One of Several Choices

In the previous section, you saw how to take one choice or another with IF . . . THEN . . . ELSE. At times, it is necessary to choose one option from among several. One way to do this with BASIC is to use the ON . . . GOSUB statement. This statement causes a branch to one of several subroutines, based on a numeric variable. Figure 16.6 shows how the ON . . . GOSUB statement is used.

If the variable *CHOICE* contains a 1, a branch is made to the first-mentioned line number (1000). If the variable contains a 2, a branch is made to the second-mentioned line number (2000), etc.

```
80 PRINT "1"
90 PRINT "2"
100 INPUT "SELECTION: ";CHOICE
110 ON CHOICE GOSUB 1000, 2000
```

FIGURE 16.6

An example of the ON . . . GOSUB statement.

To illustrate the branching concept, assume you are setting up the computer to provide information about different exhibits to visitors to a museum. The hierarchy chart of the program would consist of a Main Module labeled MUSEUM and three submodules called CHINA, IMPRESSIONISTS, and ART DECO. The submodules are named after the three current exhibits. The program design for the Main Module will consist of two statements:

1. Find out which exhibit the visitor wants to know about.
2. Perform the subroutine that gives information about the desired exhibit.

The program design for each of the submodules is the same:

1. Print information about the exhibit on the screen.

Converting the program design to the BASIC language gives the Main Module code shown in Figure 16.7. Study that code to see how the program transfers control to one of the three sub-

```
10 REM MUSEUM INFORMATION PROGRAM FOR NEARLY ALL MICROCOMPUTERS
20 REM CONWAY AND RADCLIFF
30 REM GIVES CONTINUOUS USE VISITOR INFORMATION
40 CLS  :REM (HOME ON APPLE, ?"SHIFT-CLR-HOME" ON COMMODORE)
50 PRINT "ENTER THE NUMBER OF THE EXHIBIT"
60 PRINT "FOR WHICH YOU DESIRE INFORMATION."
70 PRINT
80 PRINT "1 - CHINA"
90 PRINT "2 - IMPRESSIONISTS"
100 PRINT "3 - ART DECO"
110 INPUT "SELECT FROM ABOVE";CHOICE
120 CLS  :REM (HOME ON APPLE, ?"SHIFT-CLR-HOME" ON COMMODORE)
125 IF CHOICE > 3 THEN GOTO 40
126 IF CHOICE < 1 THEN GOTO 40
130 ON CHOICE GOSUB 1000, 2000, 3000
140 INPUT "PRESS C, THEN PRESS RETURN TO CONTINUE.....";Z$
150 GOTO 40
999 END
```

FIGURE 16.7

The Main Module code for the Museum Information program.

modules, depending on the choice of the visitor. Note the PRINT statement by itself on line 70. This just means that there will be a blank line in this position on the output. Finally, line 40 allows the module to remain on the monitor until a character is input.

On line 150 you will see a GOTO statement. The **GOTO** statement sends execution to a named program line. For this particular program, this statement tells the computer simply to go back to line 40. This will cause the menu (list of options) to again appear on the screen for the next person. The way this program is written, there is no programmed way to stop execution. Therefore, the program will continue to run until interrupted by striking CONTROL-BREAK, RUN STOP, BREAK, OR CONTROL-C, whichever is appropriate for your computer for stopping program execution manually. This is desirable behavior for this program since it should continue to operate for all visitors who come in to the museum.

With the addition of code for the modules, the program will be finished. Remembering that each module will simply print some information about the exhibit, study the coded modules in Figure 16.8.

```
1000 REM CHINA MODULE
1010 PRINT " The China exhibit comes to you"
1020 PRINT " through the efforts of Georgia Tech."
1030 PRINT " A feature of the exhibit is an"
1040 PRINT " artist who demonstrates how the work"
1050 PRINT " has been done.  Follow the signs to"
1060 PRINT " the MAIN GALLERY for a glimpse of"
1070 PRINT " the China you have never before known."
1999 RETURN

2000 REM IMPRESSIONISTS MODULE
2010 PRINT " Featuring world-famous impression-"
2020 PRINT " ists, this exhibit is sponsored by"
2030 PRINT " the Corporate Consortium for the"
2040 PRINT " Arts.  Make your way to the KLINE"
2050 PRINT " PAVILION for a new appreciation of"
2060 PRINT " these fine works of art."
2999 RETURN

3000 REM ART DECO MODULE
3010 PRINT " Art deco is an art form you should"
3020 PRINT " really get to know.  Springing from"
3030 PRINT " the playful hearts of willing artists,"
3040 PRINT " it set a new theme for many.  Follow"
3050 PRINT " the signs to LEGION HALL for sights"
3060 PRINT " you will never forget."
3999 RETURN
```

FIGURE 16.8

The coded subroutines for the Museum Information program.

STORING DATA AND REPEATING STEPS

On occasion, it is desirable to have data stored within a program for use in calculations, or to have steps repeated a number of times. Study these ideas in the following sections.

Storing and Using Data

The statements **READ** and **DATA** provide a method for storing and using data within a program. The actual data to be used is written on a line that begins with the keyword DATA. The READ statement works similarly to an INPUT statement in that both assign data to a variable. The difference is that with a READ statement, data is read from a DATA line rather than being input from the keyboard while the program is executing. Look at a very simple example:

```
40 READ A$,N
50 PRINT A$,N
60 DATA CAT,12
```

When this program is run, line 40's READ statement finds the data (which is on line 60) and assigns the first item (CAT) into variable *A$* and the second item (12) into variable *N*. The DATA statement(s) can be located anywhere in the program. A common practice is to place the DATA statements after all other modules.

Another statement that can be used with READ and DATA is RESTORE. **RESTORE** tells the computer to start over at the beginning of the data the next time it sees a READ statement. This will be illustrated for you in a program later in the chapter. If the RESTORE statement is not used, then the next READ statement will read all or part of any remaining data where the last READ statement left off.

Repeating Actions

Several methods may be used to cause BASIC to repeat actions. One of the most common methods is the loop. A **loop** involves statements being repeated one or more times within a program. One of the most useful loops is known as the **FOR . . . NEXT** loop. In its simplest form, this loop repeats all steps between the FOR and the NEXT statements the specified number of times. Here is the general form of the loop:

40 FOR *variable name* = *starting count* TO *ending count*

50 *A process such as reading or printing should be specified at this point*

60 NEXT *variable name*

As can be seen by this form, a numeric variable is picked to count the number of times the loop is executed. The starting count states where the count is to begin, while the ending count states where it will end. We can see the action of such a loop by putting a PRINT statement in it to print the value of the counting variable. Try the following lines:

```
40 FOR COUNT = 5 TO 9
50 PRINT COUNT;
60 NEXT COUNT
```

The logic of this loop is as follows: For the first run through the loop, the variable *COUNTER* prints the number 5 (the starting count for this program). The NEXT statement on line 60 then sends the program back up to line 40. The *COUNTER* is advanced to 6. Line 50 prints the 6, and the NEXT statement sends the program back up to line 40 again. For the third run, the *COUNTER* is 7, and so on. Finally, at the end of five runs, the ending *COUNTER* of 9 is printed. Since the count is at its maximum, the program exits the loop. The output of this program is the following: 5 6 7 8 9. The semicolon at the end of line 50 prevented the cursor from going to a new line after each number was printed. The starting and ending numbers, which are 5 and 9 in the example, can be variables as well as constants.

An Example Program

Suppose you want to write a program to total each customer's purchase at a hamburger restaurant. Each item on the menu is numbered, and the cashier enters the number of each item ordered. When the number is entered, the name and price of the item appear on the screen. When all items for a customer have been entered, the cashier enters a 0 to show that all items are in. At that point, the total of the purchase is displayed on the screen. For the program, data will consist of the names of the items and their prices. The data is entered on lines containing the word DATA as the keyword. Look at Figure 16.9 to see how these lines look.

Now, think about how these lines can work. The cashier may enter an item number of 3, which refers to the description and price of the third item on the list of data. Therefore, the

```
230 DATA HAMBURGER, 2.50, CHEESEBURGER, 2.75, HOT DOG, 1.95
240 DATA SMALL FRIES, .75, LARGE FRIES, 1.25, ONION RINGS, 1.50
250 DATA SMALL COLA, .45, MEDIUM COLA, .75, LARGE COLA, .99
```

FIGURE 16.9

The DATA statement provides a method of storing data within a program.

program should read three items from the data list. The third item (HOT DOG, 1.95) will be the desired one. If the cashier enters an item number of 9, nine reads will be completed. The data will then be obtained on the ninth read, corresponding to the customer's desire to have a large cola for .99. In looking up these items, the program is repeating an action over and over until some desired condition is reached.

When one thinks about the necessary actions, it becomes clear that it is not necessary to use separate modules in this instance. Rather, a simple program design can be developed as shown in Figure 16.10.

1. Clear the screen.
2. Clear the bill-totaling variable by placing a 0 in it.
3. Display the menu selections.
4. Get the menu number from the cashier.
5. If the number selected is 0, then go to Step 12 to print the total.
6. If the number selected is greater than the number of items on the menu, go back to Step 3 and get another number. (This is a safety valve in case the menu is rolled off the screen or a number over 9 is accidentally entered.)
7. Tell the computer to start reading at the first data item.
8. Read the number of menu items from data as indicated by the number selected in Step 4.

FIGURE 16.10a

Portion of a simple program design.

> 9. Print the last-read menu item and the matching price.
>
> 10. Add the price of the item to the bill-totaling variable.
>
> 11. Go back to Step 4 for the next item.
>
> 12. Print the total amount of the purchase from the bill-totaling variable.
>
> 13. End the program. (Note: By changing this line, the program could be made to run continuously, as in a real restaurant.)

FIGURE 16.10b

A simple program design continued.

Conversion of these steps to BASIC program lines gives the code shown in Figure 16.11, which will run on nearly all computers. The steps from the program design are given to help you follow the program's operation.

```
           10 REM FOODSTOP FOR NEARLY ALL MICROCOMPUTERS
           20 REM BROWN AND PARKER
           30 REM TOTALS BILL AT HAMBURGER RESTAURANT
Step  1 →  40 CLS   :REM (HOME ON APPLE, ?"SHIFT-CLR-HOME" ON COMMODORE)
Step  2 →  50 FINAL = 0
          ⎧60 PRINT "1=HAMBURGER 2=CHEESEBURGER 3=HOT DOG"
Step  3 → ⎨70 PRINT "4=SML FRIES 5=LRG FRIES     6=ONION RNGS"
          ⎩80 PRINT "7=SML COLA  8=MED COLA      9=LRG COLA"
           90 PRINT
Step  4 →  100 INPUT "SELECT MENU NUMBER (OR 0 TO TOTAL)";N
Step  5 →  110 IF N = 0 THEN GOTO 200
Step  6 →  120 IF N > 9 THEN GOTO 60
Step  7 →  130 RESTORE
          ⎧140 FOR ITEM = 1 TO N
Step  8 → ⎨150    READ DESC$,PRICE
          ⎩160 NEXT ITEM
Step  9 →  170 PRINT DESC$,PRICE
Step 10 →  180 LET FINAL = FINAL + PRICE
Step 11 →  190 GOTO 100
           200 PRINT
Step 12 →  210 PRINT "TOTAL IS: ";FINAL
           220 END   :REM FOR CONTINUOUS OPERATION CHANGE 220 END TO:  220 GOTO 40
           230 DATA HAMBURGER, 2.50, CHEESEBURGER, 2.75, HOT DOG, 1.95
           240 DATA SMALL FRIES, .75, LARGE FRIES, 1.25, ONION RINGS, 1.50
           250 DATA SMALL COLA, .45, MEDIUM COLA, .75, LARGE COLA, .99
```

FIGURE 16.11

The coded Foodstop program.

SUMMARY

By implementing additional features, you can use BASIC to program applications in just about any field. Some of the more powerful features that allow such applications are IF . . . THEN . . . ELSE and ON . . . GOSUB statements for making decisions, as well as the READ and DATA statements for storing and accessing data in a program. The FOR . . . NEXT statements allow program steps to be repeated any desired number of times, thereby making programming much easier.

REVIEW QUESTIONS

1. What is meant by an alternative action? (Obj. 1)
2. How does BASIC make a decision between two alternative actions? (Obj. 1)
3. How is data stored within a program for use by the program? (Obj. 2)
4. What are the similarities and differences between the READ statement and the INPUT statement? (Obj. 2)
5. How can BASIC be told to begin again in reading the data? (Obj. 2)
6. What is one common way for BASIC to repeat some instructions over and over? (Obj. 3)
7. Give an example of a program in which repeating instructions is a useful practice. (Obj. 3)
8. When using a FOR . . . NEXT loop, what statements are repeated? (Obj. 3)

VOCABULARY WORDS

The following terms were introduced in this chapter:

IF . . . THEN . . . ELSE	DATA
relational operator	RESTORE
GOTO	loop
READ	FOR . . . NEXT

WORKBOOK EXERCISES

Complete all exercises in Chapter 16 of the workbook.

DISKETTE EXERCISE

Complete the diskette exercise for Chapter 16.

Robot Building Can Be
Fun and Educational

At the end of Chapter 4 you learned about building a computer from a kit. In this section, we will look at some of the possibilities of building a robot. As with the computer, you can buy a robot kit if you like. There are several kits available from different companies, each performing different types of motions. Rather than looking at how to build a robot from a kit, however, let us consider some of the things to think about in designing and building a robot from scratch. It is not the purpose of this section to give you precise instructions for building a robot. However, perhaps it will start you thinking about the process. If you want to proceed with building a robot, look in some of the magazines you can find in a library. You should be able to find further guidance there.

First, let's look at the requirements for just about the simplest possible robot. As long as one mechanical movement is controlled by a computer, you can say we have a robot. Therefore, if you have a battery-powered toy car or truck and put its motor under the control of a computer, you will have a very simple robot. If you have a microcomputer that can control the motor of a cassette tape recorder, it will be easy to make such a simple robot. To do this, run wires from the toy car to a plug that will fit the computer's cassette motor control jack. The car's battery, its motor, and the plug for the cassette jack should be wired in series. Then write a program for the computer to control the car. Whenever you want the car to move, the computer program should use the statement normally used to turn on the cassette motor. Whenever you want the car to stop, the computer pro-

gram should use the statement normally used to turn off the cassette motor. The exact statements you use to write the program will vary depending on the brand of computer and the language you are using. A word of caution is in order if you want to use the cassette motor control jack to control other devices, such as a battery-powered vehicle or a light bulb. Make sure the current used by the device is no greater than that used by the cassette recorder intended for use with the jack. Too much current going through the switch in the computer can cause damage.

If your computer does not have a cassette motor control jack, you will need to use a device called a digital-to-analog converter to control any outside device, such as an electric motor or light bulb. Usually known as a D-to-A converter, such a device changes the digital output of the computer into an analog voltage. The voltage can then be used for such things as controlling a solenoid to turn a motor on or off. D-to-A converters can be purchased in the form of circuit cards that plug into the computer's card slot, printer port or other output connector.

While the use of a cassette port or a D-to-A converter will allow control of a robot's motor, it will not allow the robot to "talk back" to the computer. For example, you might want a robot that can tell the computer when it has run into something. Then the computer can tell the robot to change directions. To allow the robot to get messages back to the computer, you will probably use the opposite of a D-to-A converter; that is, an A-to-D, or an analog-to-digital converter. Such a device takes an analog signal, such as voltage that flows when a switch is closed, and turns it into digital signals that can be used by the computer.

Beyond the very simple robot capabilities we have discussed so far, what other things could be included in a home-built robot? The capabilities are really limited only by the imagination and expertise of the builder. The following paragraphs mention just a couple of the possibilities.

Freeing a robot from the wires which connect it to the computer is one thing most advanced robot builders like to do. There are two ways to accomplish this. One is to make the computer battery powered and put it inside of the robot. The other is to use radio transmission to send signals to the robot. Under this method, a transmitter will have to be connected to the computer,

and a receiver connected to the robot. If communication is to be two-way between computer and robot, both a transmitter and a receiver must be connected to each unit.

Advanced movement capabilities are also a goal of many robot builders. Many possibilities exist for various combinations of wheels, legs, arms, etc. to make the robot move in a manner required to accomplish the desired task. While most small, less expensive robots use electric motors to power their movement, other methods such as compressed air or hydraulics can be used when they are more appropriate.

Many other capabilities are also possible. To allow robots to do more and more kinds of everyday work, advanced capabilities can frequently be engineered into home-built robots. The dedicated planner and builder, by using a great deal of study and creativity, can produce a robot whose abilities rival or surpass those of many factory-made robots.

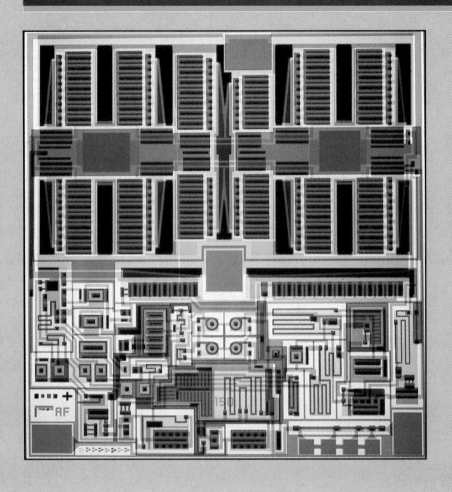

APPENDIXES

A. A Brief History of Computing

B. Computer Keyboarding

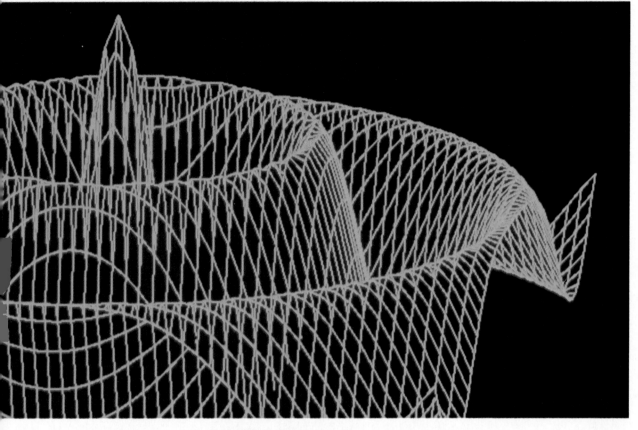

APPENDIX A

A Brief History of Computing

Objectives

1. Trace the historical development of computing.
2. Describe the different generations of computers.

FROM FINGER COUNTING TO ELECTRONIC COMPUTERS

The first digital computer used in business was installed in 1954. Although slow compared to today's computers, it made computations automatically and rapidly. What did people do before that date to speed up calculations and make them less tiresome?

Finger Counting

Before the nineteenth century, most calculations were made in a person's brain. The first computations were simple counting, and no doubt the person used all ten fingers to help. The early Roman schools actually taught finger counting and devised a method of multiplying and dividing using the fingers.

Abacus

From the use of fingers, persons moved to aids such as pebbles, sticks, and beads for computations. More than three thousand years ago the **abacus**, the first counting machine, was invented. It consists of a frame in which rods strung with beads are set. The beads represent digits and the rods represent places: units, tens, hundreds, and higher multiples of ten. In the abacus illustrated in Figure A.1, each bead in the top section has an assigned value of five; each bead in the bottom section has a value of one. The beads in both sections have a counting value when they are pushed toward the board that separates the two sections. In the illustration, the beads that have been moved represent a total of 249.

The origin of the abacus is uncertain. Some say it is a product of the ancient Hindu civilization. Others say it came from Babylon or Egypt. Some believe that the Chinese invented it. The Chinese changed and adopted it early in their history; it has, therefore, generally become known as a Chinese invention.

The Japanese also changed and adopted the abacus. The Japanese model (Figure A.2) is known as a **soraban**. It differs from the abacus in that it has only one bead on each rod in the upper section and five beads on each rod in the lower section.

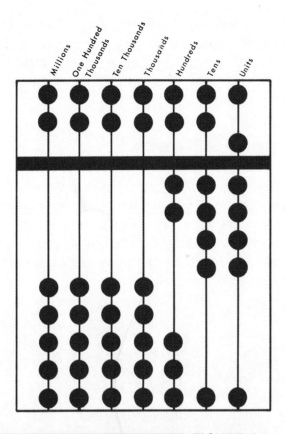

FIGURE A.1

The abacus was first used more than three
thousand years ago.

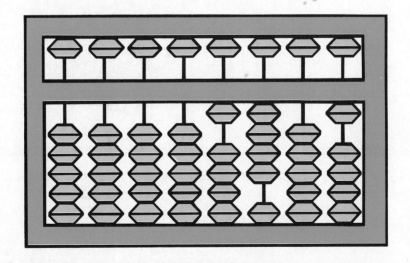

FIGURE A.2

A Japanese soraban.

Note in Figure A.1 that the abacus has two beads on each rod in the upper section and five beads on each rod in the lower section. The abacus and the soraban are still used in some countries. In skilled hands, they are amazingly rapid and efficient in making computations.

Napier's Bones

In the 1600s, John Napier invented a device consisting of bars or strips of bone on which numbers were printed. The device became known as "**Napier's bones**." By placing the "bones" at various angles and sliding one against another, computations could be performed, including the extraction of square and cube roots. See Figure A.3.

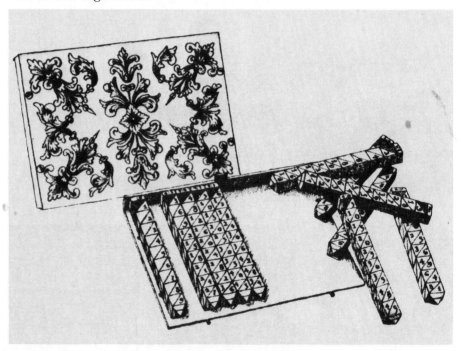

FIGURE A.3

Napier's bones could be used for computations.

Slide Rule

The **slide rule**, conceived by William Oughtred in 1622, consists of two outer rules and a central sliding rule. Both rules are divided into scales (a series of spaces marked by lines). The rules are moved either backward or forward until a selected number on one scale lines up with a selected number on the other scale. The desired result is then read from a third scale. The slide rule, shown in Figure A.4, was widely used by engineers and scientists until recently. Due to the speed and accuracy of the electronic calculator, the slide rule is rarely used anymore.

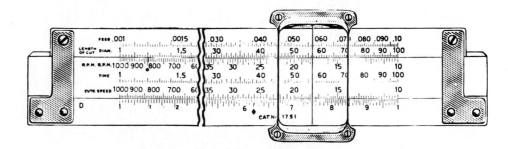

FIGURE A.4

The slide rule was made obsolete by the hand-held calculator.

Inventors of Early Calculators

The development of mechanically operated adding machines and calculators began in the 1600s. Some of the early developers are discussed in the following sections.

Blaise Pascal

In 1642, Blaise Pascal invented the first mechanical adding machine, shown in Figure A.5. It was capable of carrying tens automatically. His machine consisted of wheels with cogs or teeth, on which the numbers 0-9 were engraved. The first wheel on the right represented units; the second, tens; the third, hundreds; and so on. As the wheels were turned, the numbers appeared in a window at the top of the machine. When the units wheel was turned beyond Digit 9, the tens wheel at the left would reflect the carry. For example, to add 7 and 4, the 7 was stored on the first wheel by turning the wheel until the 7 appeared in the window. Then the wheel was turned again through four places. This procedure resulted in a carry, which was accomplished by a series of gears arranged in such a way that they turned the next wheel. As a result, 1's appeared in the windows above the tens and units wheels.

The first mechanical adding machine, invented by Pascal.

Gottfried von Leibnitz

In 1671, Gottfried von Leibnitz drew the plans for a calculator that could multiply and divide as well as count, add, and subtract. A drawing of the machine is shown in Figure A.6. In 1694, a machine was actually built using his plans, but it did not work very well. The plans were correct, but the technology capable of making the detailed parts had not yet been developed.

FIGURE A.6

Von Leibnitz's calculator.

Charles Xavier Thomas

For the next two hundred years, many attempts were made to improve on the Pascal and von Leibnitz inventions. Progress was made, although it was slow and sometimes painful. Gradually, calculators became faster, smaller, more reliable, and at least partly automatic. In the 1820s, Charles Xavier Thomas invented a calculator that was the first to add, subtract, divide, and multiply accurately. It was widely copied by other inventors and was thus considered to be the ancestor of the mechanical calculators that preceded today's electronic calculators. Figure A.7 shows a typical 1880 machine; it was capable of performing the four main arithmetic operations of addition, subtraction, multiplication, and division.

FIGURE A.7

A typical 1880 calculator.

Early American Inventors

All early calculator inventors were Europeans. In 1872, however, Frank S. Baldwin developed the first calculator to be invented in the United States. The invention of this machine, shown in Figure A.8, marked the beginning of a rapidly growing

FIGURE A.8

The first U. S. calculator, invented by Baldwin.

calculator industry in this country. The first practical adding machines which listed amounts and sums on paper were invented in the late 1800s by Dorr Eugene Felt and William S. Burroughs.

Oscar and David Sundstrand invented the ten-key adding-listing machine in 1914. This machine introduced the keyboard arrangement that became the standard for calculators used in business offices. The same basic keyboard arrangement is used on most of today's electronic calculators.

Punched-Card Machines

While development was under way on calculating machines, a new idea in processing data was being introduced in the late 1800s. It was the punched card.

Herman Hollerith

Using **punched cards** to record factual information, Herman Hollerith developed an entirely new system of processing data. Punched paper tape and punched cards had been used as early as 1728 to control weaving machines. The punched-card principle for weaving patterns in rugs on the first automatic loom was perfected in 1801 by Joseph Jacquard. The principles of these early applications were adapted by Hollerith for use by the U.S. Census Bureau. Hollerith was an independent inventor who was contracted by the Bureau in 1880 to help speed up the sorting and tabulating (computing by means of rows and columns) of census data. (It had become apparent that it would take over ten years to tabulate the next census figures without some type of automatic process.) By 1887, he had worked out a code of representing census information through a system of punched holes in paper strips. He later changed to a standard-sized card because the paper strips did not work very well. Thus, Hollerith developed the first machine capable of processing data that uses mathematical facts from punched cards. The system included the cards, a card punch, a sorting box, and a tabulator equipped with electromagnetic counters. With this equipment, cards could be sorted at the rate of about 80 cards per minute. Data appearing in the cards could be tabulated and counted at the rate of 50 to 75 cards per minute. Figure A.9 shows Hollerith's punched-card machine.

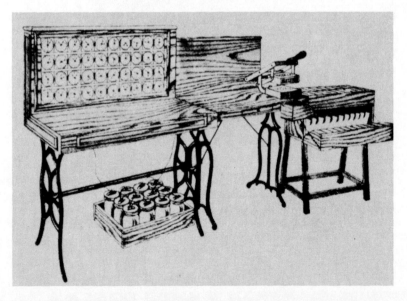

FIGURE A.9

Hollerith's punched-card machine.

The Hollerith system was used to process the 1890 census. As a result, the 1890 census was completed in one fourth the time needed to determine the 1880 census. Hollerith then organized a company to manufacture and sell his system. This company later became known as the International Business Machines Corporation (IBM).

The Punched-Card Era

Over the years many improvements were made on the original punched-card machines. The machines for punching holes in the cards were improved and equipped with a number of automatic devices. A calculator that could read the punched cards and multiply or divide the data was developed. Various models of machines were developed for sorting the cards and printing reports from data contained in them.

From the 1920s through the mid-1970s, punched card equipment was widely used for business data processing. Cards were punched on a card-punch machine (also known as a keypunch) with a keyboard similar to that found on a present-day computer or terminal. A later model **card-punch machine** is shown in Figure A.10. Cards to be punched were

FIGURE A.10

The card-punch machine is used to punch holes in cards.

placed in the card hopper and passed through the machine one card at a time as the operator entered the data on the keyboard. Each character was punched according to a certain code. The most commonly used code was known as the Hollerith code and is shown on the card in Figure A.11. The standard card was divided into 80 columns, and one character was punched in each column. Note that a digit was recorded by punching one hole in a column, while an alphabet letter was recorded by punching two holes.

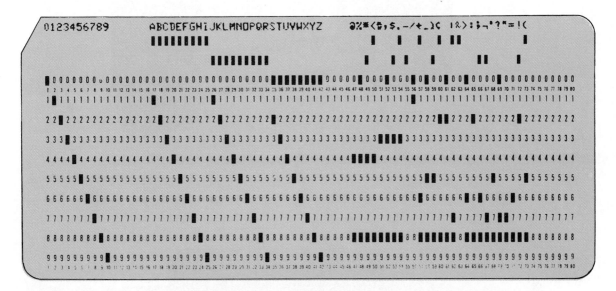

FIGURE A.11

This card shows Hollerith's punched-card code.

The different items of information in a punched card were divided into fields in the same manner that a record from a disk file is divided into fields. A card field was a vertical column or group of columns set aside to record a single fact. A field could contain a name, an amount, or a code, for example.

Once the cards were punched, they were arranged or sorted with a **sorter** such as shown in Figure A.12. A **tabulator** (Figure A.13) was then used to print reports from the data. The important thing to remember about all these machines is that, although they could do arithmetic and print reports, they were not computers. They contained many mechanical parts and did not make use of stored programs to control their operation.

FIGURE A.12

A sorter.

FIGURE A.13

A tabulator was used to print reports.

EARLY COMPUTERS

Now let's take a look at some of the developments leading up to the stored-program computer as we know it today.

The Analytical Engine

Turn your clock back briefly about one hundred and fifty years to the middle 1800s and meet another inventor, Charles Babbage. Babbage had some entirely new and advanced ideas on designing a computer. "I am going to construct a machine," wrote Babbage, "which will incorporate a memory unit system, an external memory unit, and conditional transfer. I am going to call this device an 'Analytical Engine.'" What Babbage described with startling accuracy is the computer.

Babbage was a mathematician of good reputation who spent his life and his fortune, as well as large sums of money from the British government, on the design of an automatic computer. The machine designed by Babbage was to have four basic parts. One part, consisting of the memory, was to be used to store the numeric data used in calculations. A second part, consisting of gears and cog wheels on which digits were engraved, was to be used for computing. A third part, consisting of gears and levers, was to be able to move numbers back and forth between the memory and computing units. Finally, Babbage planned to use punched cards for getting information into and out of his machine.

Babbage believed he could use cards to program his machine to handle computations automatically. He was greatly influenced by Lady Augusta Lovelace, who was the first person to create an actual computer program. As a result of this, Babbage seemed able to see the possibility of programming his machine to change from one series of steps to another when certain conditions were met. This, of course, is one of the most valuable abilities of a computer.

Babbage did not complete his machine, a drawing of which is shown in Figure A.14, but he did leave for later inventors a great many details of his plan. Due to the poor technology of the times, the various parts of his machine simply could not be made exactly as required. He was ahead of his time. Had he been successful, his machine would have been the first true computer. As it was, his work was largely forgotten until the 1940s, when new

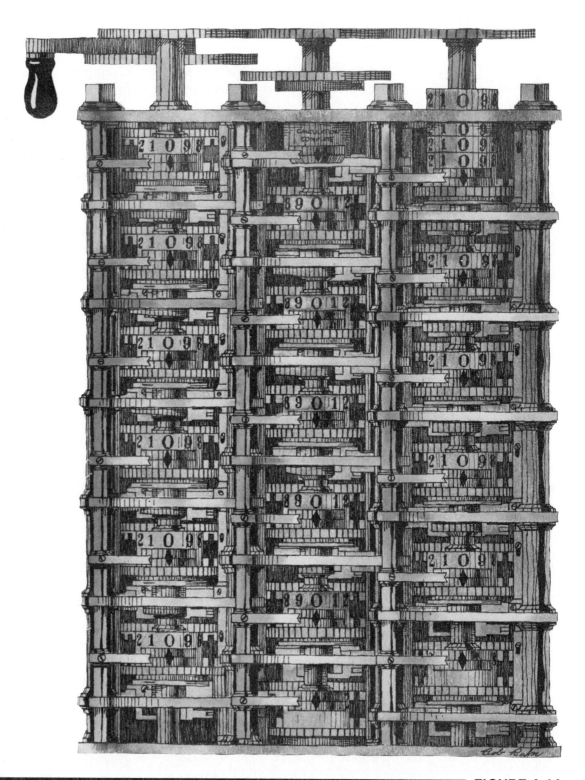

Babbage's analytical engine.

attempts were made to design and build a rapid automatic computer.

Mark I

In 1944, Howard Aiken developed a calculator called the **Mark I**. The Mark I obtained data from punched cards, made calculations with the aid of mechanical devices, and punched the results into a new set of cards. The most unusual aspect of the new machine, however, is that it was controlled automatically by instructions punched into paper tape attached to the computer. Thus, it was the first machine to use a stored program to control its actions. The Mark I, although it can be regarded as the first successful computer, was not an electronic computer. It was mechanically operated.

ENIAC

Another early pioneer working on computers was Dr. John V. Atanasoff, who can be given credit for developing the ideas on which the first electronic computers were based. Many of these ideas were used in ENIAC, developed by Dr. John W. Mauchly and J. Presper Eckert, under a contract from the U.S. Army. The first electronic computer to go into operation, **ENIAC** (the Electronic Numerical Integrator and Calculator) contained thousands and thousands of vacuum tubes. To program ENIAC required changes in thousands of wires and switches. In other words, its program was hard-wired to memory, instead of being read into memory as with today's computers. ENIAC, shown in Figure A.15, was completed in 1946 and was used for several years.

EDSAC and EDVAC

The first electronic computers to utilize the stored-program concept were the **EDSAC** (Electronic Delay Storage Automatic Calculator) and **EDVAC** (Electronic Discrete Variable Automatic Computer). Though the EDVAC (Figure A.16), developed by Dr. John von Neumann, was thought of first, the EDSAC was completed first, in 1949.

FIGURE A.15

ENIAC, the first operable electronic computer.

COMPUTER GENERATIONS

ENIAC, EDSAC, and EDVAC were largely experimental or military machines. The first computer available for data processing use was the **UNIVAC I**, a machine developed by Eckert and Mauchly after ENIAC was finished. Remington Rand bought Eckert and Mauchly's company and the UNIVAC I. Remington Rand thus became the first company in the business of selling computers. The first UNIVAC I sold to the public market was installed at the U.S. Census Bureau in 1951. In 1954, General

FIGURE A.16

EDVAC, the first computer designed to use a stored program.

Electric became the first business to use a computer when they purchased a UNIVAC I. The UNIVAC I is illustrated in Figure A.17.

IBM, which for years had controlled the market for electromechanical data processing machines for business use, announced their first computer available for the public market in 1953. They shortly overtook Remington Rand in sales. Since then, IBM has continued to be the leading company in the computer business.

UNIVAC 1 was the first commercially available computer.

First Generation

All the early computers are known as first-generation computers. They used vacuum tubes in addition to other circuits. For this reason, the machines were very large in size, were very slow by today's standards, and required almost constant maintenance.

The large number of vacuum tubes in these early computers created many problems because of the amount of heat given off by the tubes. This heat problem made it necessary to install heavy-duty air conditioning units. The first-generation computers were mostly computational machines. Their input capabilities were usually limited to keyboards and/or punched cards. Their output capabilities were usually limited to printers and/or punched cards. However, some used magnetic tape for their input and output.

First-generation computers could make over 100 thousand calculations per second. Although this may seem extremely fast, the speed of a Control Data Corporation computer introduced in 1983 is almost 800 million calculations per second, or 8,000 times faster.

Second Generation

Second-generation computers, first available in the late 1950s, used transistors in place of vacuum tubes. This change brought many improvements. The cost of computers decreased, and more businesses could afford them. The amount of heat put out by the machines was much less, reducing air conditioning requirements. The use of transistors also made it possible to reduce the size of the equipment. This change further increased the computer's computational speed. Also, the transistors proved to be much more reliable than vacuum tubes.

A typical second-generation computer was the IBM 1401 (Figure A.18). Introduced in 1959, it was designed for business use. This machine used transistors.

Removable disk storage units and magnetic tape input/output units were developed for use on second-generation computers. The speed of the line printers was increased from three hundred lines per minute, which was fairly common on first-generation computers, to one thousand lines per minute. The

FIGURE A.18

A representative second-generation computer, the IBM 1401.

speed of card readers and card punches was also increased, although not as much as the speed of the printers. These changes in the computer made it more useful as a tool in business because of the large volume of data to be processed and the long printed reports required.

Third Generation

Third-generation computers introduced the use of very small electronic circuits called integrated circuits, rather than transistors. This change further decreased the size of the computer, while increasing its speed. The speed of the first-generation computers was described in milliseconds (1/1,000 of a second). The speed of the second-generation computers was described in microseconds (1/1,000,000 of a second). The speed of the third-generation computers was described in nanoseconds (1/1,000,000,000 of a second). The speed of line printers on many third-generation computers was increased to two thousand lines per minute, while one printer could print over twenty thousand lines per minute. Figure A.19 compares integrated circuits with transistors and vacuum tubes.

FIGURE A.19

First-generation vacuum tubes, second-generation transistors, and third-generation integrated circuits.

Fourth Generation

Fourth-generation computers use what is known as **VLSI** circuitry. The abbreviation VLSI refers to *very large scale integration*. This means that extremely large numbers of electronic components are crammed into each integrated circuit chip. It is possible to place all the components required for an entire computer on one circuit chip. Figure A.20 shows a chip containing all the circuitry required for a computer.

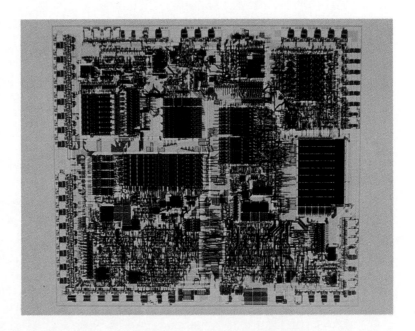

FIGURE A.20

A processor with all the circuits on one chip.

IMPROVEMENTS IN DATA ENTRY

At the same time computers themselves were undergoing tremendously fast development, the methods of getting data into the computers were also changing. As mentioned earlier, most of the first-generation computers used keypunch machines and punched cards to input data.

For years, the keypunch was the main support of data entry. A **keypunch machine** punched data into cards as punched holes and printed the meanings of the punched holes at the tops of the cards. Usually data was keyed twice: once for the original input, and again to make sure it was accurate.

The first data entry improvement over punched cards was the **key-to-tape machine**, shown in Figure A.21. This

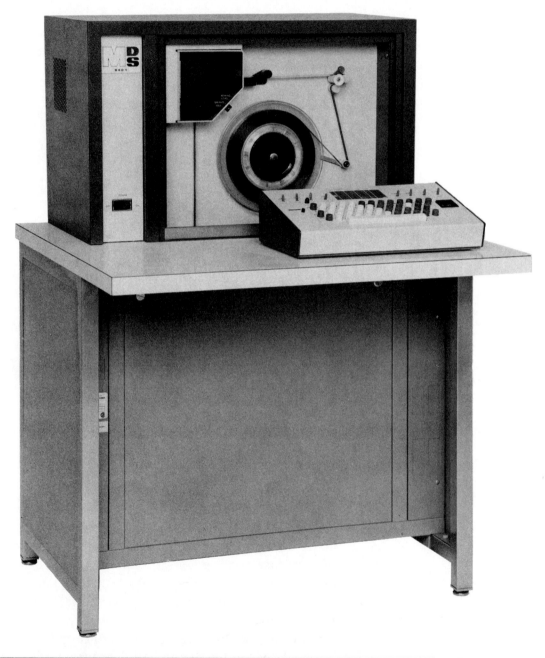

A key-to-tape machine.

machine records data on magnetic tape instead of punched cards. The machine has a keyboard similar to that of a typewriter. Data is keyed as digits, letters of the alphabet, and special characters. Data is recorded on the tape as magnetized spots in a form of binary code. Some key-to-tape machines have cathode-ray tube (CRT) displays. The data appears on the screen as it is being entered and is transferred to tape once the entry is complete.

Following the key-to-tape machine was the key-to-disk machine. The general principles remained the same. Instead of recording on tape, however, the **key-to-disk machine** records its data on magnetic disks. The present trend in data entry is toward using input devices connected directly to the computer.

Tracing the history of computational devices from the seventeenth century forward, we find that the number of devices has increased significantly in recent years. Figure A.22 shows a time-line graph of various devices which have had an impact on the development of the computer.

SUMMARY

Development of computational machines has been going on for over three thousand years, beginning with the abacus. The first machine capable of adding, subtracting, multiplying, and dividing was developed in the 1820s. Another giant step forward occurred in the 1880s when Herman Hollerith invented a punched-card method of processing data. Punched cards were the main support of business data processing through the middle part of the twentieth century.

The first electronic computer was developed in the late 1940s. From that point, development has been very rapid. Each major improvement in technology has led to the development of a new "generation" of computers. Since the first public use of the computer in the early 1950s, four different generations of computers have been developed. The fifth generation is currently under development and may become available at any time. With each generation, computers have become much faster and much more capable. At the same time, they have become very small. Large price reductions have accompanied each advance in technology. The computer has truly become a universal machine.

THE MECHANICAL ERA OF DATA DEVICES

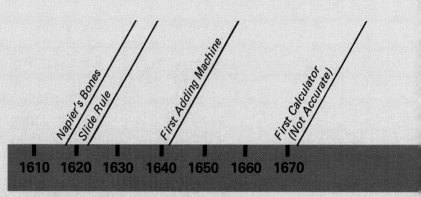

Napier's Bones
Slide Rule
First Adding Machine
First Calculator (Not Accurate)

1610 1620 1630 1640 1650 1660 1670

1750 1760 1770 1780 1790

THE ELECTRO-MECHANICAL ERA OF DATA DEVICES

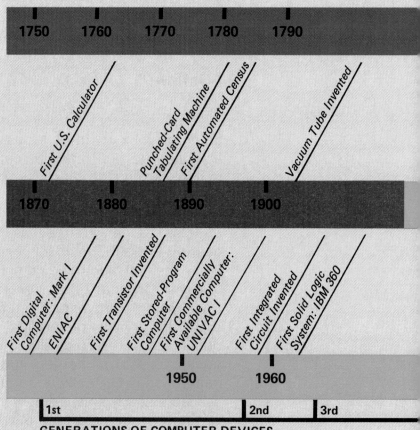

First U.S. Calculator
Punched-Card Tabulating Machine
First Automated Census
Vacuum Tube Invented

1870 1880 1890 1900

First Digital Computer: Mark I
ENIAC
First Transistor Invented
First Stored-Program Computer
First Commercially Available Computer: UNIVAC I
First Integrated Circuit Invented
First Solid Logic System: IBM 360

1950 1960

1st   2nd   3rd

GENERATIONS OF COMPUTER DEVICES

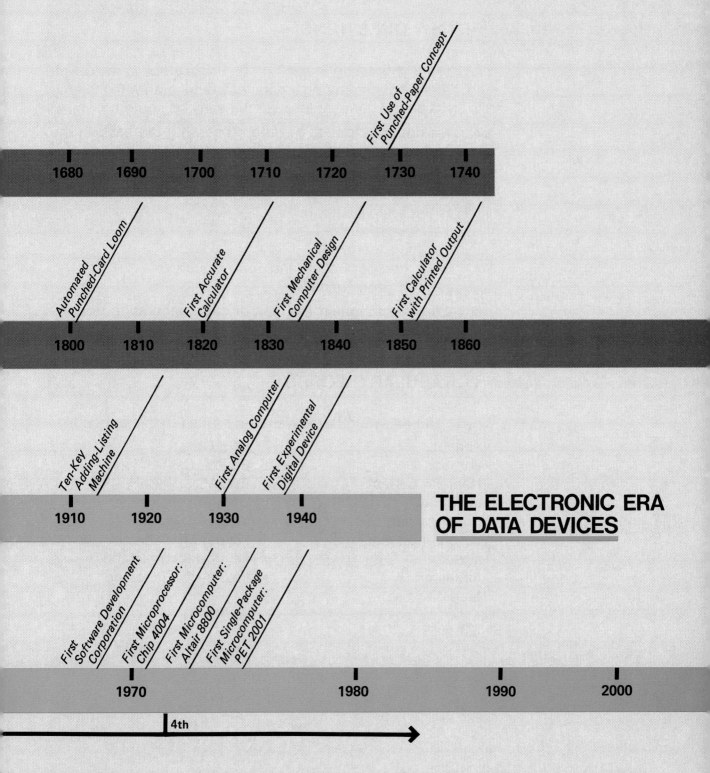

First Use of
Punched-Paper Concept

1680 1690 1700 1710 1720 1730 1740

Automated
Punched-Card Loom

First Accurate
Calculator

First Mechanical
Computer Design

First Calculator
with Printed Output

1800 1810 1820 1830 1840 1850 1860

Ten-Key
Adding-Listing
Machine

First Analog Computer

First Experimental
Digital Device

1910 1920 1930 1940

THE ELECTRONIC ERA
OF DATA DEVICES

First
Software Development
Corporation

First Microprocessor:
Chip 4004

First Microcomputer:
Altair 8800

First Single-Package
Microcomputer:
PET 2001

1970 1980 1990 2000

4th

FIGURE A.22

The recent history of calculating devices.

REVIEW QUESTIONS

1. Name and describe each of the major steps in the development of computing equipment, beginning with the abacus and continuing through the early computers. (Obj. 1)

2. In what contribution to data processing did each of the following men take part? (Objs. 1, 2)

    a. Blaise Pascal
    b. Charles Babbage
    c. Herman Hollerith
    d. Howard Aiken
    e. John Atanasoff
    f. J. Presper Eckert and John Mauchly
    g. John von Neumann

3. What are the main features of each generation of computers? (Obj. 2)

VOCABULARY WORDS

The following terms were introduced in this appendix:

abacus	ENIAC
soraban	EDSAC
Napier's bones	EDVAC
slide rule	UNIVAC I
punched card	VLSI
card-punch machine	keypunch machine
sorter	key-to-tape machine
tabulator	key-to-disk machine
Mark I	

APPENDIX B

COMPUTER KEYBOARDING

The keyboarding materials on the following pages were prepared by Dr. T. James Crawford, Dr. Lawrence W. Erickson, Dr. Lee R. Beaumont, Dr. Jerry W. Robinson, and Dr. Arnola C. Ownby. They are reprinted here with the permission of South-Western Publishing Co.

Build keyboarding speed

Key each line twice SS.

Practice hint:

Think, say, and key letter by letter.

Practice hint:

Think, say, and key each word as a word.

Practice hint:

Think, say, and key the easy words as words. Think, say, and key harder words letter by letter.

Measure and build your speed

1. Take a 1-minute (1') writing on the paragraph. See how many words you can type in a minute.

2. Read the nearest number (or dot) above the point at which you stopped. That is your 1-minute GWAM.

Practice words by *letter* response

1 you ate ink raw pop age mop tab pin

2 few|you are|pop art|get ink|oil ads

3 Lily saw him eat a crab at my cafe.

Practice words by *word* response

4 bid got man eye pay sir map but fix

5 an auto|to risk|so busy|he paid the

6 Dirk is to pay us for the map work.

Combine *letter* and *word* responses

7 eat air tax bow tie due him for you

8 my duty|as such|on fuel|we both saw

9 It is my duty to bag the best fish.

Practice an easy paragraph (all letters used)

Next you can learn to work on
the figure bank. Seize the chance
to move up in skill. The job will
not be simple, but do not quit yet.

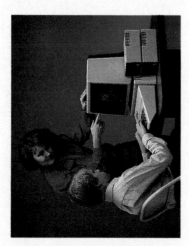

Have you ever watched in awe as a skilled person used a keyboard at high speed? Did you wonder how that person could make the fingers move so fast while an unskilled person moves slowly about the keyboard using a hunt-and-peck or a peek-and-poke system? The reason is that the skilled operator has been trained properly while the hunt-and-peck operator has not.

Since the invention of the typewriter in 1867, many millions of people have learned to operate the keyboard with skill. In the computer world of today, many more millions will learn to use a computer keyboard with speed and ease—at home, in school, or at work.

You are lucky to be one of those who will learn to keyboard in the right way—by touch (without looking at the keys). It is the purpose of this book and the computer diskettes that are available with it to see that you do so.

To learn to operate a keyboard with skill, you must learn to strike the keys and to operate other parts in the right way. This is called good "technique" (form). Good technique should be your main goal as you learn by practice the reaches to the keys. Good technique will help you to improve finger motions and to save time between motions. Improved finger motions and saved time between motions will allow you to keyboard faster than you can now write by hand. Your work will also be easier to read and will have fewer errors.

Good technique requires that the position of the hands and fingers be right because they do the work.

Sit in front of the keyboard so that you can place the fingers in a vertical (upright) position over **ASDF JKL;** (the home keys). The tips of the fingers should just touch the tops of the keys. Move your chair forward or backward or your elbows in or out a bit to place your fingers in this upright position. Do not let your fingers lean over onto one another toward the little fingers.

Curve your fingers deeply like those in the drawing. In this position, the fingers can make quick, direct reaches to the keys and snap back toward the palm of the hand as reaches are completed. A quick snap stroke is needed for proper keystroking motion.

Place the thumb *lightly* on the space bar, the tip of the right thumb pointing toward the *n* key. Tuck the tip of the left thumb slightly into the palm to keep it out of the way. Strike the space bar with a quick down-and-in motion of the right thumb. Return the thumb quickly to its home position.

Good luck to you as you learn the good techniques of keyboarding.

Keyboard review and mastery

Key (type) each line twice SS: once slowly; again at a faster speed. DS between 2-line groups.

Goals:

- quiet (steady) hands
- elbows steady at your sides
- wrists low, but not touching the machine

Practice hint:

Think and say each letter as you key (type) it.

Technique hint:

Reach from bottom row to third row (and from third row to bottom row) without moving your hands up or down the keyboard.

LESSON 18

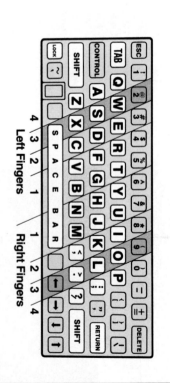

Keyboard review (all letters used)

1 have lazy jack exam dark quit signs

2 is up|to be|if we|as if to|up to us

3 Did she quit the team? I may, too.

Keyboard mastery words (all letters used)

4 fork size move coax soap want squid

5 jet lag|the hub|big play|to the zoo

6 Juan can coax them into a big play.

Practice words with long reaches

7 my any ice orb sun fun oft bum aqua

8 to my|if any|for ice|the gym|a myth

9 Cey said my unit must set the pace.

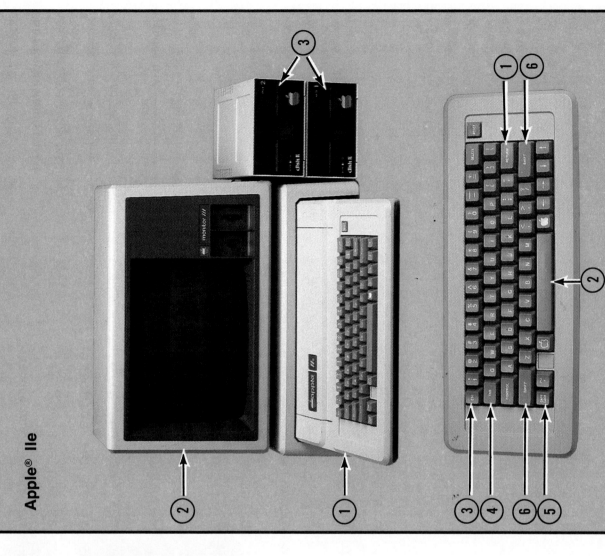

Apple® IIe

Locate:

1. Keyboard
2. Display screen
3. Disk drive(s)

Locate:

1. RETURN key
2. Space bar
3. ESC (escape) key
4. Tab key
5. CAPS LOCK
6. Shift keys

Lesson 17, Part B

Build keyboarding speed

Key each line twice SS.

Practice hint:

Think, say, and key letter by letter.

Practice hint:

Think, say, and key each word as a word.

Practice hint:

Think, say, and key the words shown in color as words. Think, say, and key the words shown in black letter by letter.

Lesson 17, Part C

Improve keystroking speed on sentences

Take three 15-second (15″) writings on each line. Your rate in gross words a minute (GWAM) is shown word by word above the lines.

NOTE: If you finish a line before 15″ are up, start over.

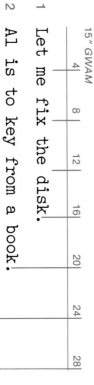

Practice words by *letter* response

1 cat you are pop see him was joy far

2 a mop|as far|we are|was red|saw him

3 As my dad saw, you were on a barge.

Practice words by *word* response

4 and the end she but odd cut too off

5 he did|is off|if she|of all|the end

6 She is to go to the lake to fix it.

Combine *letter* and *word* responses

7 do we of ad to my an be the him and

8 to be|if we|to add|of him|is my own

9 I was to see him on the bus at six.

15″ GWAM

| 4 | 8 | 12 | 16 | 20 | 24 | 28 |

1 Let me fix the disk.

2 Al is to key from a book.

3 Roz went to use it at the lab.

4 Vic did a quick jig at their party.

Commodore™ 64

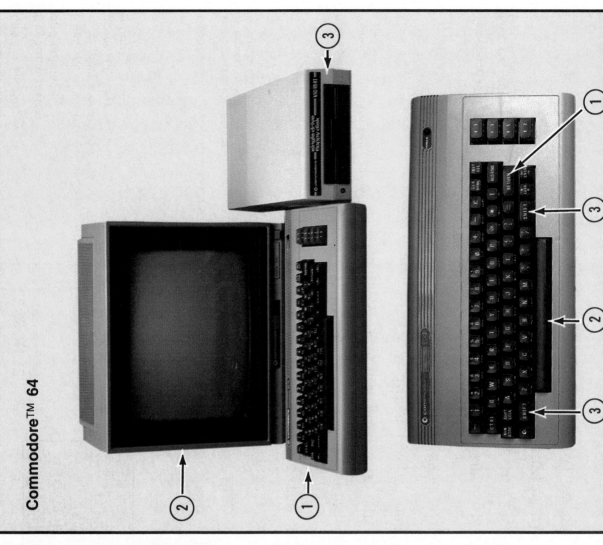

Locate:

1. Keyboard
2. Display screen
3. Disk drive

Locate:

1. RETURN key
2. Space bar
3. Shift keys

Lesson 17, Part A

Keyboard review and mastery

Key (type) each line twice SS: once slowly; again at a faster speed. DS between 2-line groups.

Goals:

- quiet (steady) hands
- elbows steady at your sides
- wrists low, but not touching the machine

Practice hint:

Think and say each letter as you key (type) it.

Technique hint:

Keep the fingers upright (straight up and down over the home keys).

LESSON 17

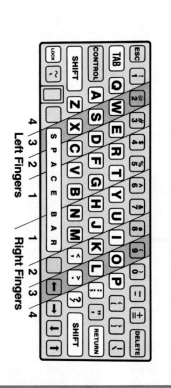

4 \ 3 \ 2 \ 1   1 / 2 / 3 / 4
Left Fingers   Right Fingers

Keyboard review (all letters used)

1   by odd off fix too all sit did sold

2   clam park quiz next give when major

3   Good form is the key to high speed.

Keyboard mastery words (all letters used)

4   firm push very grow your jerk squad

5   a jet|a box|an oak|the zoo|her luck

6   Set a new goal if you wish to grow.

Practice words with side-by-side reaches

7   as wet oil top buy elk ore her open

8   as we|to say|an elk|did try|the top

9   As you said, we can try a top goal.

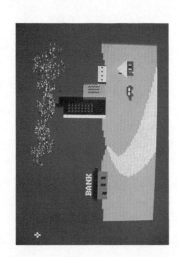

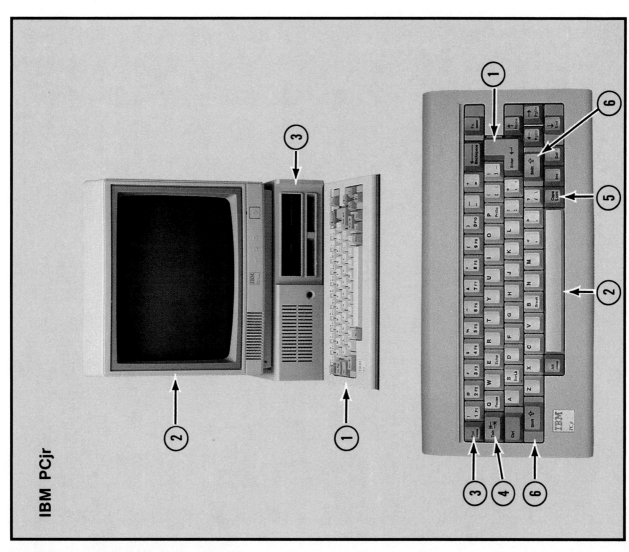

IBM PCjr

Locate:

1. Keyboard
2. Display screen
3. Disk drive

Locate:

1. ENTER (return) key
2. Space bar
3. ESC (escape) key
4. Tab key
5. CAPS lock
6. Shift keys

Lesson 16, Part B

Improve keyboarding technique

Key each line twice SS.

Practice hint:

Think, say, and key the words at a brisk pace; space quickly.

Practice hint:

Shift, strike the key, and release both in a 1-2-3 count.

Practice hint:

Keep up your pace to the end of the line; return quickly; start next line without a pause.

Lesson 16, Part C

Build keyboarding speed

1. Take a 20-second (20") timed writing on each line. If you finish a line before time is called, start over. *GWAM* is shown word by word.

2. Do the drill again.

Goal: To get to the end of the line just as time is called.

Space bar (Use a down-and-in motion.)

1 am an by so it ah or of do me to go

2 I am|in it|to me|if so|is an|by the

3 Kent is to go to the zoo with Mala.

Shift keys (Shift; strike key; release both.)

4 Labor Day|Joji or Aida|April or May

5 Pam and Zoe will play Hal and Theo.

6 May we go with Evan, Jae, and Rosa?

Return (Finish line; return; start new line quickly.)

7 Xica has set a high goal.

8 Key the names at a high speed.

9 Try to key the word with good form.

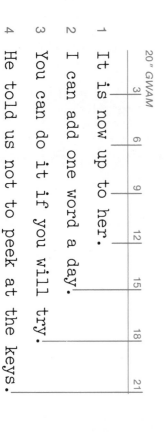

20" GWAM
| 3 | 6 | 9 | 12 | 15 | 18 | 21 |

1 It is now up to her.

2 I can add one word a day.

3 You can do it if you will try.

4 He told us not to peek at the keys.

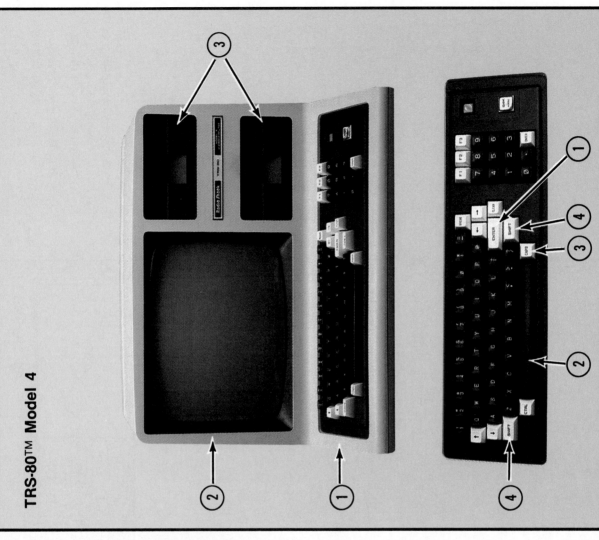

TRS-80™ Model 4

Locate:

1. Keyboard
2. Display screen
3. Disk drive(s)

Locate:

1. ENTER (return) key
2. Space bar
3. CAPS lock
4. Shift keys

Lesson 16, Part A

Keyboard review and mastery

Key (type) each line twice SS: once slowly; again at a faster speed. DS between 2-line groups.

Goals:

- curved, upright fingers
- finger (not hand) reaches
- quick, snap keystrokes
- down-and-in spacing

Recall:

- Space twice after end-of-sentence punctuation marks (. and ?)
- Space once after within-sentence marks ; , . but twice after :

Practice hint:

Think and say each letter as you key (type) it.

LESSON 16

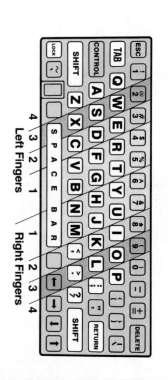

Keyboard review (all letters used)

1 me us if am ox is or it go all dogs

2 by cup jar zoo the van oak wig quit

3 Oki, Al, and Su will go. Will you?

Spacing with punctuation marks

4 Is it Jay? I know it is; he spoke.

5 Major, my dog, has gone to the vet.

6 Key these names: Ed, Jo, and B. J.

Keyboard mastery words (all letters used)

7 fix man sit can pad for tow zoo vim

8 by fox jam fog his lob ski den aqua

9 I call my cat Paws; my dog, Caesar.

YOU LEARN
THE LETTER KEYS

Lessons 1-15

YOUR GOALS

In this unit of fifteen lessons, you will learn:

1. The keyboard location of each letter key
2. The correct finger to use to strike each key
3. How to strike each key properly (good technique)
4. How to move from key to key quickly and smoothly
5. How to space, shift for capitals, and return
6. How to use the computer to help you learn

LESSON 1

STARTING LINE

Get ready to keyboard

1. Get to know your machine by studying the material on page 367 for the Apple, page 368 for the Commodore 64, page 369 for the IBM, or page 370 for the TRS-80.
2. Compare the computer pictures with the machine you have.

Arrange your work area

1. Be sure the front edge of the keyboard is even with the front edge of the table.
2. Stand your book at the right of the keyboard; move all other books and materials out of the way.
3. Be sure the keyboard and display screen are directly in front of you.

YOU BUILD SKILL ON THE LETTER KEYBOARD

Lessons 16-18

YOUR GOALS

In this unit of three lessons, you will:

1. Improve the technique (form) with which you key or type copy
2. Improve the speed at which you key or type copy
3. Improve the control or accuracy with which you key or type copy
4. Increase the number of words that you can key (type) with ease

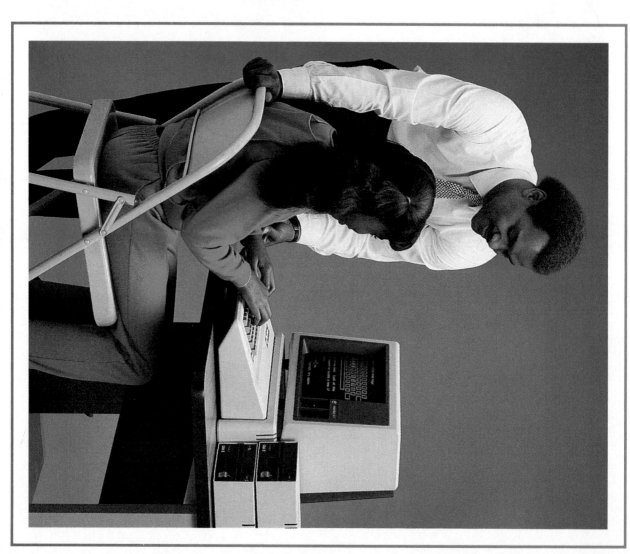

Lesson 1, Part A

Take keyboarding position

1. Study the picture of correct keyboarding position shown at the right.
2. Take good position directly in front of the keyboard. As you do so, observe each step listed at the right of the picture.

Position points

1. Sit back in chair; back straight; lean a bit forward from your waist.
2. Place both feet on the floor (if possible) for body balance.
3. Place your hands over the middle row of letter keys — left index finger on **F**, right index finger on **J**.
4. Keep fingers well curved, the wrists low.

Desks or tables and chairs should be adjustable for proper position.

Lesson 1, Part B

Place your fingers in home-key position

1. Find on the chart the letters **A S D F** (home keys for left hand).
2. Using your left hand, place
   index finger on **F**
   middle finger on **D**
   ring finger on **S**
   little finger on **A**
   on your computer keyboard.
3. Find on the chart the letters **J K L ;** (semicolon). These are the home keys for the right hand.
4. Starting with your index finger, place the fingers of your right hand on **J K L ; ***
5. Place the right thumb lightly on the space bar.

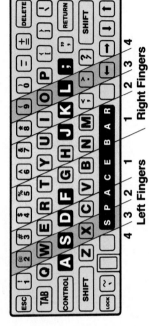

Fingers upright

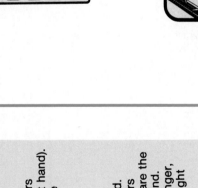

Fingers curved

*On Commodore 64, place the right little finger on **:**

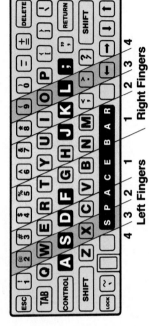

Left Fingers   Right Fingers

Lesson 15, Part B
Improve keystroking speed on sentences

1. Take a 20-second (20″) timed writing on each sentence. Your rate in gross words a minute (GWAM) is shown word for word above the lines.

2. Take another 20″ writing on each line. Try to increase speed.

Lesson 15, Part C
Learn to indent paragraphs

1. Learn how to indent the first line of a paragraph. (Ask your teacher to show you, or use the diskette for Lesson 15.)

2. Practice each of the paragraphs shown at the right.

3. If time permits, practice them again.

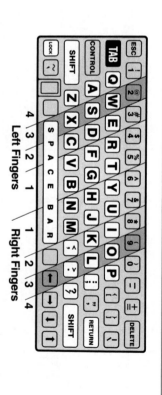

20″ GWAM						
3		6		9		12		15		18		21	

Six of the girls fish off the dock.

She lent me a map of the busy city.

It is up to them to fix their sign.

Gig owns an auto that is aqua blue.

Vi may come by jet in a week or so.

Set a goal and use zest to make it.

Indented paragraphs

Tab On some computers, you strike the space bar five times to indent the first line of a block of copy.

Tab On other machines, you can set a tab stop five spaces to the right of left margin and tap the tab key.

Lesson 1, Part C

Learn to strike keys and space bar

1. Study the keystroking and spacing drawings shown at the right.
2. Practice twice each of the drill lines shown below the drawings.*

*Commodore 64 users must reach to the right to strike ; key.

To end one line and start the next one:

Reach to the right with the little finger of the right hand and strike the RETURN or ENTER key. Doing this will move the cursor (enter point) or typing element to the beginning of the next line down.

Keystroking technique

Strike the key with a quick, sharp tap of the finger. Snap the tip of the finger slightly toward the palm of the hand as the keystroke is completed.

Spacing technique

Strike the space bar with the thumb of the right hand. Use a quick down-and-in motion (toward the palm of the hand).

GOAL: Learn to strike home keys and space bar.

Strike space bar once between pairs of letters.

```
ff jj ff jj ff jj dd kk dd kk dd kk   Return

ss ll ss ll ss ll aa ;; aa ;; aa ;;   Return

fj fj dk dk sl sl a; a; jf kd ls ;a   Return
```

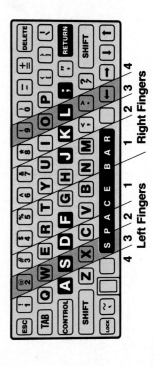

Left Fingers   Right Fingers

Reach review

Practice each line twice SS: once slowly; again at a faster speed. DS between 2-line groups.

Technique goal:

• Hands and arms quiet; reach with the fingers. →

Technique goal:

• Key (type) words as units; space quickly between them. →

Technique goal:

• Key words at a steady pace, letter by letter; keep elbows steady. →

LESSON 15

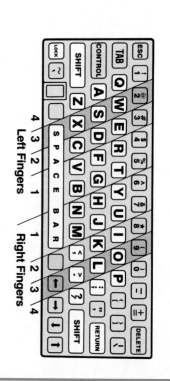

Left Fingers   4 3 2 1   1 2 3 4   Right Fingers

Reach review (all letters used)

1 uj ws p; ed ol qa nj za ik rf .l ed

2 cd ,k tf mj xs hj vf yj bf ?; gf LF

3 ox am zoo jet pow irk fog vie quits

Practice easy words (all letters used)

4 an if ox so me is am it or go by he

5 cut zoo fix pen map but did got jam

6 both work lake down such quay visit

Practice harder words (all letters used)

7 we up ad in as on ax my was pop are

8 pin bet you saw ink tax him gas oil

9 cave milk were look faze jump quits

Lesson 1, Part D

Practice
home-key letters

1. Practice each drill line once as shown. If you forget the location of a key, find it on the chart; *do not* look at your keyboard.

2. If time permits, repeat the drill. Try to strike the keys at a faster speed.

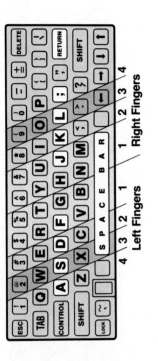

Left Fingers   **Right Fingers**

4 3 2 1   1 2 3 4

GOAL: Curved fingers; quick-snap keystrokes

Space once for each blank space.

1 f ff j jj d dd k kk s ss l ll a aa   Return

2 f j fj d k dk s l sl a ; a; fj;   Return

3 fj dk sl a; jf kd ls ;a ds lk a;fj   Return

4 sa jk ds lk df kj sd kl fd jk a;fj   Return

Lesson 1, Part E

Practice words using
home-key letters

1. Practice each drill line once as shown.

2. If time permits, repeat the drill at a faster speed.

3. When you stop practice, TURN OFF the machine.

GOAL: To improve keystroking and spacing

Space once after ; and between words.

1 a a as as ask ask a a ad ad lad lad   Return

2 all all fad fad jak jak ads ads ask   Return

3 as; a jak; as all; ask dad; all ads   Return

4 as a lass; ask a lad; all lads fall   Return

Lesson 14, Part B
Improve keystroking technique

1. Practice each line twice SS: once slowly; once more at a faster speed.
2. If time permits, practice each line again.

Space:

- once after ; and ,
- twice after . and ? at end of sentence
- once after . at end of initials and abbreviations; but do not space after . within small-letter abbreviations

Lesson 14, Part C
Combine sentences into a paragraph

Practice the paragraph twice DS: once slowly to get the feel of the words; then again to speed up keystroking.

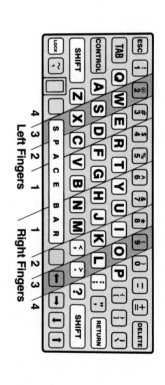

Practice sentences (all reaches learned)

1 Mrs. Van made a quick trip to Troy.

2 She, he, and I fixed a party snack.

3 R. J. will send the credenza c.o.d.

4 I used qt. for quart; yd. for yard.

5 Is he going? If so, may I go, too?

6 THINK, but do more than that. ACT.

Practice a paragraph (all letters used)

The size of a word helps to make it hard or easy to key in. Over time, you will be able to enter all words quickly. Try this major goal next.

LESSON 2

Plan for learning new keys

1. Find the new key on the keyboard chart.
2. *Look* at your keyboard and find the new key on it.
3. Study the reach-technique drawing at the left of the practice lines (see page 376).
4. Learn which finger strikes the key (see reach-technique drawing for the new key).
5. Curve your fingers; place them in home-key position.
6. *Watch your finger* as you reach it to the new key and back to home position a few times (try to keep it curved as you reach).
7. Practice twice each of the 3 lines at the right of the reach-technique drawing:

   slowly, to learn the new reach;
   faster, to improve keystroking.
8. If time permits, practice each line again.

Strike the space bar once.

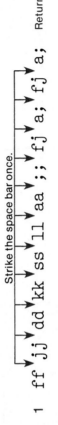

1   ff jj dd kk ss ll aa ;; fj fj a; a;   Return

2   dk sl kd ls sa kl ds jk df sd lk a;   Return

3   as as ad ad jak jak fad fad all all   Return

4   a; a jak; a jak; all fall; all fall   Return

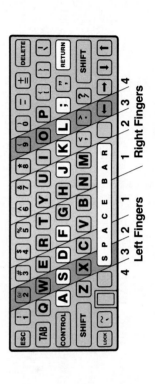

Left Fingers   4 3 2 1   1 2 3 4   Right Fingers

Lesson 2, Part A

Get ready to keyboard

1. Get ready to keyboard as directed on page 371 or as directed by your teacher.
2. Arrange your work area as directed on page 371.
3. Take keyboarding position as shown on page 372.

Lesson 2, Part B

Review home keys

1. Curve your fingers and place them on the home keys:

   left   right
   ASDF   JKL;

2. Practice each line of the drill shown at the right.
3. If time permits, repeat the drill at a faster speed.

RECALL: Strike the space bar once after a letter standing alone, after groups of letters, and between words.

Strike RETURN or ENTER at the end of a line to move the cursor (enter point) or typing element to the beginning of the next line.

Learn new keys: LOCK and ? (question mark)

1. Learn the location of new keys SHIFT (CAPS) LOCK and ? by following the standard plan.

2. Practice each drill twice SS: once slowly; again at a faster speed.

Reach technique for LOCK

Reach left and down with left little finger.

Reach technique for ? (question)

Left shift; reach down with right little finger; space twice after ? at end of sentence.

NOTE: Depress the LOCK and leave it down until the ALL-CAP combination has been typed. Strike the LOCK again to return to regular capital-and-lowercase typing. On typewriters, strike a shift key to release the LOCK.

LESSON 14

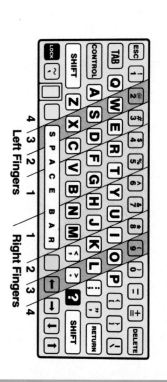

4 3 2 1   1 2 3 4
Left Fingers   Right Fingers

Learn LOCK (Find CAPS or LOCK; use closer little finger.)

1 NBC and CBS|WLW or WKRC|WGN and USA

2 The USPS asks us to use a ZIP Code.

3 The UCLA game will be shown by ABC.

Learn ? (question mark)

4 ; ? ? ?; ?; Who?   Who?   Who is she?

5 When did she go?   Shall we go, too?

6 Do you know why Masami is not here?

Combine LOCK and ?

7 Did you use the UP ARROW or ESCAPE?

8 Does she use the LOCK for ALL CAPS?

9 Did you read the book OLIVER TWIST?

Lesson 2, Part C

Learn new keys: E and H

For each key to be learned in this lesson and the lessons that follow, use the "Plan for learning new keys" given on page 375.

1. Study the plan with your teacher's help. Follow the steps in the plan to learn correct reaches to **e** and **h**.
2. Practice each drill (set of 3 lines) twice: once slowly; again at a faster speed.

Reach technique for e

Reach *up* with *left second finger.*

Reach technique for h

Reach to *left* with *right first finger.*

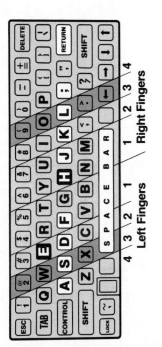

Left Fingers   Right Fingers

Learn e

1 d e ed ed el el led led eel eel fed   Return
2 ed el led led eke eke lee lee fee e   Return
3 a fee; a lake; a desk; a jade sale;   Return

Learn h

4 j h hj hj ha ha ah ah had had has h   Return
5 hj hj ah ah ha ha has has ash ash h   Return
6 ha ha; ah ha; has had; has ash; had   Return

Combine e and h

7 he he she she shed shed held held e   Return
8 he had; she has; a shed; he has ash   Return
9 he asked; she has jell; he had jade   Return

Lesson 13, Part B

Improve keystroking technique

1. Practice each line twice SS: once slowly; once more at a faster speed.
2. If time permits, practice each line again.

Technique goals:

- Reach with the fingers; keep the hands in place.
- Shift, strike letter to be capped, and release both keys (1-2-3).

Lesson 13, Part C

Combine sentences into a paragraph

Practice the paragraph twice DS: once slowly to get the feel of the words; then again to speed up keystroking.

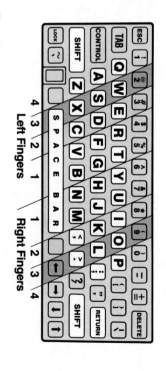

Left Fingers   Right Fingers

Practice sentences

1 Vi can pave the way to a big party.

2 Quent dived in to save their lives.

3 Vivian wrote a verse of high value.

4 Jacki may have won a seventh prize.

5 Lex won the diving medal in Denver.

6 She has two horses: Veda and Vida.

7 Goal: curved fingers; quiet hands.

8 Viva has a very good view of Dover.

Practice a paragraph

You have done a good job. You know each letter. If you work on and do not quit, the big prize comes next.

Lesson 2, Part D

Improve keystroking technique

1. Practice each set of 3 lines twice: once slowly; once more at a faster speed.
2. As time permits, practice each set of lines again.

Technique goal:
- Fingers curved and upright (straight up and down over home keys)

Technique goal:
- Keystrokes quick and snappy

Color verticals (which are not to be typed) divide the lines into phrases.

Technique goal:
- Space quickly and smoothly between words
- Make returns without stopping at ends of lines

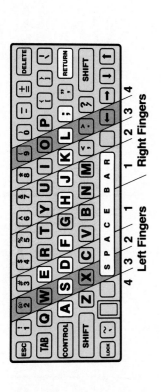

Left Fingers   Right Fingers

R = Return

Practice words

h/e 1 | hj ah ha he he ed led led heel heel R

a 2 | a ah ha as had ask ash jak lad fake R

e 3 | e he she led elf fed dell lake jade R

Practice phrases (word groups)

4 | a shed|a hall|a sled|a lake|as half R

5 | a dash|a jade|he had|as she|she led R

6 | she fed|he has|a jak fell|ask a lad R

Practice key words

7 | a as he she has had ask led all add R

8 | he see sea seek lake half jell fall R

9 | has a lake; he had jell; he fed all R

Lesson 13, Part A

**Learn new keys:
V and : (colon)**

1. Learn the location of new
keys **v** and **:** (colon) by
following the standard plan.
2. Practice each drill twice SS:
once slowly; again at a faster
speed.

Reach technique for v

Reach *down* with
left first finger.

Reach technique for : (colon)

Left shift and strike **;** key;
space twice after **:** used
as punctuation.

On Commodore 64 and TRS-80 it
is not necessary to shift for **:** key.

LESSON 13

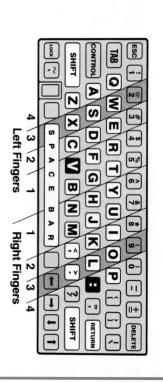

Left Fingers   Right Fingers

Learn V

1 f v v vf vf vie vie have have vowel

2 v v vf vf five five dive dive views

3 vie for; has vim; to dive; the view

Learn : (colon)

4 ; : : : :; :; Dear Jo: Shift for a :

5 : : :; :; Date: To: From: In re:

6 Dear Dr. Su: Follow the ten steps:

Combine V and **:**

7 Enter these words: vie, vim, have.

8 Pick the right word: let or leave.

9 Marv read: Shift to enter a colon.

LESSON 3

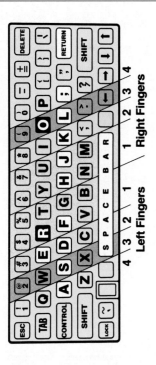

Lesson 3, Part A

Learn new keys: O and R

1. Learn the location of new keys **o** and **r** by following the steps in the "Plan for learning new keys" on page 375.
2. Practice each drill (set of 3 lines) twice: once slowly, again at a faster speed.

Reach technique for o

Reach up with right third finger.

Reach technique for r

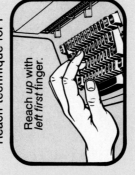

Reach up with left first finger.

Learn o

1 l o ol ol do do of of so so old old   Return
2 o o ol ol of of off off do do doe doe   R
3 do so; a hoe; of a doe; so old; off   R

Learn r

4 f r rf rf re re jar jar her her are   R
5 r rf rf jar jar her her are are ear   R
6 a jar; her jar; a jerk; a real jerk   R

Combine o and r

7 o or or for for rod rod fork fork   R
8 a rod; of her; he or she; for a jar   R
9 jar of roe; for a doe; are for her;   R

Lesson 12, Part B
Improve keystroking technique

1. Practice each set of 3 lines twice SS: once slowly; once more at a faster speed.
2. If time permits, practice each set of lines again.

Technique goal: →

● Reach up to **q** without moving the elbow out.

Technique goal: →

● Curl the middle finger down to , without moving the hand toward you.

Lesson 12, Part C
Combine sentences into a paragraph

Practice the paragraph twice DS. At the end of a line, do not stop; return quickly and begin the next line.

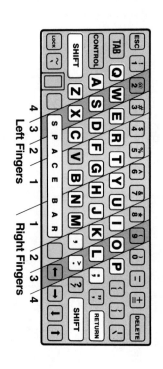

Left Fingers   Right Fingers

Practice phrases (word groups)

1 they quit|an easy quiz|is not quite

2 a quart of|a big quilt|a quick stop

3 may call it quits|am to take a quiz

Practice sentences

4 During the quiz, we all kept quiet.

5 His step is quick, but so is yours.

6 When I say quite, I may mean quiet.

Practice a paragraph (all letters learned)

Keep on. Do not quit now. You are doing fine; the prize is just a bit ahead. You can make the next goal.

Lesson 3, Part B

Improve keystroking technique

1. Practice each set of 3 lines twice: once slowly; once more at a faster speed.
2. If time permits, practice each set of lines again.

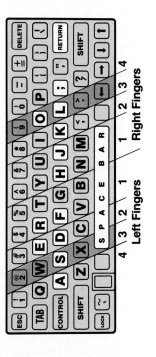

Left Fingers   Right Fingers

Practice words

1 a ah as ask has had lad ash jak dad   Return

2 he or of so doe she for rod her ear   R

3 are oak old hoe jar fork fold sells   R

Practice phrases (word groups)

4 a lad|a jar|a rod|a hoe|a fee|a doe   R

5 do so|or so|he has|she led|a jar of   R

6 a lad led|of old oak|he or she rode   R

Practice key words

7 a he of do or so as she for oak all   R

8 off jar has had ask her are old led   R

9 as a hero; look for her; add a jar;   R

Technique goal:

● Reach with one finger at a time; keep other fingers over their home keys.

Technique goal:

● Space quickly between the words of each phrase.

Technique goal:

● Keep the cursor or typing element moving steadily, word by word.

Lesson 12, Part A

Learn new keys:
Q and , (comma)

1. Learn the location of new
   keys q and , (comma) by
   following the standard plan.
2. Practice each drill twice SS:
   once slowly; again at a faster
   speed.

Reach technique for q

Reach *up* with
left little finger.

Reach technique for , (comma)

Reach *down* with
right second finger;
space once after ,
used as punctuation.

LESSON 12

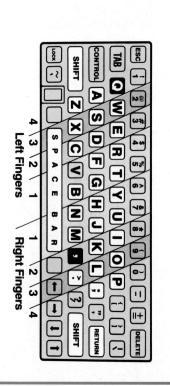

Learn **q**

1 a q q qa qa qt. qt. quit quit quiet

2 q q qa qa quit quit quiz quiz quick

3 the quiz; he has quit; quite a bit;

Learn **,** (comma)

4 k , , ,k ,k Jan, Kit, or I will go.

5 Bea, go with Sue; Jo, come with me.

6 Pick to, too, or two and key it in.

Combine **q** and **,**

7 Enter quit, quiz, quite, and quiet.

8 Quin took the quiz, but Quent quit.

9 If you are quite sure, use a quote.

LESSON 4

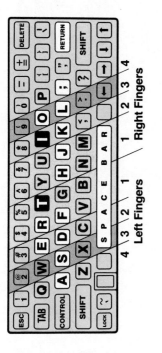

Left Fingers   Right Fingers

Learn i

1   k i i ik ik is is if if fir fir die

2   i i ik is is fir fir die die rid

3   he is; if she; is rid; a fir; a kid

Learn t

4   f t t tf tf to to at at the the toe

5   t t tf tf to to the the dot dot too

6   to do; the toe; to toss; to dot the

Combine i and t

7   i t it it fit fit sit sit tire tire

8   he is fit; dot the i; if the tie is

9   it is his; if the toe; the hat fits

Return

Lesson 4, Part A

Learn new keys: I and T

1. Learn the location of new keys i and t by following the steps in the "Plan for learning new keys" on page 375.
2. Practice each drill twice: once slowly, again at a faster speed.

Reach technique for i

Reach *up* with *right second finger.*

Reach technique for t

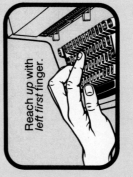

Reach *up* with *left first finger.*

Lesson 11, Part B

Improve keystroking technique

1. Practice each set of 3 lines twice SS: once slowly; once more at a faster speed.

2. If time permits, practice each set of lines again.

Technique goals: ⟶

- Reach up to **y** and down to **z** with the fingers; keep your hands steady.
- Avoid twisting your hand in at the wrist as you reach to **z**.

Lesson 11, Part C

Combine sentences into a paragraph

Practice the paragraph twice DS. At the end of a line, do not stop; return quickly and begin the next line.

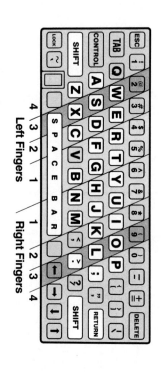

Left Fingers   Right Fingers

Practice words and phrases

1 zip yes zoo you zap may fuzzy plays

2 yell zinc year zoom yawn zone yours

3 she got a zero; will send it to you

Practice sentences

4 Zoe asked me for ten yards of yarn.

5 Zeno zipped to the new zoo by bike.

6 Cy and Mazie may get a bus to Zapp.

Practice a paragraph (all letters learned)

It is too soon to go for zero error now. Aim next to build speed with good form. Just pace your work.

Lesson 4, Part B

Improve keyboarding technique

1. Practice each set of 3 lines twice: once slowly; once more at a faster speed.
2. If time permits, practice each set of lines again.

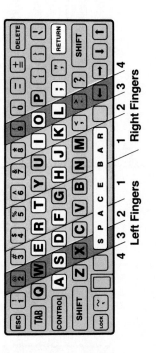

Left Fingers   Right Fingers

Practice words

1   at to if so is do of or it ad he as

2   ask jet the for kit did aid dot toe

3   idle fish jade lake said talk flake

Practice phrases (word groups)

4   if it is|to do so|is to do|to do it

5   the jet|as a kit|is a hit|as a talk

6   had a hit|fit for a|ask for the jet

Practice key words

7   or as he of it do is to if so at ad

8   for the all old are ask fit she did

9   ask for the jar; all are at the jet

Technique goal:

● Reach with one finger at a time; keep other fingers over their home keys.

Technique goal:

● Space quickly between the words of each phrase.

Technique goal:

● Keep the cursor or typing element moving steadily, word by word.

Lesson 11, Part A

Learn new keys: Y and Z

1. Learn the location of new keys **y** and **z** by following the standard plan.

2. Practice each drill twice SS: once slowly; again at a faster speed.

Reach technique for y

Reach up with right first finger.

Reach technique for z

Reach down with left little finger.

LESSON 11

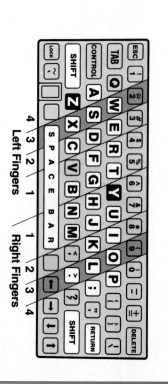

Left Fingers 4 3 2 1   1 2 3 4 Right Fingers

Learn y

1 j y y yj yj jay jay lay lay hay hay

2 y y yj yj may may hay hay eyes eyes

3 a jay; an eye; is to pay; he may be

Learn z

4 a z z za zap zap zip zip zoo zoo

5 z z za za zap zap oz. oz. zone zone

6 zap it; zip it; the zoo; for an oz.

Combine y and z

7 jay zap eye zoo yes zip boy oz. yap

8 yell haze says jazz days lazy fuzzy

9 by a zoo; a lazy day; buy the pizza

LESSON 5

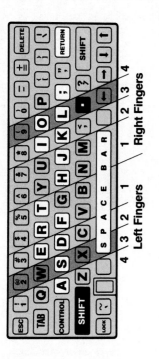

Left Fingers   Right Fingers

Learn **left shift key**

1 Ja Ja Ha Ha Hal Hal Kae Kae Jae Jae Return

2 Kae fell; Hal has jade; Jake did it

3 I see Hal is to aid Jae at Oak Lake

Learn **.** (period)

4 l . . .l .l ed. ed. ft. ft. fl. fl.

5 . .l .l ed. ed. fl. fl. rd. rd. ft.

6 hr. hr. rt. rt. ord. ord. fed. fed.

Combine **left shift key** and **.**

7 I do. I did. Jae is. Ike has it.

8 I see. Hal said it. Ola has fish.

9 Les has a kite. Ida lost her skis.

Lesson 5, Part A

Learn new keys: left shift key and . (period)

1. Learn the location of new keys **left shift** and **. (period)** by following the steps in the "Plan for learning new keys" on page 375.
2. Practice each drill twice: once slowly, again at a faster speed.

Control of left shift key

Reach down with left little finger; shift, type, release.

Reach technique for . (period)

Reach down with right third finger; space twice after. at end of sentence.

NOTE: Space **once** at the end of an abbreviated word and after periods following first letters of names (initials). Space **twice** after a period at the end of a sentence.

Lesson 10, Part B
Improve keystroking technique

1. Practice each set of 3 lines twice SS: once slowly; once more at a faster speed.
2. If time permits, practice each set of lines again.

Technique goal:

● Keep the hands steady; avoid moving them forward (away from you) or downward (toward you).

Technique goal:

● Keep the elbows still; avoid moving them in or out as you key (type) the copy.

Lesson 10, Part C
Combine sentences into a paragraph

Practice the paragraph twice DS. At the end of a line, do not stop; return quickly and begin the next line.

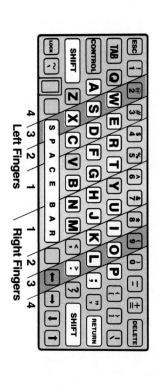

Left Fingers   Right Fingers

Practice words and phrases

1 ox me ax am fix man dam fox map mix

2 make flax some flex mark oxen times

3 fix a map|mix the jam|mark the flax

Practice sentences

4 Pam can fix the map as I mark flax.

5 Max saw six oxen at a dam in Macao.

6 Suma made me a jacket of blue flax.

Practice a paragraph (all letters learned)

Jack can fish off the dock near his home. I am to go there next spring to fish with him. It will be fun.

Lesson 5, Part B

Improve keystroking technique

1. Practice each set of 3 lines twice: once slowly, once more at a faster speed.
2. If time permits, practice each set of lines again.

Space once:

- after ;
- after . used with abbreviations and initials

Space twice:

- after . at the end of a sentence except at the end of a line; there, return without spacing.

Technique goal: ↑

- Move from word to word quickly; do not stop between words.

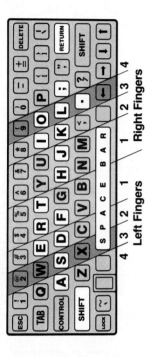

Left Fingers   Right Fingers

Return

Practice abbreviations and initials

1   O. J. has a sled; he lets Kae ride.

2   He said ft. for feet; rd. for road.

3   Lt. Oakes let K. L. take his skiff.

Practice sentences

4   I like Lee a lot.   I also like Ila.

5   I let her talk; I like to hear her.

6   Oki had a fish dish; Ida took hash.

Practice key words

7   or he to if of ha is do as el it so

8   led old for ask jet dot aid off the

9   Jo said he is to take the old road.

Lesson 10, Part A

Learn new keys: M and X

1. Learn the location of new keys m and x by following the standard plan.

2. Practice each drill twice SS: once slowly; again at a faster speed.

Reach technique for m

Reach down with
right first finger.

Reach technique for x

Reach down with
left third finger.

LESSON 10

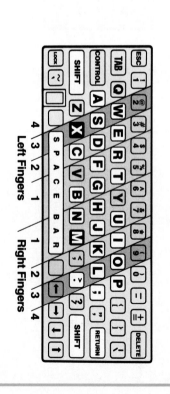

Left Fingers   Right Fingers

Learn m

1 j m m mj mj me me am am ma ma jam j

2 m m mj mj am am jam ham ham dam

3 to me; am to; for jam; and ham; man

Learn X

4 s x x xs xs ox ox ax ax six six fix

5 x x xs xs ox ox six six fix fix fox

6 an ox; an ax; a fox; to fix; at six

Combine M and X

7 m x am ox me ax jam six ham fox men

8 a jam; a fox; an ax; a man; for six

9 am to fix; ham for six; mix jam for

LESSON 6

Right Fingers

Left Fingers

Learn U

1   j j u u uj uj fur fur due due sue sue   Return

2   u u fur fur due due jut jut hue hue

3   to us; is due; for us; the fur; sue

Learn C

4   d c c cd cod cod cot cot tic tic

5   c c cod cod cot cot tic tic col col

6   a cod; a cot; has a tic; at the cot

Combine U and C

7   c u cue cue cut cut cur cur cud cud

8   a cut; the cue; his cud; at the cue

9   is a cur; of the clue; cut the cake

Lesson 6, Part A

Learn new keys: U and C

1. Learn the location of new keys **u** and **c** by following the standard plan (see page 375).
2. Practice each drill twice: once slowly, again at a faster speed.

Reach technique for u

Reach *up* with *right first finger.*

Reach technique for c

Reach *down* with *left second finger.*

Lesson 9, Part B

Improve keystroking technique

1. Practice each set of 3 lines twice SS: once slowly; once more at a faster speed.
2. If time permits, practice each set of lines again.

Technique goal: →

- Make up and down reaches with the fingers without moving the hand or moving the elbow in or out.

Technique goal: →

- Use a 1-2-3 count in shifting: (1) shift; (2) strike key to be capped; (3) release both keys.

Lesson 9, Part C

Combine sentences into a paragraph

Practice the paragraph twice DS. At the end of a line, do not stop; return quickly and begin the next line.

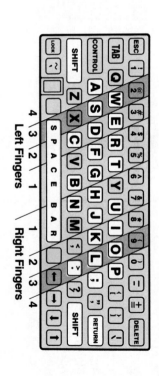

Left Fingers 4 3 2 1   Right Fingers 1 2 3 4

Practice words and phrases

1 pa up pi be bow pep bit pal rub bop   Return

2 but pig bid pen bud paw cub cup sip

3 a big cup|to pet a cub|is a big pal

Practice sentences (all letters learned)

4 Bobbi will sign the bid with a pen.

5 Beth kept top spot in the pep club.

6 Jack did a good job for Dr. Frisch.

Practice a paragraph—(all letters learned)

I set a goal and go for it. This   Return

is how to push for speed. I just   R

keep at the job till I reach goal.   R

Lesson 6, Part B

Improve keystroking speed

1. Practice each set of 3 lines twice: once slowly; once more at a faster speed.
2. If time permits, practice each set of lines again.

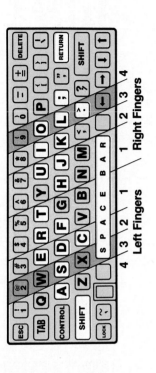

Left Fingers 4 3 2 1

Right Fingers 1 2 3 4

Return

Practice words and phrases

1 cut fur cod due dude duet code luck

2 clue rush such just lock sick ticks

3 is due; a clue to; just as the lock

Technique goal:

- Curl the middle (left second) finger under to strike **c**. Try not to move elbow out.

Practice sentences

4 J. L. has a lot of cod at the dock.

5 Lt. Judd cut the cost for the furs.

6 Ola is due at four; she told us so.

Technique goal:

- *Reach* down to strike **shift key** and . without moving hand down.

Practice key words

7 the for due cut did she fit off kit

8 ask jet aid old jut cue led all are

9 sure this luck jack surf cull thick

Technique goal:

- Speed up between letters within words; space quickly between words.

Lesson 9, Part A

Learn new keys: B and P

1. Learn the location of new keys **b** and **p** by following the standard plan.

2. Practice each drill twice SS: once slowly; again at a faster speed.

Reach technique for b

Reach *down* with *left first finger.*

Reach technique for p

Reach *up* with *right little finger.*

LESSON 9

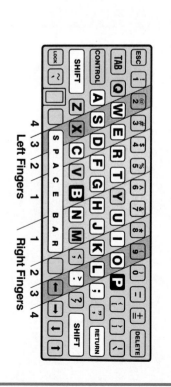

Left Fingers 4 3 2 1 | Right Fingers 1 2 3 4

Learn b

1 f b b bf bf fib fib fib rib rib rob rob

2 b b bf bf fib fib big big jobs jobs

3 to fib; or rob; and bid; the job is

Learn p

4 ; p p p; p; pa pa; pep pep; tap tap

5 p p p; p; pa pa; up up lap lap peep

6 apt to keep; take a nap; kept it up

Combine b and p

7 b p but put bit pit rib rip bid dip

8 a pan; a bus; to dip; the bid is up

9 apt to be; a big pen; to pick a job

LESSON 7

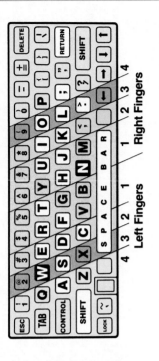

Left Fingers   Right Fingers

Learn n

1   j n n nj nj an an and and land land   Return

2   n n nj nj an an in in no no end end

3   an oak; an end; and so; in one line

Learn w

4   s w w ws ws ow ow wow wow sows sows

5   w w ws ws ow ow low low how how jaw

6   so low; we sow; to owe; to show how

Combine n and w

7   n w own own win win won won now now

8   a win; we own; she won; he owns it;

9   to win it; a new inn; is an old law

Lesson 7, Part A

Learn new keys: N and W

1. Learn the location of new keys **n** and **w** by following the standard plan (see page 375).
2. Practice each drill twice: once slowly, again at a faster rate.

Reach technique for n

Reach down with right first finger.

Reach technique for w

Reach up with left third finger.

Lesson 8, Part B

Improve keystroking speed

1. Practice each set of 3 lines twice SS: once slowly; once more at a faster speed.

2. If time permits, practice each set of lines again.

Fingers curved   Fingers upright

Strike down   Snap toward you

Lesson 8, Part C

Combine sentences into a paragraph

Practice the paragraph twice DS. At the end of a line, do not stop; return quickly and begin the next line.

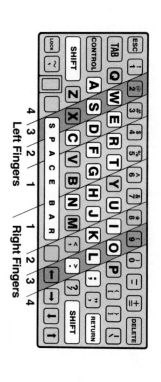

Practice words and phrases

1 go got cog fog ago rug wig dig gold   Return

2 golf frog goof good flag clog goals

3 in the fog; goes to jog; a week ago

Practice sentences (all letters learned)

4 Chuck is to go to the dock to fish.

5 Di is a cute girl who is also nice.

6 Jan got a red skirt and gold shirt.

Practice a paragraph (all letters learned)

Alf works for his uncle. Nan works   Return

for her aunt. Each wishes to get a   R

gift for their sick friend Jud.   R

Lesson 7, Part B

Improve keystroking speed

1. Practice each set of 3 lines twice: once slowly; once more at a faster rate.
2. If time permits, practice each set of lines again.

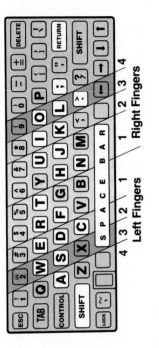

Keep fingers curved

Keep fingers upright

Lesson 7, Part C

Combine sentences into a paragraph

Practice the paragraph twice; double-space (DS) between lines each time. At the end of a line, do not stop; return quickly and begin the next line.

Practice words and phrases

1 an we in ow and own end owe hen how   Return

2 land work lend worn wood nice towns

3 a law; an owl; in a wok; she won it

Practice sentences

4 Jan Kuri can work at the town hall.

5 He had cake and cola near the lake.

6 I will lend her the cash for a fur.

Practice a paragraph

June and he took the wok to a fire   Return

at the shore. Lake fish will soon   R

send a fine odor into the cool air.   R

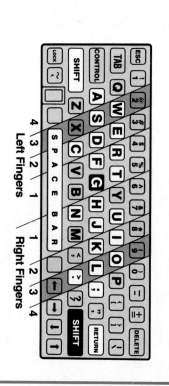

Lesson 8, Part A

Learn new keys:
G and right shift key

1. Learn the location of new keys **g** and **right shift** by following the standard plan.
2. Practice each drill twice single-spaced (SS): once slowly, again at a faster rate.

Reach technique for g

Reach to *right* with *left first finger.*

Control of right shift key

Reach *down* with *right little finger;* shift, type, release.

LESSON 8

Learn **g**

1 f g g gf gf go go go fog fog fog golf golf
2 g g gf gf go go fog fog fig fig got
3 to go; he got; the fog; gone to jog   Return

Learn **right shift key**

4 A; A; Al Al; Ali or Flo; Di and Sol
5 Ada lost to Elsa; Dale lost to Ron.
6 Tish was in Tulsa; she was with Al.

Combine **g** and **right shift key**

7 Gif has gone to Rio; Al got a note.
8 Gina got an A for golf; so did Rog.
9 Gigi can go ahead with a good shot.

388 ■ Lesson 8

GLOSSARY

abacus: an ancient calculating device consisting of a frame in which slender bars strung with beads are set; by sliding the beads, computations can be done.

Apple DOS: an operating system developed by Apple Computer, Inc.

applications programmer: a person who writes instructions for the computer that solve specific problems.

applications software: programs designed to solve specific problems for the user.

artificial intelligence: a field of study in which people are attempting to develop computers that can be used for intelligence and imagination; it can be used to simulate thinking processes.

ASCII: American Standard Code for Information Interchange; a commonly used code to represent data.

assembler: the program that translates assembly language programs into machine code.

assembly: putting together different parts of text to form a new document.

assembly language: a language in which the instructions to the processor are expressed in short alphabetic terms.

auxiliary storage: additional storage devices that are connected directly to the computer, such as a disk drive.

backspace: to move the cursor to the left one space using the back arrow key.

backup: a copy of data placed on an auxiliary storage medium to serve as a safety copy should the original be destroyed.

band printer: an impact printer that contains characters on a rotating band.

bar-code scanner: an input device that reads bars of varying width that are printed on the package of a product; the various widths of bars and spacing are translated to a unique identification number.

BASIC: Beginner's All-Purpose Symbolic Instruction Code: an easy-to-learn high-level language generally used on microcomputers.

binary number: a number system which uses only the digits 0 and 1.

bit: either a 1 or 0 in the binary number system; it takes eight bits to equal one byte on most microcomputers.

boot up: to start up; it is usually a process within the operating system which depends on information from the disk to be transferred to memory.

bubble memory: an auxiliary storage device consisting of a chip containing a surface across which magnetic "bubbles" move in patterns representing information.

byte: eight switches, or bits; it generally represents one character of information on most microcomputers.

CAD/CAM: computer-aided design/computer-aided manufacturing.

CAD: computer-aided design; the use of computers to create, evaluate, and test new designs.

CAM: computer-aided manufacturing; the use of computers to control machines or automated environments.

calculating: the process of computing in order to arrive at a mathematical result.

canned software: software produced to be sold to the public without need for custom applications.

card-punch machine: a machine used to put information on a card by punching holes in a coded pattern.

cashless society: a society that uses credit cards and electronic mediums rather than cash to buy and sell items.

chain printer: an impact printer that contains characters on a rotating chain.

channel: a recording path along magnetic tape.

character: the smallest element of data processed by a computer system.

character variable: a variable that holds data which cannot be used for math; it is recognized by a dollar sign at the end of the variable name.

CLS: a keyword used to clear the screen on the IBM and TRS-80 computers.

COBOL: COmmon Business Oriented Language; a high-level language designed for use in business applications.

coding: (a) the process of assigning certain symbols to stand for something else; (b) the process of converting program designs into computer language.

command: any keyword that is normally not preceded by a line number; it is used for the computer's immediate action.

communicating: the process of sending information from one point to another.

compiler program: a program that translates an entire high-level language program into machine code before the processor carries out any of the instructions.

components: different parts of the computer that work together; consisting of hardware, software, and data.

computer-assisted instruction: learning aids that allow each student to learn at his or her own pace and that provide immediate feedback.

computer-assisted retrieval: the technology that assists office workers in finding records that have been microfilmed.

computer ethics: a code of conduct that promotes honesty when using the computer.

computer output microfilm: a technology used in offices where files are placed on microfilm to save space.

computer service technician: a person who repairs computers.

constant: any number not written in quotes.

control key (CTRL): a special key that is pressed while striking another key; usually used to perform special internal functions.

CP/M: an operating system that was developed by Digital Research, Inc.

cursor: the location on the screen where the next letter, number, symbol, or space can be entered; it may be a dot, line, box, or blinking square.

customer engineer: a person who repairs or modifies computers.

custom-written software: software written exactly for the job that needs to be done.

cylinder: an imaginary cylinder shape on a disk pack consisting of each track at the same location on all the disks; for example, Track 3 on every disk surface.

daisy wheel printer: a letter-quality printer that uses a print wheel that is shaped like a daisy.

data: the information that is processed by the computer system.

DATA: a statement used to specify that the remainder of the items on a line consist of information that can be used by the READ statement in BASIC.

data base: a group of information that may be accessed by a computer.

data base program: a program for the entry, storage, and retrieval of data.

data processing: the job of putting facts into usable form.

debit card: a bank card that causes the amounts of purchases to be immediately subtracted from the checking account.

debug: to find and correct errors in a program.

decision support system: a data processing system that helps managers make decisions.

deferred execution mode: a mode in which an entire set of instructions are saved by the computer and executed at once when commanded to do so by the user.

digitizer: an input device used to draw or trace shapes; it changes shapes into numbers for storage by computers.

direct access: another name for random access.

direct machine control: a process in CAD where the designer draws and tests designs on a VDT.

disk drive: the most common form of auxiliary storage; it uses round, flat plastic or metal disks coated with a magnetic surface.

disk pack: a group of disks housed in a single canister.

diskette (or disk): a magnetic, Mylar-coated, record-like platter (encased in a square protective envelope) used for recording or reading data by computer systems.

dot matrix: a row and column arrangement of dots used to form characters on a screen or printout.

EBCDIC: Extended Binary Coded Decimal Interchange Code; a commonly used code to represent data.

edit: the process of rearranging, changing, and correcting copy; includes proofreading but is not limited to it.

EDSAC: an acronym which stands for Electronic Delay Storage Automatic Calculator; the first stored-program computer to be finished.

EDVAC: an acronym which stands for Electronic Discrete Variable Automatic Computer; the first stored-program computer to be designed.

electronic mail: a method of sending messages by computer; it has affected the way many office workers communicate.

ENIAC: an acronym which stands for Electronic Numerical Integrator and Calculator. It was the first electronic computer; however, it did not use a stored program.

ergonomic: a term used to describe devices that are comfortable and non-tiring to use, resulting in increased productivity.

escape key (ESC): a key found on some computers which lets the operator leave one segment of a program and go to another.

feedback: the ability of the computer to sense; in some uses of computers this allows the computer to make decisions based on physical changes.

field: an individual item of data made up of characters, such as a person's last name.

file: a collection of related records treated as a unit, such as a list of students and their grades.

flexible disk: a disk made from thin plastic which is used to store data. This medium is sometimes known as a floppy disk.

floppy disk: another name for a flexible disk.

FOR...NEXT: a pair of BASIC statements that form a controlled loop; a way of forming a loop so that certain program statements will be repeated a specified number of times.

function keys: special keys that are used alone or in combination with other keys to perform special system functions such as setting margins, stopping operation, centering, and so on.

GOSUB: a statement that tells BASIC to go to a subroutine or module and perform the work found there.

GOTO: a statement that sends execution to a specific program line.

graphic: a chart, drawing, or picture.

graphics program: a program that represents the output data in the form of a picture.

GWAM **(gross words a minute):** a measure of the rate of keyboarding speed; *GWAM* = total 5-stroke words keyed divided by the time taken to type them.

hard disk: a nonflexible disk which is capable of very high amounts of data storage.

hardware: the physical equipment that makes up a computer system.

hierarchy chart: a diagram used to write down the different functions that a program must perform and to show the relationship of one function to another.

high-level language: a language in which instructions are expressed in English and English-like terms.

HOME: a keyword used to clear the screen on the Apple microcomputer.

IF...THEN...ELSE: a way of making a decision in BASIC by selecting one of two actions based on a logical relationship.

immediate execution mode: a mode in which each instruction is executed immediately upon entry from the keyboard.

impact printer: a printer that strikes the paper to form images.

information center: a center which provides information and assistance in using the computer to people other than data processing personnel and managers.

information processing: the job of putting data into usable form.

information system: a system that processes data.

information utility: a business that has huge groups of information stored in its computers and makes this information available to subscribers who pay a fee for the service.

ink-jet printer: a nonimpact printer that shoots ink onto the paper.

input: data that enters an information system.

INPUT: a statement used to get data from the keyboard and assign it to a variable.

input device: a device that receives data and feeds it to the processor.

insertion: new text that is added to existing text.

integrated circuit: a single electronic chip that contains large numbers of electronic components.

integration: the process of bringing together.

interactive: a term used to describe a program or computer system that performs two-way communication between the user and the computer.

interpreter program: a program that translates a high-level language into machine code one statement at a time; the processor then carries out each instruction as it is translated.

keyboard: a device that sends data to the processor each time a key is struck.

keypunch machine: another name for a card-punch machine.

key-to-disk machine: a data entry machine with which data is recorded directly on magnetic disk for later input to a computer.

key-to-tape machine: a data entry machine with which data is recorded onto magnetic tape for later input to a computer.

keyword: any word that the computer recognizes (this is usually accomplished by a CPU-controlled matching technique).

kilobyte: 1024 bytes of computer memory; computer manufacturers express the capacity of memory in terms of the letter K, which is short for kilobyte.

laser disk: an auxiliary storage medium in which characters are represented by coded holes burned in the disk by a laser beam.

laser printer: a nonimpact printer that uses a laser beam to "write" characters on a drum that is sensitive to photographic images; the drum then transfers the characters to paper.

LET: a statement used to assign data into a variable.

letter quality: refers to print where the characters are made from unbroken lines and look as if they were produced by a good typewriter.

light pen: a device used to point out locations on a video display; the pen is pressed against the screen and the computer calculates the position against which it is pressed.

LIST: a command that displays a program line by line on the screen.

literal: any character or numeral written between quotation marks in a program.

LOGO: a high-level language widely used in education for understanding logic.

loop: statements being repeated one or more times within a program.

machine language: a language in which instructions are written in the binary number code that is directly understood by the processor.

magnetic disk: an input, output, or auxiliary storage medium on which data is magnetically recorded on a round, flat surface.

magnetic ink character recognition: an input system used to process data printed in magnetic ink with specially designated numbers and symbols; it is primarily used by banks on checks and deposit slips.

magnetic scanner: an input device that reads magnetically coded data from a short strip of magnetic tape such as the tape used on the backs of credit cards.

magnetic tape: a long strip of flexible plastic covered with magnetic material used to store data.

Main Module: the first module in a top-down designed program; the first module for which a program design is prepared.

main storage: another name for memory.

mainframe: a computer that is large in size and very fast.

Mark I: the first programmable calculating device.

media: the materials that data is recorded on before it is sent to the computer.

medium: the singular form of media.

megahertz: a million cycles, or pulses, per second; a term used to rate computer speed.

memory: storage locations in the computer.

menu: a list of operations from which the user may choose.

merging: (a) the process of combining text and data into the same document; (b) the process of combining one program or file with another.

microcomputer: the "computer on a chip"; a small-sized computer, generally a single-user device with a keyboard, a screen, and auxiliary storage. Its central processor is usually a single CPU chip.

microfiche: small rectangular sheets of microfilm.

microprocessor: a processor that has all of the processing circuits contained in one piece known as an integrated circuit.

minicomputer: a medium-sized computer, generally used with several terminals.

mode: a way of operating.

modem: a device that enables communication between computers through telephone lines.

module: part of a program; a specific part of the program which performs a given task.

monitor: a televisionlike screen used for output on most microcomputers.

monochrome: a term used to describe a video output device that uses only one color.

mouse: an input device which when rolled about a surface sends signals to the computer which can direct a cursor on the video display screen.

MS-DOS: an operating system developed by Microsoft Corporation.

Napier's bones: an early calculating device consisting of slender bars or strips of bone on which numbers were printed.

natural language: a programming language which uses ordinary English to instruct the computer.

natural language processor: a processor that provides a way to communicate with the computer as though communicating with another human being.

NEW: a command used to erase a program from the computer's RAM memory.

nonimpact printer: a printer that forms characters without striking the paper.

numeric address: the numeric label or name applied to a location in memory.

numerical control: CAM technology in which holes in paper tape represent numeric information to control automated machinery.

off-line: a term used to describe computer-related activities which are not physically connected to a computer; an example would be keypunching of cards.

omnipresence: the state of being present everywhere; it is appropriate in describing computer usage.

on-line: connected directly to a computer.

operating system: a series of programs that control the operation of the computer system.

optical-character reader: an input device (scanner) that recognizes written letters, numbers, and symbols.

optical-mark reader: an input device (scanner) that can sense the presence or absence of marks made in specified locations on input cards; it is often used in true/false or multiple-choice testing.

optical scanner: a device that sends data to the processor as it "looks at" data in printed or written form.

original data: data to be processed, also referred to as raw data.

output: useful information that leaves an information system; usually presented to the user as a screen display or a printout.

Pascal: a high-level language especially well suited for structured programming.

PC-DOS: an operating system developed by International Business Machines Corporation (IBM) for use on IBM's Personal Computer.

personal productivity tool: a computer program that allows work to be done with less effort or in less time than would be required without the computer.

pixel: a dot that appears on the screen; many pixels together form an image on the screen.

plotter: an output device that uses pens to draw output on paper.

points of reference: specific locations on a workpiece which can be represented mathematically; used with numerical control.

print: to produce, using a printer, a paper copy of information displayed on a computer screen or stored in computer memory.

PRINT: a statement that displays data on the screen.

printer: a device that produces output in the form of written characters on paper.

printhead: the part of a printer that actually does the printing.

printout: the printed paper output of a computer.

processing: steps set up to make sure everything that should be done to the data is completed.

processor: the computer system unit that receives and carries out instructions.

program design: an English description of the steps to be performed by a module.

program mode: same as deferred execution mode.

programming language: a series of instructions used to communicate with the computer.

prompt: a message displayed on the screen telling the user that the computer is awaiting a specific response.

pseudocode: another name for program design.

punched card: a card in which data can be represented by punching holes.

random access: a term used to describe a device that can go directly to the location of particular data without having to read through all the data in front of it.

random-access memory (RAM): a temporary location in memory while processing is taking place; it is erased when the computer is powered down.

rate: the speed of doing a task, as in *keyboarding or typing rate*—usually expressed in words a minute or lines per hour.

raw data: data to be processed, also referred to as original data.

READ: a statement that reads data from a DATA line and assigns it to one or more variables.

read-only memory (ROM): memory which does not lose its data when the computer is powered down.

real-time controller: an output device that converts computer output to some kind of action that controls a process.

real-time sensor: any input device that constantly monitors a situation, as opposed to an input device that sends data to the computer only when ordered to by a person.

record: a group of related fields.

recording: the process of writing, rewriting, or reproducing data by hand or electronically.

relational operator: a symbol used to tell BASIC what relationship should exist between two data items in order for some action to be taken.

REM: a statement used for entering comments into programs.

replacement: a function of most word processors which enables the user to change one word to another, either in one place or throughout a document.

report spacing chart: a sheet used for planning the way the output of a program should look.

RESTORE: a statement that tells the computer to start back at the beginning of the DATA so that the READ statement can use the data over again.

retrieving: the process of making stored information available when needed.

RETURN: a statement used to tell BASIC to return from a subroutine or module to the statement following the GOSUB statement from which it left.

revision: changes made in text, such as correcting misspellings, adding or deleting words or characters, or rearranging the text.

robotics: a current technology used extensively in manufacturing that deals with the construction, maintenance, and use of robots.

RUN: a command that causes the computer to execute a program.

scanner: a device that "reads" the Universal Product Code (other scanners can read other things, such as printed words and numbers).

sector: a segment on a disk which contains the smallest amount of data that can be read or written at one time.

sensor: an electronic device that detects changes.

sequential access: a term used to describe a device that records and reads back data only in a one-after-the-other sequence.

shift key: a key used to make capital letters and certain symbols when struck at the same time as another key.

SHIFT LOCK (CAPS lock): a key that when depressed causes all letters to be capitalized (ALL-CAPPED).

slide rule: a calculating device consisting of two outer rules and a central sliding rule which slide in relation to one another.

software: instructions, or programs, that tell the computer what to do.

soraban: a Japanese version of the abacus.

sorter: a machine used to sort punched cards into the desired order.

sorting: the process of arranging information according to a logical system.

source documents: forms on which raw data may be written.

speech recognition device: an input device that recognizes human speech, allowing voice command or voice response.

speech synthesizer: a device that imitates the human voice.

spelling checker: a program that looks up the words of a document in its dictionary; any word not found in the dictionary is called to the attention of the operator.

spindle: a vertical bar on which disks are stacked in a hard disk drive.

spreadsheet: a program that uses a table (row and column arrangement) of numbers to perform calculations.

statement: a keyword preceded by a line number for use in a program to be executed in deferred mode.

storing: the saving of information so that it may be used later.

string variable: same as a character variable.

structured programming: a sequence of steps designed to make programming as easy and effective as possible.

subroutine: a module within a program which is entered by use of the GOSUB statement and exited by use of the RETURN statement.

summarizing: the process of changing processed data into brief, meaningful form.

supercomputer: a very fast and powerful computer.

system: a group of devices and procedures for performing a task.

systems programmer: a person who writes instructions that tell the computer how to operate.

systems software: programs designed to keep the computer functioning and programs to perform many everyday tasks related to the operation of the computer system.

tabulator: a machine used to record data from punched cards and print reports.

technical writer: a person who prepares written manuals that explain how to use the computer and how to run programs that may come with the computer.

technology: refers to applied science (a way of achieving a practical purpose).

telecommuting: a term used to describe the worker that uses a computer at home to perform a job.

teleconferencing: the term used to describe a way to hold a business meeting using the telephone system and the computer without people leaving their offices.

terminal: a keyboard and screen (or printing unit) used to access a computer.

text entry: the process of getting words from the mind of the writer or from a written document into the computer system.

three-dimensional: a term used to describe an object having depth as well as length and width.

top-down design: a process of beginning with the "big picture" and gradually refining the design, adding more detail at each step.

track: a path on which data is recorded on a disk or tape.

TRSDOS: an operating system developed by Radio Shack Division of Tandy Corporation.

two-dimensional: a term used to describe an object having length and width.

UNIVAC I: the first computer sold to the public market.

Universal Product Code: a bar code printed on products (especially grocery items) to identify the items.

UNIX: an operating system developed by Bell Laboratories.

user-interface shell: a program that makes the use of operating system commands easier.

utility program: a program designed to do a routine job, such as copying data from one disk to another.

variable: a named memory location for data.

variable data: data that is entered from the keyboard, or data computed during program execution.

video display: an output device which displays output on a televisionlike screen.

video display terminal (VDT): an input and an output device which consists of a keyboard and a display.

VLSI: very large scale integration (refers to the technique of combining many integrated circuits into one chip).

windowing: a process that allows the user to have different applications displayed in different areas of the screen at the same time.

word processing: the writing and storing of letters and reports on a computer.

writing-style checker: a program that checks a document for such things as overused words or grammatical errors.

XENIX: an operating system very much like the UNIX; it was developed by Microsoft Corporation.

INDEX

in the wake of chaos

Science and Its Conceptual Foundations

David L. Hull, Editor